OUR FUTURE SELVES

Love, Life, Sex, and Aging

MERRILY WEISBORD

Published in Canada in 1991 by Random House of Canada Limited, Toronto.

Canadian Cataloguing in Publication Data

Weisbord, Merrily
   Our future selves

ISBN 0-394-22194-X

1. Aging — Psychological aspects. I. Title.

BF724.55.A35W4 1991   155.67   C91-093991-8

COVER AND TEXT DESIGN: Brant Cowie / ArtPlus Limited
FRONT COVER PHOTOGRAPH: Wayne Grady
TYPE OUTPUT: TypeLine Express Limited

Printed and bound in Canada

Every effort has been made to ensure that permissions for all materials acknowledged below were obtained. In the event of any inadvertent omissions, formal acknowledgments will be included in all future editions of this book. In addition to the permissions listed below, full credit for sources may be found in the Bibliography.

From *Women and Aging: An Anthology by Women*. Edited by Jo Alexander et al. Copyright © 1986 Calyx Books.

From *Simone de Beauvoir: A Biography*, by Deidre Bair. Copyright © 1990 by Deidre Bair. Reprinted by permission of Summit Books.

From *Sister Age*, by M.F.K. Fisher. Copyright © 1983 by M.F.K. Fisher. Reprinted by permission of Alfred A. Knopf.

From "Not for Women Only," by Betty Friedan. Copyright © 1989 by Betty Friedan. From *Modern Maturity*, April/May, 1989. Reprinted by permission.

From "The Aging Mind Proves Capable of Lifelong Growth," by Daniel Goleman, February 21, 1984, and from "Erikson, In His Own Old Age, Expands His View of Life," by Daniel Goleman, June 14, 1988. Copyright © 1984/88 by The New York Times Company. Reprinted by permission.

From *The Hite Report*, by Shere Hite. Copyright © 1976 by Shere Hite. Reprinted by permission of Macmillan Publishing Company.

From *Bricks to Babel*, by Arthur Koestler. Copyright © 1980 by Arthur Koestler. Reprinted by permission of Random House Inc.

Contents

Acknowledgements

I am grateful to the many people who spoke to me — whose example and reflection carried me through a misplaced fear of aging. Because of them, I am now clearer about what may be difficult and what may be full of wonder.

I wish particularly to thank Ted Allan, Lea Roback and my father, Sydney Weisbord, who entertained and guided me through years of research and writing.

I wish also to thank the people who helped me in various ways throughout this work: Mark Achbar, a true gentleman, eased me into the writing marathon; Penni Jaques carefully transcribed the interviews; Phyllis Amber compiled thorough research for the Mind/Body chapter; Josh Freed, a writer who knows what a story is and what it takes to tell it, was my first reader; Linda Gaboriau, Betty Jane Wylie and Yosh Taguchi provided helpful comments on the manuscript; Colette Lebeuf painstakingly assembled end notes, permission letters and bibliography; Bernice Eisenstein did the copy-edit.

My sincere appreciation to the Canada Council without which this book would not have been possible; to Kim Kachanoff, Cleo Paskal and Anna Paskal for their encouragement; to Lee Davis Creal and Noona Barlow for their support; and to Ed Carson for recognizing my aspirations, and for his incisive substantive edit.

For Arnie Gelbart,
whose respect and care bless my work space.

ONE

Identity

MY DAD PHONES to ask if he can come to my house for a visit. I am rushing to prepare my daughter Anna's sixteenth birthday. Twenty of her friends will be arriving soon and expect to be housed and fed. "Sure," I say. "See you soon."

I put down the phone and resume sweeping. And when Dad appears, bare-chested, in shorts, sporting a peaked cap and his Mexican tire sandals, I am sweeping still. He sits and I sit. He asks about the children and my work. I ask about the trip to Stratford and Molly's wedding. I am half-listening to a scene from the wedding and half-planning the chili when all my attention focuses on, it seems to me, *new* quarter-inch-diameter spots on Dad's arms and shoulders. There, on the swimmer's muscles, in curls of white hair, clearly visible, are markings I have never seen before.

"Look at that, Dad, you got new brown spots," I say, interrupting his story.

My dad looks without much interest.

"They aren't new."

"Yes they are. They're new spots. Look at them." I am fixated and a little upset. "Hey, Dad, am I going to have spots like that, too, when I'm old?"

My dad extricates himself from the wedding description, a scene in which "a weird woman" asks him to dance her past her daughter and then yells, "Karen, look at me dancing. Look at me dancing." He doesn't look at the spots again. Instead, he leans back, cocks his head, and his eyes twinkle.

"You have to get old first, Merrily, you have to get to *be* seventy-five before you can have these spots."

When I began this book, I knew almost nothing about old age. I saw that my father, my aunts, the older people in my community, and the people I interviewed for an earlier book did not fit the popular stereotype of old age. But all around me — on billboards, TV, magazine covers, in my friends' minds — were paeans to youth and depressing, pervasive images of old people as people in decline. Like most North Americans, I feared what aging portended: loss of intellect, attractiveness, independence. Loss of love.

Ours is not an encouraging culture in which to grow old.

And that is what I am in the process of doing. Growing older.

Already, ageist ripples lap at my flanks. Women, in their thirties, discovering I have grown children, ask my age. When I say "forty-seven," they protest gleefully that it is not possible, I look so young — "How do you do it?" Their comments make me feel uncomfortable, freakish. If I were 35, not 47, Anna would be 4, not 16. My first book would not yet be written. I would not have visited Sardinia, or Tuscany, or made love with the trust and joy I have grown into, or watched my daughters ski moguls and do surgery, or felt so close to my women friends . . . I am beginning to know myself. I have a stake in life. And a seriousness and levity that come from a place that I've earned. When these younger women say, "You look so young," they know nothing of all this. They think 47 is old. And they are afraid of age.

So few older people live in the midst of our daily lives that most of us are totally out of touch with what it means to be old. Old people are retired, shunted into place in a growing aging industry, and ostracized further by governments that chose to subsidize segregated institutions for the aged rather than people themselves.

We may begin to know our parents. Some of us may even know our grandparents. But, for the most part, we are cut off from regular contact and friendship with older people — strangers to what we will become.

I see the pervasiveness of this split when I instruct students in a junior college writing class to interview someone over 65, to learn firsthand about aging. Half the students are unable to locate an old person to interview. The other half is as estranged as Joyce, 18, with her 69-year-old neighbour, Mr. Smith.

Joyce quickly establishes that Mr. Smith is married, has three children and six grandchildren, worked forty-eight years in a distillery and was retired four years ago.

"How does it feel to be old?" she asks.

"You just slow down a bit but you never realize that you are slowing down."

"Are you afraid of it?"

"Everybody's afraid of growing old, but it's not as bad as you think."

"Do you hang around with people your own age?"

"Well, obviously, it seems like young people these days are afraid of old people."

Out of the blue, Joyce asks, "How about senility? Do you see any signs of it in you or your wife?"

Mr. Smith hesitates. "Not really. Do you see senility in me?"

"Mmmm, well, I haven't really spoken to you for that long to see it. But I've known you for a long time and, no, I don't actually, but maybe it's because I know you so well."

The tape clicks off. When it resumes, Joyce says, "Okay, let's get off the question of senility. I think I insulted you by asking you that question. Okay. What I want to ask you is what you care about now that you didn't think about before."

"Every day," Mr. Smith answers.

"What do you mean by that?"

"Every day matters now . . ."

"What is your greatest fear?"

"My greatest fear definitely is of being alone. If, God forbid, my wife passed away, I'd pray for death."

"Well, I don't think any person should ever do that."

Finally, Mr. Smith raises his voice. "It's something that you could never understand. You don't have a person that you're used to for fifty years."

But Joyce is not interested in what Mr. Smith would die for. She has fulfilled her assignment.

"Well, that's great. Well, it was really nice talking to you, Mr. Smith, and I'm really glad to see that there are old people with brains around like you," she laughs. "No, I'm just joking, but you're very healthy and I wish you the best in the rest of your life."

Unless there is a major shakeup in cultural attitudes, it will be harder and harder for me, as I age, to believe that what is important to me has value and that what I value about myself is real. Mediated images have oozed into the vacuum left by real-life models. Stick figures on a greeting card hold a banner saying "Don't feel old! We have a friend your age," and the text inside reads, "And on good days he can still feed himself." A TV commercial portrays the competitor's employees as slow, clumsy older men. The advertiser's punch line comes when the older worker drops the box marked Fragile.

The Gray Panthers, an American activist organization, monitors media nationally to make the public "critically aware of the elements of ageism perpetuated through the media." The L.A. rep tells me she looks for "silly old fool" and "doddering old idiot" types. She and her fellow watchers have found that nearly all old characters — on TV, in magazines, greeting cards, and children's books — are inaccurate and unattractive stereotypes. A pamphlet published by the watchers of Greater Boston elaborates:

> PHYSICAL TRAITS — frail, infirm, deaf, toothless or with dentures, stooped, constipated, incontinent, small, quivering voice, timid, sexless or lecherous
>
> ATTITUDE — indecisive, depressed, unstable, disruptive, irresponsible, cranky, dissatisfied, meddlesome, passive, inactive, blissful, serene, slow (as drivers or workers, especially), useless, lonely, childish, incapable, intolerant, unbending

"*Stereotypes encourage and permit ridicule,*" warns the pamphlet. They limit possibilities and isolate older people from the mainstream of society — "This indignity works to the disadvantage of all of us."

In 1981, when the Gray Panther Media Watch Task Force first reported to the White House Conference on Aging, they had a thick file of complaints about ageism and stereotyping. Coordinator Lydia Bragger, eighty-two, recalls an example of stereotyping from "All in The Family": "The bride was a very old woman, very bent over, and she came down the stairs in this white gown, with a white veil on and, of course, everybody laughed. Another old woman, sitting at the table with the wedding cake, was also dressed in a ridiculous manner and she kept going to sleep. And the groom couldn't hear well and kept asking the minister what he was saying."

For Lydia Bragger, whose priorities are "love, caring, warmth," this stereotyping was "simply horrendous. If old people were hard of hearing, or couldn't see well and bumped into things, everyone laughed. This was supposed to be very funny but people who had these impairments didn't find them funny. It was painful to have to watch people laughing at these things."

And it is painful still. Comedian Phyllis Diller begins her act with a run of colonized one-liners: "I'm so wrinkled, I could screw my hat on . . . If I have another lift, it'll be a cesarean . . . I went to the airport with my broom and they tried to sell me flight insurance." Bill Cosby says TV uses old people like it uses Afro-American people, Asians, or Hispanics: "They're there for the joke."

That is, if they're there at all. Older people constitute 12 percent of the total population, but only 3 percent of the characters on TV. As magazine consultant James Kobak explains: "Who wants to look at old people? It's an environmental thing — same reason I don't want to look at old Coke bottles . . ." Convinced that old age is a turnoff, enterprising advertising experts suggest the "camouflage" publicity method. *Grandparents* magazine focuses on readers' situations — that of being grandparents — rather than age. Publisher Jerry Ward explains that in this way "*Grandparents* gave us the opportunity to approach the market out of joy rather than on the basis of age."

To be old is a cultural concept. Until recently, North American popular culture associated old people with sick, lonely, nursing home, Alzheimer's, impotent, resource drain — *problems*. Lately, a new mythology conjures up the fountain of age, future youth, the gift of life, sex after 60, painters over 80, mountain climbers of 93. The new, positive mythology is as intolerant of the vicissitudes of aging as the old, negative one. And it is a daunting thought that even when my generation reaches 65 and there are 54 million Americans and 6.5 million Canadians over 65, there may be no more accurate or richer conceptualization of what it really means to be old.

As long as stereotyping and discrimination exist, they will be part of my aging process. And how the culture treats me will be part of how it is for me to grow old. If I am to live in a society that allows me to see myself as a full person, with an ongoing life, something has to change.

For a year, I talk to people between 65 and 97 years old, looking for ways to understand what growing older is really like. I find people who have written about aging and others whom I think can teach me something. Most of the people I meet are what gerontologists call "the well-aged," which is apt since most older people *are* well. Seventy-four percent of Canadians over 65 (including those over 80) say their health is very good or excellent for their age and eighty percent live without need of "health service support," or "with only periodic care." Over seventy percent of older U.S. citizens rate their health as good, very good, or excellent and ninety-five percent live in the community, alone or with other people.

I start by broaching my own rather typical concerns and let people take me into their way of seeing. I am often surprised by what they say and so are they. Old people are asked to talk about the past but rarely about the present, even though they are pioneers in a new demographic mindscape. I ask questions about how to cope, whether new values emerge, if sex and love change. My mind is open but I am alert for clues to my potential. I don't want to grow up like the first old person ever born.

Soon after I begin researching, I hear Betty Friedan is writing a book on aging and I decide to start in-depth interviewing with the great debunker of the feminine mystique. She agrees to see me on the condition that I drive her from her dinner at the Cock and Bull, on Sunset Boulevard, to her apartment in Santa Monica "because I don't like to do this sort of thing unless I get something out of it too." I borrow a car, wedge the tape recorder in the seat divider, and pick up a short, white-haired woman with glossy pink lipstick and large white sunglasses. Ms. Friedan slumps in the passenger seat, safe behind her opaque lenses. "Go right down to the ocean is what you want to do." I get in gear, hit the freeway, whirr, keep up, pass, go, squeezed and quietly terrified by the traffic and the speed. Ms. Friedan, unmoving, either trusts my driving or is asleep. I drive, straight ahead on the Santa Monica Freeway, without screaming.

Finally, magnanimously, Ms. Friedan speaks. "What's this for?"

"Your new work on gerontology."

And then, because she is brilliant and can do this sort of thing in her sleep, Ms. Friedan growls. "It's not on gerontology. I'm interested in breaking through the age mystique. Nobody looks at age, in this hemisphere, at least, except as a decline from the standards of youth and male youth at that. And there's such an *over*evaluation, in America, of certain characteristics of male youth, macho in a way. Dating from the frontier and with a certain amount of reality, American society has, in some ways, worshipped macho. And age is so *feared* by people seen only in these terms. There's an *enormous* denial of age. Whole fortunes are made in dyeing of hair. Men in panic fleeing from age, starting all over again with young wives and new babies. Women have their face lifted four and five times. And there's no, there is *no image* of what happens in the new sort of life that people have now as a result of the dramatic change in the aging process. None, other than this *terrible* decline. There is a denial of the personhood of people over sixty-five. What values emerge if you don't measure everything in terms of youth? What is that human being like?"

"What values do emerge?" I ask.

"Well, I'm not going to tell you my book. That's as much as I want to say about that. You want to talk to me about anything else . . ."

I don't really. Ms. Friedan volunteers that she retains her commitment to the women's movement, which is threatened by fundamentalists and the isolation of women with the double burden of work and home.

"So you find yourself interested in a new subject and pulled back to the old one."

"I don't give up my commitment to the women's movement, but I'm pursuing the fringe of my own thinking having to do with breaking through the age mystique."

"What drew you to that?"

"Observations that I made over fifteen to twenty years — the dramatic change in the aging process, why men are dying so much younger than women. Then I decided to work on this, and as I got immersed in the state of the art I suddenly thought I've been there before, and I saw there is this false stereotype of age, distorted, that creates a self-fulfilling prophecy."

I tell her that I'm glad she's writing the book because even now I'm getting age flack and, hopefully, it will help change attitudes.

No response. The car is silent except for the roar of the freeway. I think maybe I've put her to sleep. But hark, "This mystique, this stereotype, is so great that people say to me, 'Oh, I hear you're working on a book about aging,' and the eyes glaze over and I hear myself saying, 'Oh no, no, no. I'm not writing a book about aging. I mean, I've got some far-out hypothesis . . . woman . . . man . . .'"

"They don't want to know, do they?" I commiserate. "Nobody wants to know. It's the last taboo, isn't it?"

"Yep."

"Masters and Johnson broke through the taboo against talking about sex and Kübler-Ross did it for death."

"Death. All right, death," Betty Friedan says. "Death happens and that's that. Age is worse, in a way."

And with that clunker, she laughs, a disconcertingly friendly laugh.

I have spent almost all the summers of my life in a community made up of people of all ages: naked babies, obstreperous ten-year-olds, fascinating teenagers, new parents, struggling adults, family and family friends who have gotten old. This place is my touchstone. I know where the frogs live and where the crayfish feed. I've walked the paths since I was a kid, as my grandparents and parents did. As my children do now.

Today, my companion and I played tennis with my father and Ralph, who, when they won, boasted the combined ages of 150 years. Because I have known Ralph since I was born, I would no more dismiss him as "senior citizen" or "golden ager" than he would categorize me as a middle-aged divorcée. Especially not after tennis. But I haven't ever talked to him, or the others here, about what it means to be older. And when I begin to read and to pay attention, I hear echoes of Ms. Friedan, decrying the prejudice and discrimination that so insidiously erode a sense of self.

"Take me," says writer Baba Copper, "I will soon be sixty-seven. I am becoming invisible. I am seen as asexual, although that is not how I feel. I am condescended to and socially segregated, as if I had a condition that was catching . . . It is not physiological aging or psychological aging that is troubling me. I am experiencing social aging — agesim. A generalized image is being projected on me that does not correspond with my self-image. I must continually internalize this feedback, or adjust to it, in order to retain my sanity at all. It is disorienting, and very hard not to lose confidence and blame myself."

"A producer bought something I wrote, a book I wrote," says my friend Ted Allan, seventy-one. "And he gave it to a young writer because, even though I wrote the book, he was afraid I couldn't have the point of view of the young person in the book. Which is quite hilarious inasmuch as I wrote it. It's taking an idea to its ultimate absurdity, isn't it? Where the man who buys this book that I wrote says that he has to hire a young writer to show the young point of view. As if I write 'old' now. So I started laughing. I said, 'Who the hell created that young character? It was me. I created him. It was *me*. Young.'"

So widespread is discrimination against media writers based on age that the Age Discrimination Committee of the Writers' Guild of America West presents a seminar to dispel the prejudice that "creativity diminishes with the onslaught of gray in one's hair." And veteran Hollywood agent Mike Zimring, finding aging especially hard "in business," decides to chuck it.

"I left the company because I had the feeling that I was being treated as a second-class citizen," he says. "This is a young man's business, it always has been. You see all those young executives, they're all young. And all of a sudden these young people, even at a talent agency, they know everything, right? They really haven't had any experience but they know everything."

"Were you being humiliated by the way you were treated?"

"Well, there were things, like they started suddenly making people members of the board of directors and they were inviting people to come to corporate meetings, and here I was — I was already seventy, and they just didn't include me. I stayed but I was very unhappy. I'd been handling Karl Malden for forty years, Carl Reiner for over thirty, Katharine Hepburn for twenty.

And I thought to myself it's humiliating for me to walk in here like this. And Karl Malden sensed it, and he and Carl Reiner said, 'Come on, screw them, get out of there and we'll go with you.' So I did it."

"When you opened your own 'boutique,' as I'm told you call it, did you feel better?"

"Oh yeah. Of course. Sure. People see me now, people in the street, they say, 'Hey, you look different, you look happy.' I didn't realize it but I must have worn it on my face somehow."

"If you get to be eighty or ninety," says Alex Comfort, an authority on geriatric psychiatry, "you won't feel any different. But you'll be surprised that other people treat you as if you turned into another person. The waitress asks the person you're with: 'Does he have cream in his coffee?' ignoring you as if you're some sort of zombie or idiot."

For a while, I think about redefining *old* and *young*, so that "old at heart" is a preferred state. I experiment with the word *old*, capitalized and uncapitalized: *Old* is a condition inflicted by society and *old* is a simple chronological description. It is driving me nuts how nobody who feels well, feels *old*. How everybody wants to *act young*.

Not that I don't understand the impulse.

Once I open my eyes, I see the corpses of *Old* in various stages of putrefaction. Even on the pages of books for children.

I am reading *How Does it Feel to be Old*, a picture book "filled with love," according to the *New York Times*, when my daughter Anna announces her impending visit to eighty-year-old Auntie Katie. In the book, Grandma takes her grandchild to the mirror and says, "You begin to resemble this old grandmother . . . Oh, not this wrinkled prune that I am! Who I was back *then!*" I am at the part where Grandma worries about falling and looking like "a silly old clown," when Anna returns to report, "Auntie Katie said, 'The reason I am so happy is I have people who love me.'" The storybook ends with Grandma's self-effacing "Soon you'll be knowing / that Grandma has died / while you are still growing / in inches and pride."

All gone, Grandma. But not, thank goodness, Auntie Katie.

Baba Copper writes about "that virulent stereotype, the age/death connection." She tells of a younger woman, with many loved ones dead, who assumed she and Baba had a great affinity since Baba was old and, therefore, well versed in death. But she was wrong. Except for her mother who had died at ninety-three, Baba Copper's loved ones were all still kicking.

"Unique to our culture is its rejection of the old," Alex Comfort reminds us. "Their exclusion from work and their accustomed social space, their premature burial by society as 'unpeople,' and a rich and erroneous folklore of mental decline, infirmity, asexuality, ineducability, and the normality of causeless mental disorder in the old."

Yet most old people are and feel themselves to be the same people they were in their youth. The Baltimore Longitudinal Study of Aging concludes that personality dispositions are extraordinarily stable in adulthood: "At any point in time, a person is more like he has always been than he is like peers of his age group." My dad is still a jock at heart. Ralph, building little museums, the world in his backyard, remains a steadfast disciple of Thoreau. Ted is a storyteller. My friend Lea, at eighty-six, still can't keep quiet.

If there were no societal prejudice, we would be freer to deal with the real and difficult enough challenges of aging — the vagaries of physiological change and the demanding existential imperative of making sense of the lives we've lived.

Margaret Ritter, seventy-one, painter, cross-country skier, tap dancer, puts her arm up on the couch, looks incredulously at her own wrinkled skin and says, "I don't own a crepe blouse."

Barbara Macdonald presents herself, full-face and time-etched, on the cover of *Look Me in the Eye*. Lines extend from the sides of her nose, down her face, past the corners of her mouth. Other lines crisscross her neck and cheeks. Skin hangs loosely from her forearm. "It seems disconnected from me; it is someone else's, it is the arm of an old woman. It is the arm of such old women that I myself have seen, sitting on benches in the sun with their hands folded in their laps; old women I have turned away from. I wonder now, how and when these arms I see came to be my own — arms I cannot turn away from."

Lying on his bed, Ted scours his beard in a hand-mirror, looking for white hairs. He thinks they make him look old and debates the merits of artificial coloring. I sit at the foot of the bed pointing my Sony 640 omnidirectional mike at him, knowing his dilemma is relevant to a discussion of image and identity. But I am having trouble relating to him as an old person. He *is* over seventy. I guess he looks old. But the *being* of him is so present, so full of a hilarious, compelling black humor, that age seems an unreal and contrived frame. Fortunately for the interview, Ted is momentarily obsessed with looking "like an old man." I ask what *old* means to him.

"Old means ugly and girls won't go for me. Unattractive and off-putting."

I have watched my friends struggle to accept themselves with five more pounds. And then say defiantly, This is me. I have stared into mirrors obsessed with my own wrinkles and now choose to concentrate on flexibility, muscle tone, weight — physical attributes that I can control. I tell myself that to grow old is a normal part of the life cycle. Traditional societies have rituals and rites of passage to mark changes and help people encounter *otherness*. In modern society we have lost the systems for transforming ourselves. Marian Jarvis Lewis can't believe she's ninety-seven. "I've never been ninety-seven before. So I have no way of judging these things, no guidelines of *any* kind. Why that's an old, old person and, you see, I don't think I'm old." My dad can't believe he's seventy-five. "I don't know what it's *supposed* to feel like but I don't feel like that."

Old people, demystified, have lost their place as the guardians of social health, as the ones with ritual access to sacred powers. Now, as psychologist Marvin Frankel says, "Old people are considered garbage because they don't produce. Society doesn't have a script for them."

Writing about women who try to deny age, Cynthia Rich says, "Without a history, without a literature, without a politic, they find it impossible to reconcile their sense of themselves — as real women, whose lives are ongoing — with the new, degrading ways in which they find themselves seen [or rendered unseen], or with their own lifelong training in ageism." They color their hair, lift their faces, hide their age. As Rich says bluntly, "The old woman tries to pass."

"It becomes rather puzzling to you as you grow older," muses writer Morley Callaghan. "Pretty women seem to become kindlier to you. To have a pretty woman have no hesitation to rush over, throw her arms around you and start kissing you. You know, this is vaguely, sort of, disquieting. It is odd."

"They don't think you have a sex urge anymore."

"I don't know. I never want to raise this subject because there's such genuine warmth and friendliness there, you see, and I fear that I would sort of spoil something, you know . . . Well, they're strange things. But this has never been written about. This is a strange business. And I've never read anything on this subject."

"On the subject of sexuality as you're older?"

"Well, say on what is involved in, say, a male and female relationship where the woman is, say, thirty and a man is eighty. That is, in the relationship, is there any sex involved at all? Is the woman *utterly* confident there's none involved at all? Does the man *actually* assume that none can be involved at all? This is a little area of exploration. Because people laugh about it."

The body changes.

Society cuts the older person loose.

He or she is alone with the enormous task of making profound and personal sense of it all.

In this situation, says writer Malcolm Cowley, "the aging person may undergo another identity crisis like that of adolescence."

"This situation is enough to make anyone ill," says Alex Comfort.

Between 1981 and 1984, cosmetic surgery increased 61 percent. Most of the procedures were face-lifts — despite the normal risks of surgery, including infection and nerve damage, and the additional risks with plastic surgery of scarring, hemorrhage, and blood vessel blockage. Plus the possible effects on the heart of the accompanying anesthetic. Plastic surgery is currently one of the fastest growing medical specialities in North America. And 90 percent of the patients are women.

"You will look outside how you feel inside," the plastic surgeon says to Eroca Coty, an elegant, attractive seventy-year-old. For Eroca, this is a seductive thought. As a widow, she is becoming socially isolated. Her freelance work has dried up. Women her age don't invite her to dinner parties because she is single. And she can't go to dinner dances at the club without an escort even though "the men are all dead or hiding." She says, "When you start to lose attractiveness, you don't know what to do. It's kind of devastating. You think, I shouldn't look like that because I don't feel like that. And if people don't know your age and you look younger, they think you're younger."

I tell Eroca about "Youthenasia," an Anne Noggle portrait of a woman fresh from plastic surgery, her face black and swollen, raw scars around her eyes.

"Do you think plastic surgery is self-abuse?" I ask.

"No. I think anything that can help you, go for it. If it's going to make you feel better, why not?"

"How long does it last?"

"Maybe five years. Seems five years is the big number."

"I understand correcting deformities by plastic surgery. But I don't think of old age as a deformity."

Eroca looks at me with her cool blue eyes. "Well. Think of it as a deformity to your psyche. It's what you can't see that's hurting. Maybe the face isn't really so bad, but it all contributes to making you feel unwanted and unattractive and un-every-thing. Because, let's face it, women have to be attractive, *have* to be attractive."

I call my friend Anne Silverstone, seventy-one, married to Ralph. She is ironing on the porch in the sun. Mother of seven, inveterate collector, and graduate phys ed teacher, Anne was a vivacious, red-haired athletic woman and is now a vivacious, white-haired athletic woman. I have known Anne all my life. She and Ralph have summered for over fifty years in our Laurentian community of family and friends. Several of the children from the community have built homes nearby, and it is here that I live year-round. I leave my desk, walk past Aunt Sue's winterized house, past Auntie Katie's summer cottage, past the counsellor's shack, the tennis court, the men, women, and children at the pool, across the bridge, up the hill, to Anne. I hope she is going to tell me her life is full and she is quite happy with how she looks.

What she says is, "Sometimes I look in the mirror and I say, 'Yech. Yeuch,' and I know that a visit to a plastic surgeon would just be great. But then it's a question of time, recuperation, the element of pain deters me. If I was going to face a public, or compete for companionship, I wouldn't hestitate. I don't really want a drastic job. Just take a little twitch around the mouth to take out the sour look, and a little twitch in the neck to take out the chicken look. Because, as you grow old, you don't look pleasant. I think the lines around your face make you look sour. Don't you think?"

"How does my father look to you?"

"Your father looks very good. He looks very fit. Extremely fit. Don't you think?"

"But he has wrinkles."

"You don't notice those in a man. A wrinkle in a man is almost a handsome attribute. Whereas a wrinkle in a woman does nothing to soften or beautify her."

"But you are accepting that only the young can be beautiful."

"Yes, I accept the woman's attempt to alleviate the growing-old condition. I don't think that any woman after sixty-five is happy with how she looks. The only standard is what the ads are going to make. It's only the ads that make the lumpsous [*sic*] girls — they're the ones that sell products and they're the ones that are in the forefront — the beautiful, young luscious girls. It's not the old. Although you see *some* older women in ads now. My friend is in an ad for a senior citizens' residence. They didn't take her au naturelle; they dyed her hair, fixed her up a bit, but still, she's there."

I tell Anne about *Future Youth*, a 646-page, large-type guide on "How to Reverse the Aging Process," which fetes the hundreds of thousands of men and women who yearly "put guilt and self-consciousness aside and knock on the doors of surgeons' offices in hopes of finding ways to lift sags and bags and erase wrinkles."

I tell Anne I'm scared of needles. I don't want my face cut into. I'm concerned that there is no standard of older beauty.

"Well, there's all these nice, old actresses that have shown up now with their wrinkles. The Hepburn girl and Helen Hayes.

They're made up and everything else, but they're not afraid to let people know they're around and they're there."

And, to this strange consolation, Anne adds, "To start being afraid of age, you're on the wrong road right away. It's inevitable and it's universal. It's a process that you have to face. I'm just grateful that I can do what I do. There's nothing seriously wrong with me, which would be a worse thing than growing old."

Anne doesn't like how she looks but she's happy she's not sick. I recall Alex Comfort's comment that "our social image of age is so negative that many old people are agreeably surprised on reaching it to find that they are not demented, sick, incapable of learning, asexual, unemployable, and lonely."

I want more than that. When I get older, I want people to treat me with the same respect they would any normal person. And look *at*, not through, me, to see the beauty that there is. Currently, beauty in North America, especially female beauty, is synonymous with youth, something that perplexed me until a conversation I had with Will Allister and his wife, Mona. The conversation begins with Will's discomfort at turning seventy and "aging ten years." He is "startled" when he looks in the mirror because he doesn't feel like he looks. He doesn't feel any different in his thinking but he looks old. I ask Mona how she feels when she looks in the mirror. She says even though she used to be "pretty," she's "at peace" with herself, so looking old doesn't matter.

"But you are beautiful," I say to Mona, whose dark eyes, full lips, and finely sculpted face make her a classic beauty. "I think so and my children think so. Don't you?"

"No. I look okay for an older woman but I am not beautiful."

"Why can't we say Mona is beautiful?" I ask Will. "She is."

"Mona means sexual beauty," Will explains. "You have different kinds of beauty — a flower, a tree — she is referring to sexual beauty."

Finally, I get it.

Old women are not considered sexual by most men. Since men no longer consider them of any sexual interest, their appearance does not count. Therefore, they cannot be beautiful.

Not beautiful, not sexual, and, of course, not strong. As Barbara Macdonald describes, this kind of garbage can pollute the wellsprings of sexuality.

It is raining in Kenmore Square, Boston when Barbara joins a parade of women, six abreast, in close ranks for a March to Take Back the Night. Monitors in bright yellow slickers move back and forth along the lines. Barbara feels like a racehorse at the gate: "The exhilaration, the oneness with the women around me, the sense of at last doing something . . ." At some point, she notices her lover Cynthia is no longer beside her but a few feet away with a monitor. Barbara goes over. The monitor is evasive at first. Then, choosing her words with care, she says to Barbara, "If you think you can't keep up, then you should go to the head of the march."

Barbara is shamed and helpless. She chants with the other marchers:

> *"We are angry, proud and strong*
> *Freedom is our righteous song."*

But how, she wonders, can she feel strong when she's being told she's weak. "I wondered what Cynthia was feeling," she writes, "and if I would ever have the confidence to make love to her again."

So far are we from a conceptualization of strength and beauty in older people that I can only grasp at how these qualities might be seen and how an alternative esthetic will evolve.

"Look, my dear, I'm glad I have wrinkles," says my friend Lea Roback, eighty-six, needle-trade organizer and activist. "It shows I've grown up. This is what we went through. We have wrinkles of laughter around the eyes, wrinkles on the forehead from thinking, wrinkles around the mouth from when we had to clench our mouths when we had things we had to overcome. We have *lived*. I love to see Inuit women, their faces crinkled, their eyes smiling. And those beautiful women from Crete. And Anna Magnani. You can tell what they are feeling.

"Blond, rouged up, face scraped — it's stupid. Such torture to take away character. If that is all they have to worry about, it's their pleasure. But what pleasure can you get if it's not really you. My face is an open map. I've got wrinkles and I'm proud of them. So, we're older. As long as the mind is working and the feet walk. That's us."

I recall that, after a poetry reading, Lea said eighty year-old poet Dorothy Livesay was "so beautiful."

"Why did you say that?"

"Her animation. When she laughs, her head goes back just a bit. She's more beautiful now than she was in the thirties. There's something bubbling within her. She is herself. And she's beautiful, just beautiful, because she's a real person."

I go to see Dr. James Birren, one of the foremost gerontologists in North America, to ask him about beauty and the identity crisis in old age.

"I don't think it's so much an identity crisis of old age as of middle age," he says, "fifty to seventy-five, what Allan Pifer calls 'the third-quarter of life.' In that quarter you realize you are not omniscient and you have to come to terms with some limitations. But by very old age, that's been taken care of. Middle age is that shifting of gears between striving against the discontents of youth and coming to terms with what we might broadly call 'the meaning of life.'"

"It seems very difficult for people when their appearance changes. There seems to be no image of older beauty, especially for women."

"That's true. In Japanese culture, there is a concept that is called *sabi*, which takes into account adaptations to the passing of time and events. If you imagine a Monterey pine buffeted by winds off the Pacific, you see that it takes on a shape depending upon the prevailing winds and in time it looks windswept. It has a configuration which becomes pronounced with time, and what you do is admire that. Now the American approach to esthetics would be that something that's beautiful should be symmetrical and not show differences.

"If you think again of a redwood house, exposed on one side to the sun, you see it becomes more silvery on the side. One approach would be to sandblast it to make it even all over, to get rid of any blemish. The other is to say no, we should have the subtlety of observation to appreciate the adaptations with time and that's where the beauty is. As a younger culture, we haven't come into this.

"Let's now translate this into interpersonal relationships. As relationships mature with years, they take on a life of their own and you can allude to things in the heart without speaking directly of them. There's a subtlety there of expression. And the duration of the relationship creates an esthetic and a quality of its own. In North America, generally, we have a fresh-from-the-factory view of esthetics. As soon as you take the cellophane off, it begins to change downwardly. The newness is more important. In contrast, we can have the esthetics of adaptation and change."

I ask Dr. Birren if the esthetics of change transmits into sensuality.

"Yes. This is reflected in a doctoral dissertation done with me by Margaret Reedy. She had couples nominated as having close, intimate relationships — young, middle-aged, and old couples. The older couples rate loyalty and companionship higher than some other qualities. Youth emphasizes candidness, honesty, the immediate, because they're establishing a trust relationship. Late in life you count on those, those have been established. What you place value on is the companionship in the relationship. Sexuality per se diminishes somewhat, but there is this other form of sensuality which has to do with companionship."

"Does this companionship and trust transmit into a sensual feeling. Because you love your wife in this way, do you want to touch her?"

"Yes, I think so. I've been doing a fair amount of travel recently and I like my wife to travel with me. It is not complete without her being there to share the events, to have her with me when we're on the airplane, that type of intimacy, of being *next to* someone. When I was younger, I was go, go, go and impatient. Now it's more a quality of a mutual appreciation of what is jointly experienced, trying to talk about what the meaning of what that experience was. This is part of sensuality. Sensuality isn't only the experience of the senses but the interpretation we put on the experiences of the senses.

"It seems more subtle than people think," I say.

"We don't have yet a language for this kind of thing, and I think as we mature we will come to have a language for it. We have the capacity for it. It's just that when you're establishing yourself as a pioneering culture, a young culture, you don't take the time; therefore, you don't create words to describe these things we're talking about."

At a theater opening in Montreal, I tell a friend of my research into ageism and my growing interest in how older people perceive themselves. She refers me to Dr. Edith Wallace, eighty, a painter and practising Jungian analyst, who she thinks will contribute to the discourse.

Dr. Wallace greets me at the door of her Central Park apartment with a direct, assessing gaze, a small woman in light spring colors. She gives me a poem written for my friend's wedding and I tell her why I have come. I tell her I and my generation, with arguably the longest, most protected adolescence in human history, are beginning to realize it is time to face our own aging. And when we try, we find ourselves woefully ill prepared.

Dr. Wallace asks my age.

"Forty-seven."

"There is a time in life when we have to come to terms with the fact that life is not endless. And your age is just the time — there's a much earlier time also — when you see all the horrors of growing older. When you get there, it isn't like that at all. The body wears out. That's the instrument; it doesn't last forever.

"But my work and my belief is the more you develop your creative potential, the healthier you are. And if you don't, if you start mourning, you get sick. When you get older, you're free to do things you may not have had the chance to do when you were doing things that circumstance dictated. And when the creative source has a chance to show itself, and when we are connected to it, that's the best part of life."

I tell Dr. Wallace that many people worry about getting old and losing what is conventionally thought of as good looks or beauty.

Dr. Wallace says when she was young, she was a very beautiful girl, and it got her into a lot of trouble.

"And men wanted things from me I wasn't ready and willing to give. And it didn't interest me. And now there are many people to whom I can give love and who can give love to me. It's warm. It's a mutual recognition, and seeing beyond what appears. Physical beauty is what's on the surface. I wouldn't want to settle for being attractive just physically. I want to be recognized as me, as a woman. And that increases when you grow older, it doesn't decrease."

"Aren't there new frustrations as you get older?"

"It depends on your attitude. If you say, 'Oh, my beauty's going and I won't be sexually attractive and I won't be able to do physically what I used to do,' then you will have more frustrations. But let me tell you a story: "When the Jungian trainees met in Sardinia, we explored the island, and one day we decided to climb the mountain. I've been a mountain climber all my life, especially in Italy, and when I see a mountain I've got to reach the top, and I take other people with me. Well, it got very windy up there, and when we got to a certain point just below the *chima*, the peak, I said, 'This is as far as I can go. I'm not doing the last part.' And I was very, very pleased. I thought I had conquered something. It was a great experience. It was a spiritual feeling if you want to call it that."

"What did you think you had conquered?"

"The need to get there. The need to reach the top. It's not good anymore, that kind of concern. Other things are happening. Precious things that I have to focus on. There is a difference in what is *needed* at my age. And I'm quite happy with what is needed right now."

"What is the difference in what's needed?"

"The kind of preoccupation one wants to live fully. When you come to my age, you look at that other side and you want to know a little more about it. You are closer to the other shore — closer to the end of your mission — and you want to think about that. What you have been working toward all your life is somehow coming toward fruition and other things are incomplete and cause pain, but it's a needed preoccupation and a rewarding one as you grow older."

"Why rewarding?"

"You can let go. And you get a vision of something and are close to something that has very little to do with everyday life — although it can happen at any moment, anywhere, in everyday life."

"So it allows a spiritual perspective that you didn't have before."

"Right. And that is very precious to me."

When I first started researching this book, I was caught in the cobwebs of North American stereotypes about old people. Then, I was struck by the effects of subtle and overt discrimination on people's feelings about themselves. As my dialogue with older people continues, I begin to see that *my* concerns — about looks, power, and the kind of sexuality that I am familiar with — may be beside the point. And since I learn best from talking to people, I accept Aunt Sue's invitation to visit her, Uncle Joe, and their "Florida family," in the winter when Montreal is cold and Hollywood, Florida, is hot.

I take a Nordair flight to Fort Lauderdale Airport, rent a car and drive it through a traffic jam to Highway 441, pass Taco Bell, Pantry Pride, Pizza Cabaret, Boatarama, the Conquistador rental apartments, brown naked torsos in shorts, to my destination: Seminole Park for Mobile Homes and Recreation Vehicles.

A neighbor stops mowing his postage-stamp lawn and directs me to Uncle Joe and Aunt Sue's thirty-two-foot Holiday Rambler. Joe takes my bags, Aunt Sue offers me juice. I sit at a table, which will lift so my bed can come down. They point to their room thirty feet away and assure me that they live in this space with Auntie Katie for a month every winter.

Sue and Joe perform a domestic pas de deux and food is quickly on the table. As we finish eating, Lora Allaire, four trailers over, leaves her Florida room and La-Z-Boy chair, picks up her buddy Millie Rawinski, and saunters over to where we are sitting. I take in Lora, with her blond tight curls, dark round glasses, legs long and knobby. Millie is right beside her — another blond with a round Slavic face, gold jewelry and two-tone glitter glasses. Lora whisper-talks, fast, right at me. "Hi. How you keepin'. What you up to . . ." Fingers going, hands fluttering. They invite me to join them, and Sue, Lora, Millie, and I hit the three-mile path, out for the nighttime stroll.

Up and down the rows of tree-lined paths we walk, past trailers, Chevys, Pontiacs, to a turn graced by the sweet, sticky smell of jasmine. Under the street lamp, a group of older people are laughing. Hands on hips, chin jutting into the action, Lora reports, "Ralph, here, has a problem. He has a bleeding colon. So he says he has to wear a napkin. So Beth, here, goes, 'That's not so bad. You know how many years I wore a napkin?'" They laugh again. A man coughs and my aunt says, "Don't bark like that." I look up at trees three times my width, trees so high the sodium lights of the Ford Agency make strange clouds of their tops. Illness isn't a dirty secret here. It's out in the open. It's funny.

Sunday afternoon.

Can't interview any men. They're all watching the football game. Yesterday was the Thunderbird Fair, tonight there's an evening dance class. Monday is a cocktail party. Then square dancing, golf, the track, bingo, cards, fifty laps on the three-wheeler, bring your own hot dogs, build the shed, the flea market and the soaps — which Uncle Joe calls "As the Stomach Turns" and "John's Wife's Other John."

These guys are busy. Finally, Millie, Lora, and I take the Chevy to Hollywood Beach. "The girls," on an outing, are in an infectiously good mood.

"You have to work to make life joyful," Millie says, as we spread our towels. "If you want to be depressing, your life will be that way, but if you want joy, you have to make it. Nobody's going to make it for you."

"I'm sixty-eight but I don't feel it," says Lora. "It's a person's attitude. Look at my sister — she's seventy-seven and right in there all the time. You can't be with your man or even with your children constantly. You have to get away and do what pleases you. You've got to love people."

Millie tells me she worked at a woolen mill, her husband at a steel mill, then they bought a hog farm. "Start at eight in the morning, pick up garbage to feed three hundred hogs, be back at noon. After that, take it to the animals. At home, do the baking and cooking and cleaning in the meantime. And the washing, needless to say."

"No time for holidays," says Lora who had a dairy farm. "We had to exclude our fun in the summer. Nothing did we do. We worked."

"When my mother was fifty, she was old," says Millie. "She worked all her life. And she cooked. That's all she did is cook."

"Right," says Lora with glee. "If we don't like cooking, we say, 'Hey, what do you say, let's go out.'"

Millie's husband, Joe, moves his sizable potbelly with a hop and some grace and welcomes me into the carpeted trailer. The conversation, slow going at first, becomes surprisingly animated on the subject of grandchildren. "My own kids — you ask her — I never had time to play with 'em. Because I worked like eighteen, twenty hours at a time. With my grandchildren, I make enough time. When we come down there and they see us comin' in, they open their door, the oldest one's head is stickin' out through and the little guy's on the bottom . . . the way they adore you. I mean that's somethin' they can't take away from ya," says Joe with a sense of discovery.

Irwin Smalley, seventy-three, slender jowls like a dachshund, worked forty years for the Prudential Insurance Company and retired to the park. Irwin "babied" his wife, bringing her breakfast in bed, relishing the happiest years of their life. When she died, horribly, both legs amputated, Irwin went out of his mind. "Even after all these years, I still moan and cry about it internally. It's like living without an arm and a leg. So living in a trailer park, there are people around here who were able to recognize I was partly insane for years. There is a sympathy in the park with people that get to know you and like you. It helps you to carry the burden."

Joe and Gertrude Kuhl, married fifty years, have ailments that ease up in the park. Square and muscled, Joe worked ten to twelve hours a day, six days a week, as a tool-and-die maker for Continental Can until he had ulcers, thirteen operations and a chunk of his stomach removed. Pear-shaped Gertrude has such bad arthritis that up north she'd be housebound. Like many others in the park, they see their family back home in the warm months and their Florida family in the winter. They live in a $15,000 trailer for under $700 a month.

"When I retired, I couldn't believe it when I woke up," Joe says. "I didn't believe I wouldn't have to account for some kind of inefficiency or plan how to make things faster the next day. After I went trailering, I realized I didn't need a doctor so much as I needed gettin' away from what was causing it."

"When I'm sick, he can take care of me better down here," Gertrude says. "An ambulatory person stuck in a nursing home is no good. This is far better. When my arthritis is bad, I go to bingo and my mind gets occupied and it doesn't hurt so much. There are eight widowers here and they can cope better. In a condo or a separate apartment, you're not among people and that makes a difference. It's just the idea that you're able to get out among people, that you're not cut off."

"A man can continue to be a man. Fix things, build, help people, continue to have your pride that you can do things . . . You can still be a man in the park," says Joe.

I say goodbye at a "cocktail" outside Sue and Joe's trailer where I have lived happily for a week. Joe Rawinski and George Allaire, two overstuffed bad boys on folding chairs, throw peanuts across the astroturf into Lora's blouse. "You think I'm a basketball court?" she says, barely interrupting her conversation with Millie. Behind me, someone tells a joke as another voice yells, "Funnier, funnier." I ask a man about retirement and he looks at my tape recorder and says, "Is it on? I don't want to talk for nothing." Irwin puts his arm comfortably around Millie. Beside me, Uncle Joe tells someone, "The bracket was rusty so I suggested a squirt of WD-40. I WD-40 everything. Even my wife."

As she leaves, Millie gives me a big bosomy hug and some advice, "You should ask yourself questions like you ask us."

Nordair Flight 151.

I am not elated as I am after a real holiday but I am relaxed and pleased. Whatever the uninitiated think of older people, the gang I just visited have a totally different concept of themselves.

They don't feel useless, even though they are no longer in the system. In fact, after years of hard work, most are relieved not to be in the system. It's their time, they say. They don't have to prove themselves anymore. And they don't need roles, hierarchies, or guilt. They call themselves "boys" and "girls" and want "to just live and enjoy this life."

As a community, they support each other, respect each other, flirt, share philosophies and coping strategies, keep sharp with wit and repartee. They are each other's mirrors, reflecting personhood in a way that could teach society a lesson. Nobody here suggests that older people should be shunted off or herded into segregated living spaces, but given the options of residential senior housing, isolated retirement communities, or nursing homes, they chose the more autonomous and community-minded trailer park. It is an antidote to the societal assault on identity, a modest countercultural resistance. You can still be a person in the park.

Malcolm Cowley reinforces the concept of an informal cultural alliance of older people. When his article "The View From 80," was published in *Life* magazine, Cowley received a flood of letters and felt:

> a burst of affection for those in my age group; for all my coevals, to use a word from "the literature." Each of them has found his or her own sort of wisdom, an individual way of adjusting to circumstances, and some have displayed a courage that puts me to shame. We octogenarians form a loose and large secret order, with many members in each city and with representatives in almost every village.

Cowley considered his contemporaries "comrades in age."

When Giff Gifford, sixty-seven, retired professor of social work and Second World War bomber pilot, began interviewing leaders of activist senior citizens' organizations for his book, *Canada's Fighting Seniors*, he, like most people, was "absolutely ignorant" about the one million Canadians and five to six million Americans who belong to seniors' activist organizations. "I didn't know what was going on. I had no real conception that there was a whole senior citizens' culture out there." Then, in 1985, when the Canadian government tried to cut back the indexation of the old-age pension, seniors from all over Canada marched to Ottawa. "I kept seeing people I'd interviewed across the country appearing on television with broad grins on their faces. They had been plugging away for years and the media paid no attention. Then, suddenly, they were discovered. The media seemed to think they'd 'sprung' the organizations but it's a real grass-roots movement."

At a private rehabilitation center, healing from a nerve operation on her hand, my friend Lea prepares for an interview with a Radio Quebec TV personality, who Lea says "smiles all the time about things, like where to invest your money." Lea has agreed to the interview on the condition that she can talk about underpaid nurses, the parking of old people, the disintegration of the health-care system. She wants to praise workers like her physiotherapist — "The strength of that young woman's hands flows into mine." She thinks nurses should get a medal or, at the very least, be well paid. "We need them and they have to have time to nurse, not run like rabbits from one to another." She is ready with clippings, comments she's collected from the staff, and her own old, tough credibility. "Some oldsters say, 'Oh, what can we do?' I tell them when Baloney [Prime Minister Brian Mulroney] was running for election, he said he'd never cut our pension. Then, the first thing he does when he is elected is cut. In twenty-four hours, with the oldsters' groups, the trade unions, the phones ringing, we had a hundred people on their way to Ottawa. Mme. Lebrun stood in front of Baloney, wagged her finger right in his face, and said, 'Tu as menti.' She called him 'tu' [the familiar form of you] not 'vous' [the polite form]. 'You lied.' We all stood around her and clapped. And, P.S., he didn't cut our pensions."

In 1970, Maggie Kuhn and five others, forced to retire at sixty-five, started the Gray Panthers, now a nationwide American organization of 60,000 members. They looked at the ways in which age stereotyping creates "self-doubt and rejection and all the rest of it." They looked at government-funded social programs to see "to what extent there is self-determination . . . . to what extent older people are being made into 'wrinkle babies,' infantilized and dependent." Like educators Joan and Erik Erikson, both over eighty-five, Maggie Kuhn chose to live in an intergenerational cooperative household, believing that "shared housing makes loneliness obsolescent. There is companionship, there is a sharing of household responsibilities, there is safety." Her housemates are younger since "being part of society means being involved in the lives of children and people of other ages — the elimination of age segregation."

The first time I meet Maggie Kuhn, she is at the tail end of one of her demanding talk-and-travel schedules. She has given a stirring speech about the need for "radicals like us who have participated in America's social movements to write autobiographies, to celebrate our history, to celebrate life, to provide a needed historical perspective." When she finally sits, I ask a visibly exhausted Maggie how she does it.

"I get my energy from the people around me."

She gestures to the people nearby and, as if on cue, a woman facing us cradles her hand. "And from the value of association. The reason loneliness is so lethal is that you're deprived of the energy that comes when you interact with others. We energize each other constantly."

In old age, Maggie Kuhn claims the freedom to speak out and take risks. When she sees image makers consciously manipulating the image of age (such as pharmaceutical companies that reinforce people's feeling about the decrepitude of their aging bodies to sell tranquilizers), she no longer tries to be diplomatic. Or to say things with a minimum of tension. "We've got to create some new structures and new models and new mind-sets. It's as simple as that . . . because we have such a rampant malaise about ageism and gerontophobia. It's an epidemic. People are afraid and anxious and they are also denying their own history. When you lie about your age, you're just throwing away whole chunks of your life that ought to be part of your affirmation, your history, your own self-esteem.

"You take the risk and there's a community of risk taking. And that makes a tremendous difference. I'm not put down for my outlandish ideas as a kooky old woman, because there are more people who are saying the same thing. And we can't all be crazy."

Dr. Birren attended the first public meeting of the American Gerontological Society in 1948 and began building the Andrus Gerontology Center in 1965, when the field was a sleepy backwater. "You have to remember," he says, "that North America was settled relatively recently, by young people who had to make their own way. They wanted to get a piece of the land, have a family, settle down, get those security things. We didn't *have* older people. In Holland I visited an old people's home that was founded when the Pilgrims were still in England [before 1620]. They've had institutions for the aged there for over three hundred years, while North America is just coming off its pioneering spirit. We're better at doing than reflecting on the meaning of what we're doing."

"You have been dean of the Andrus School of Gerontology for twenty-two years," I say. "Why have you chosen to retire?"

"I expect to do something else, including writing children's books. I've just written one called *King Later and the Gift of Time*. Because the king is annoyed with time, he says, 'Time, time, I'm always under the pressure of time. People respect time more than they do me and I'm the king.' So he wants to do away with time."

"And you hope to be less pressured now."

"Yes. There again, it goes back to the issue of what's a desirable pattern. More control over the flow of time, more control of our options. That's what we want to do. Erik Erikson had much the same idea of getting it together late in life — he talked about the theme of integration. Carl Jung had the same idea, of putting your life together a bit."

"A revolution is implied if we begin to look at the years after sixty as simply another period of human development when *we* start to define the terms," writes Betty Friedan, years after our tryst on the Santa Monica Freeway. "As we move into our sixties, seventies and eighties, my generation and the generation that follows will show that these can indeed be new, vital years of life, satisfying in ways that we, as pioneers, will define."

At the Blue Heron Center for the Arts, in Washington, Meridel Le Sueur introduces her poem "Rites of Ancient Ripening."

"The title of this comes of the fact that I'm doing away with the word 'age.' Aging? You've heard of that? Aging or age or death? Aging? You never hear of anything in nature aging, or a sunflower saying, 'Well, I'm growing old,' and leaning over and vomiting. You know, it *ripens*, drops its seed, and the cycle goes on. So I'm ripening. For 'age' you can say 'ripening.'"

"Parts of the aging process are scary, of course," writes M.F.K. Fisher, "but the more we know about them, the less they need be. That is why I wish we were more deliberately taught, in early years, to prepare for this condition. It would leave a lot of us free to enjoy the obvious rewards of being old, when the sound of a child's laugh, or the catch of sunlight on a flower petal is as poignant as ever was a girl's voice to an adolescent ear, or the tap of a golf-ball into its cup to a balding banker's."

The current generation of long-lived old people is the first wave of the so-called demographic revolution. And my generation, should the world survive, is next. Many of those now old are developing an existential wisdom that allows them not only to withstand physical disintegration, but to be open to life in a way that their generation is just beginning to find the words to say. In succeeding chapters, I will talk with them, hoping in that way to comprehend the possibilities of my future self.

Already I understand Barbara Myerhoff who worked for years with elderly immigrants from Eastern Europe and then said, "I consider myself very fortunate in having had, through this work, an opportunity to anticipate, rehearse, and contemplate my own future. This has given a temporal integration to my life that seems to me an essential ingredient in the work of maturing. I *see* old people now in a new way, as part of me, not 'they'."

For me, Myerhoff's understanding and acceptance of the continuity of the life cycle is key to retaining a functional sense of self. If we are lucky, we will age. And if we think of old people as "the other," we will not grow up to be ourselves.

The Old Are Us, says professor Ruth Weg's T-shirt.

The portrait of my daughters dances on the wall beside my desk. The clipping of La Pasionaria, ninety-seven, her skull prominent, features androgynous, faces them across the emerging pages of this book. I will try to get from hither to yon — to an understanding of a future where I am able to live fully with love, meaning, and the multitudinous equivalents of my father's little brown spots.

TWO

Mind/Body

I phone my friend Lea who has been sick with a pernicious respiratory illness for over five months. It has kept her from marching. It has kept her from Mary Two-Axe Early's seventieth birthday party. When I spoke to her before my vacation, she sounded uncharacteristically weak and cowed and I have worried about her all the time I was gone. She is, after all, eighty-six.

She answers the phone with the welcoming, energetic voice I am used to and I relax.

"It's so good to hear you better," I say. "You did it."

"Yes, Merrily," she answers, "some people get this and they don't pull through. They go out in a box. I guess I'm not ready yet to go out in a box."

It will take a while before I appreciate Lea's succinct insight into the metaphysics of staying alive. My mother intoned "mens sana in corpore sano" (a healthy mind in a healthy body) as other mothers intone prayers. I trained as a dancer and swam competitively. When I had a problem, my father told me to wash my face in cold water and "take a brisk walk." Good health, it was assumed, was the reward of a disciplined, physical regime.

As the years went by, this simple, familial philosophy was overlaid with existentialism, art, experimentation. I had children and rode on my youth, active but not self-consciously so. I seemed all right. Fine. Until my marriage broke up and I was alone with three small children and no bank account. Reflexly, my father bought me a membership to the Y. Thirty laps in the pool left me feeling better. Everything around me might be falling apart but I could still control the shape of my body. And that's the way I saw it — esthetically, pragmatically. I felt better but I thought it was because I looked better.

Improved nutrition followed lap swimming. Dad's new wife taught herself to cook a low-fat, vegetarian diet, which tasted good, kept Dad's prostate normal, digestive system clear, and blood with a healthy, low level of cholesterol. Dad took over sloganeering where Mom had left off.

By age forty, I was quite sure I knew what was required to stay alive.

I was not surprised to find that most healthy older people eat what Dad eats: large quantities of fresh vegetables and fruits, complex carbohydrates, high fibre, fish, some fowl, a small amount of lean red meat, low fat, very limited sugar, moderate alcohol, no smoking.

I was perfectly comfortable with the many statistical studies showing that

- Physical exercise has a measurable effect on psychological well-being among older adults.
- Physical activity in old age increases life expectancy even into advanced old age.
- Exercise helps people with chronic disease (arthritis, hypertension, heart disease) experience improvements in cardiovascular fitness, strength, and flexibility.
- Even men and women between eighty-seven and ninety-six, on a weight-training regime, can increase their strength by almost 160 percent.

Or, as Dr. Michael Freedman, director of geriatric medicine, New York University Medical Center, says, "Exercise seems to retard what was once thought to be the aging process."

Great — nutrition and exercise. It seems like old-home week to me.

But when I reread the many relevant interview transcripts, I see this mechanistic approach to health just won't do. Too many people I interview mention "attitude." Too many insist on a vital connection between the body and the mind.

As Meridel Le Sueur tells it, "I went to a doctor when I was about seventy and he said, 'Oh, just take these tranquilizers.' I said, 'Are you kidding? I'm going to do my best work between seventy and eighty.' 'Oh,' he said, 'that's ridiculous!' And he gave me the most brilliant description of decay you ever heard. He described sclerosis, and cutting off your wind, and total decay, stroke, and so on. 'Just take these tranquilizers.' I said, 'No, I'm not going to do that. I'm really going to do my best writing before I'm eighty.' In three years he was dead."

I file my background research, put my conditioning on hold, and plan an interview trip to the mecca of contemporary health research — the American West Coast. Between Zen Fast Foods and the smog are the Andrus Center of Gerontology, the Linus Pauling Institute, the UCLA Department of Psychoneuroimmunology — pioneering research centers rigorously documenting what used to be thought of as the mystical, granola fringe of health care — vitamins, minerals, and the mind/body connection.

On the plane, I read early stress research, starting with neuroendocrinologist Hans Selye who in the mid-fifties established the important role of certain stress hormones in the development of nervous breakdown, ulcers, and heart disease. "Each period of stress, especially if it results from frustrating, unsuccessful struggles, leaves some irreversible chemical scars, which accumulate to constitute the signs of tissue aging."

Damaging stress or "distress" produces "insoluble waste products that clog up the machinery of the body until it is no longer usable."

As biologist Ruth Weg describes: "Stressors that are continuous and unabated are translated into an increased flow of certain stress hormones, mainly from the adrenal and some from the pituitary glands. If we're at high levels of stress for continuous periods, these stress hormones will finally do damage to certain very precious tissues like the blood vessels in our heart. And we can't afford that as we grow to be middle-aged because these systems are already less efficient."

The more often we are overstressed, the more likely we are to get sick, warns Selye. The more often we get sick, the more we use up our body's natural resources because "the body's adaptability, or *adaptation energy*, is finite." On the other hand, personally rewarding, enjoyable activity provides us with "the exhilarating feeling of youthful energy even at a very advanced age." That is because pleasure is the counterbalance to stress in our lives, explains Ruth Weg: "It helps us deal with the stresses more effectively by calling out hormones which have a positive effect on our systems. So pleasure should also be a goal in our lives."

In L.A., I drive to the Beverly Hills duplex Ted Allan shares with his daughter. I spot his granddaughter's bags in the living room and Ted typing on a metal table in the bedroom. The kitchen doubles as a feature film office. Three house phones ring. Ted and I talk until 2:00 A.M. my time when I crash on a couch beside an answering machine — "Hi, I'm at Danny's for twelve minutes, then I'll be at Suzie's, we'll be joining Fred, I really need to see you, call me at Ned's, if not at Jed's, we're all going to . . ." I'm in mid-doze when Ted's daughter returns from "the most stressful week" of her life, coughing her lungs out. The next morning, I scurry about, making calls, taking notes, as obtrusive as a windup toy.

By the second day, I too am sick.

Ted, however, is fine, typing on his metal table, stretched out talking on the phone. The world in one room, just like his third-floor walk-up in New York, or any room he inhabits. Given the two major coronaries, the quadruple bypass operation, and this current living situation, he obviously knows something I don't.

"After my heart attack, I realized the attack was not only due to my fatted arteries but also to an incredible repressed rage that I didn't know how to cope with. A physician in London taught me a mild form of self-hypnosis akin to some of the meditative procedures I had tried. In meditating one repeats certain sounds like 'Ommm, ommm, ommm,' breathing in and out deeply and rhythmically. But I found this difficult. This doctor taught me to send my mind to the various parts of my body — beginning with my toes — ordering my toes and the muscles in my toes to relax, then the soles of my feet to relax, then my heels, my ankles, my calves, knees, thighs, groin, buttocks, pubic area, lower intestine, higher intestine, diaphragm, chest, heart. I have worked on this and now I talk to my heart — 'goodheart, sweetheart, greatheart' — telling it I like it and I'm very pleased that even though I have abused it and it has suffered, it is now trying to keep me going.

"Relaxing myself from toe to scalp puts me into a mild self-hypnosis. And then I say, 'Every day, in every way, I'm getting better.' In other words, I instruct the area of my mind that one usually reaches only in dreams. I tell it I'm better. And my body behaves better. My sclerosis gets less. My arteries are more open.

"I do this when I have the slightest evidence of angina, of the tightening of the arteries and not enough oxygen and blood coming to my heart, which happens when I am tense. I lie down and do this self-hypnosis or listen to a relaxation tape, and within minutes, the chest pressure goes. By releasing me and relieving me of the stresses around me, it makes me healthier. I feel better for it. I am convinced that we contribute to our illnesses with the stress, the anxiety, the rage."

I snake up Mulholland Drive to a peak overlooking the canyons of the Hollywood Hills. Ted has told me how positive emotions can affect health and help fight back disease. I'm now on my way to find out more about how the body can affect the mind. I call to say I will be fifteen minutes late, and when I arrive, Laura Huxley, seventy-eight, greets me wearing an Italian tracksuit, looking like she's just got off the dance floor. I comment on her high spirits and she points to the treadmill in the entrance hall.

"In the fifteen minutes you were late, I could run a mile. It was wonderful. And you know how it is when you run: ten minutes after, you're still running."

She invites me into a high-ceilinged, windowed sitting room with a desk in one corner and the out-of-favor ski and rowing machines in the other. The treadmill faces a TV so Laura can walk or run as she watches, moving her arms and upper body to stretch her torso at the same time.

Four years ago, when I was here, I studied her slim, muscular back as she stood, hands on hips, poised and lithe as an athletic young boy. I've returned knowing that for over thirty years, since she married Aldous Huxley in 1956, she's been practising methods of body work I've only read about. Both she and he, by different paths, came to Aldous's conclusion that "the life-problems of a multiple amphibian are many faceted and, if they are to be solved, must be attacked simultaneously from many different angles." They worked with pioneering mind/body teachers such as the late F.M. Alexander and Moshe Feldenkrais, whose schools continue to train students throughout the world. They studied yoga and autosuggestion and asked themselves how much the body affects the mind and how much the mind affects the body. In the beginning of "Recipes for Living and Loving," written when she was a successful therapist, Laura suggests people imagine themselves to be "a diamond . . . each recipe that you experience completely will clear one or more facets of the diamond and let more and more light shine through the others. The difference between being merely not dead and fully alive is the difference between being opaque and being translucent."

Laura leans forward, compelling in her attention. I tell her I've come to learn how she takes care of herself.

She answers with a sweep of her hand. "So many different ways. I've been a vegetarian for decades, but in the last two years I have realized the more things I eliminate from my diet, the better it is."

She describes her simple diet and then says, "And, of course, I have to move. Sometimes I have to do it when I really don't want to start. I say, 'I'm tired, I have to lie down.' But, instead of lying down, I try to just run five minutes on the walker or go up and down the steps — something strenuous and quick that doesn't require much awareness. It pushes and my energy goes up by itself."

"Anything else?" I ask, expecting a discussion of alternative body work.

"I try not to let negative emotions accumulate. Because it is this unconscious pain which is tucked away that does tricks to our health. All of a sudden we are sick and it's difficult to know why. I think it saps the immune system. Life pain. I had proof of that in '75, after a period of great difficulty, when I got a grave case of herpes zoster, a neurological illness, usually called shingles. And I know that it was just that the nerves couldn't take it anymore and so it burst into this illness. Of course, there is always the combination of stress and picking up a bacteria, or some germ. But I might have picked it up fifty times before and rejected it. Sometimes we are able to reject it and sometimes we cannot do it anymore and they get us."

I prod Laura, telling her I know about walking, running, swimming, stretching, but I don't know about the alternate methods of body work she uses. I remind her that on my last visit, she had hurt her knee in a fall, and instead of doctors and X-rays she had called her Rolfer.

"He came and it was just a question of making a little adjustment, a little space in the knee, nothing was broken," she recalls. "You see, there is something around our body called *fascia*, which is like a bandage that keeps the muscles together. When a child falls, when one has little accidents, the body naturally tries to compensate by going away from the pain. And then the fascia holds the body in this position which is not quite equilibrated. Then, even if you want to correct your body, it's difficult because it has a bandage around it. So Rolfers have to do some heavy massage, which is sometimes painful, to give space again. They try to make space between the muscles, to loosen up the fascia, so the body can be made more free."

"This is after an accident?"

"Yes. But even for breathing. Breathing should go down the back and to the stomach. But most of us don't do that. Most of the time we breathe from our chest. So, the Rolfers try to make you a space in the ribs, so you breathe much deeper. They massage between the ribs, they massage all over the body beginning with the feet . . ."

Laura uses Rolfing techniques when she needs it, and Feldenkrais, Alexander, yoga, and T'ai Chi, as well. She doesn't do each one every day, but they are methods of body work she can call on when she wants a particular experience. In fact, a man who does Alexander, a friend, is due that evening for a session.

"Alexander was an Australian actor who would get very emotional and lose his voice when he had to go on stage," she recalls. "He went to all the doctors and nothing worked, so he began to study himself in front of a mirror. He noticed that when he spoke with passion, he made a little movement in the head and then would come the sore throat. He studied for fifteen years, and according to him, the most important thing is the relationship between the head, the neck, and the trunk.

"Alexander practitioners hardly touch you, just a little, subtly, here and there until you become aware of what you're doing and what not to do. It is more a study in consciousness than a physical thing in that you have to stop what is habitual and permit the natural thing to come. For example, if we are anxious, we tighten up and sometimes we don't untighten. If we are scared, we hunch up our shoulders. So the whole body, particularly the whole spine, is influenced. There is so much backache now in our culture, it is an epidemic.

"Alexander teaches you a posture where first of all I remember this kind of going forward and up. According to Aldous, the Alexander system changed his life in the sense that he was very shy and was stooping because he was so tall. John Dewey did it, Bernard Shaw, all these people who were into consciousness were the ones that sustained and supported F.M. Alexander. When I first did it, I was in a specially bad situation having played and practised the violin six hours a day for twenty-five years. I was totally twisted, holding my violin no matter where I was. I don't need it so much now, but I have a lesson once in a while to make me aware again . . ."

As she gets older, Laura does even more body work. She uses the methods she described, as well as Feldenkrais, "which puts your body in a more straight line situation"; yoga, "which goes to the mind though the body"; and T'ai Chi, "which gives you an equilibrium — a contact with the earth and also a feeling of the above, so you feel between heaven and earth."

"Why do you want to do these things?"

"Because as we get older, the body needs rituals more and more to better use all the resources possible. When I am strong enough, I try to keep my body in a way where at least that part is taken care of, and when that is taken care of it's very reassuring. Because otherwise, sometimes, there is this tiredness which is like death. You feel, 'I cannot think, I cannot move.' Sometimes I cannot do anything and, then, as soon as I start a little bit, then things begin to move again. Some people maybe take care of their mind first; I think I begin first taking care of my body and then my mind can take care of the problems, whatever they are, much better. And there is enjoyment in some of this, and if it's enjoyable, it's good. Then, the earth just gently pushes me to the next step and gravity, instead of pulling me down, sustains me."

I ask Laura if she has much to do with doctors and she says she's afraid of doctors. "I'm afraid to be sick and be in the hands of a doctor without someone else who is intelligent and knows my feelings watching out for me, since if I am sick I cannot watch."

"So you try alternate ways of healing."

"All the things that I tell you, they're all things to avoid doctors. I hear so many stories from my friends: they go to doctors and the doctors give them pills and the pills make them sick. Instead, if they would do some of these things — there are so many possibilities . . . All these things are a little bit different. And when we do many things in our body we see what an incredible universe the body is. Merely doing things like this, we get to know that there is always something else."

I leave smiling. I'm pleased to have met a seventy-eight-year-old who can put her foot behind her ear and I'm happy to know about a whole new world of body work. I career down Mulholland, along Pico, to Ted's couch and another sleep punctuated by the hoots and calls of Beverly Hills teenagers searching for a place to alight. The next morning, despite my best intentions and more vitamin C, my throat hurts and I find myself in a minor panic — tired, pressured, worried that I will not be able to go to Palo Alto to interview Dr. Linus Pauling, which has been arranged for months, for which I have come so far, at great expense, with such meticulous prepreparation, HELP!

I get up, eat — trying not to use dishes with germs, trying not to breathe where anyone has coughed — and drive my Rent-a-Wreck to the ocean, where a friend gives me the keys to an empty apartment for a whole blessed weekend. I bathe, stretch, and breathe deeply and rhythmically, in and out, until I fall peacefully asleep.

The next day I am better. And very much looking forward to going to UCLA to see Dr. James Birren, Monday, 8:00 A.M., the only time he can fit me in.

I arrive a little before eight to collect Dr. Birren's eight-page curriculum vitae and his twenty-six-page list of publications. Birren was the founding director and dean of the state-of-the-art Andrus Gerontology Center at the University of Southern California. His "retirement" from Andrus, at seventy, was merely a change of venues to direct a new center of gerontological research at UCLA.

Birren's secretary hands me a report from a conference in which frail elderly people in a nursing home count privacy — not food, family, or nursing care — of prime importance. I start to tell her how much I empathize when I see a spare, craggy-faced man with a shock of white hair striding toward us. Birren lopes in, shakes my hands, gives his secretary notes, turns on the heater, bustles about, and seems a bit odd until I learn that he's taken the stairs three at a time and is, like Laura Huxley, still running.

When we sit, I tell Dr. Birren I am inundated by fact and fancy about health. He confesses he is too. Over the weekend he discussed approaches to health with an old friend who had been told that apple cider vinegar and honey, drunk twice a day, would relieve his terrible arthritis. His friend tried it and was able to walk and play golf once a week, attributing his relief to the new remedy.

"Whether it's true or not I don't know," admits Birren. "There is a great deal of struggling to get an objective handle on health and what to do about it."

"It's hard to work one's way through it," I agree. "When I heard about UCLA's Department of Psychoneuroimmunology, I didn't know how to pronounce it, let alone what it was . . ."

Birren nods. "When I was in the navy in World War II, I worked on motion sickness, then thought to be primarily a psychological affliction — a fear of death at sea that made people ill. As we looked at it more, we discovered that horses and dogs also get sick: if you put a dog in a swing and swing him, he will get sick, just like many a young child. So, where's the fear? We began to realize that if fear were there, it would modulate a basic mechanism. But the basic mechanism was a neurological response to conflicting sensory input. We went all the way, then, from a view that it was primarily psychogenic to one that it was completely physiogenic.

"Now we recognize that things can have a physical cause and yet be manipulated by psychological factors. Or be primarily psychological in nature. The epidemiologists in Sweden have done an excellent job of examining psychological effects by looking at bereavement. They studied every death in Sweden for a five-year period to look at the survival of the spouse. Death of the spouse will accelerate death rates in men 46 percent during the first six months following the death — a dramatic increase in death rate, almost double. And it goes up 22 percent in women. So you are getting a real bereavement effect.

"It was very difficult for the older generation of scientists to accept that you could initiate physiological events with psychological factors. Now I think we accept that. There are issues of mixed causality. So if I have hypertension, say, I expect some gain by reducing my salt intake and some gain from relaxation therapy. There are levels of influence, and that thought is rather new. And now with new studies on the nervous system and the neuropeptides [hormone-like substances, produced by neurons and other cells in the body, which carry messages to the brain and throughout the body to control a wide variety of bodily functions], we realize it's just not a telephone line from A to B. There are modulators of the messages, neurotransmitter messages, that enhance, or detract, or inhibit, or facilitate. So now you think of all these different modulators. And it's perhaps multiple causation you believe in with a hierarchy from major to minor causes."

I thank Dr. Birren and I tell him I am going to see Linus Pauling, who is eighty-nine years old and is busy studying crystals, atomic nuclei, and the methodology of biostatistical analysis. I ask Birren if there is anything he would like me to ask Pauling.

"Yes," says Birren. "Ask him how his head works at this age. Is there any difference in his attack on problems?"

I fly to San Francisco where I am met by Sophie and Mitch Van Bourg, friends my father has made, on holiday, in Mexico. The Van Bourgs take me to the Planetree Health Resource Center, a large book-lined room where people can order or find medical texts, articles, bibliographies, treatment options, and support groups for any illness. An older woman double-checks her husband's treatment — "It makes me feel better to know exactly what's going on." An older man researches his medication — "To know what I'm putting in my body for my own self-confidence."

"Empowerment," explains Sophie, the mental health consultant: "Good medicine now is open to giving people the power to take care of themselves. It's a way of getting your attitude healthy, to think that you are really anxious to survive and are willing to try whatever people have found to be helpful to the body — visualization, imagery, relaxation, whatever. That's hope. Hope has to do with feeling you have some power to do something about what's bad. And there's proof that people who are hopeful live longer."

What will Linus Pauling make of this?

Mitch drives me to Palo Alto, to the large warehouse building on which is written Linus Pauling Institute of Science and Medicine. Founded in 1973 to investigate the importance of the nutritional approach to health problems, the institute is a non-profit research organization with about twenty Ph.D.s or M.D.s and fifteen research support staff.

The atmosphere is friendly but I am nervous. I have heard about Dr. Pauling since I was a teenager. When the hydrogen bomb tests began in the early fifties, the Atomic Energy Commission issued reassurring public statements: no abnormal incidence of birth defects in Hiroshima, vigorous, hardy fruit flies raised in radioactive containers . . . . My mother, a biochemist and a peace activist, didn't buy this whitewash of atmospheric nuclear testing. What she believed instead, and what motivated her to action, were the urgent warnings of Dr. Linus Pauling, Nobel laureate in chemistry, 1954. In Quebec, in the fifties, she could be jailed for handing out leaflets and she knew that he, too, was threatened — his passport restricted, called before the Internal Security Subcommittee of the U.S. Senate in 1955 and again in 1960, threatened with jail for refusing to reveal names of those who helped him collect signatures for his 1957 appeal to end nuclear testing, and tarred with McCarthyite opprobrium that affected his family and friends.

In 1963, on the same day the American/Soviet ban on atmospheric testing went into effect, Dr. Pauling was awarded the 1962 Nobel Peace Prize and my mother celebrated. It vindicated him and it vindicated her. In Pauling's words, "It made working for peace respectable." Like F.G. Banting, one of the discoverers of insulin, and Dr. Norman Bethune, who developed mobile blood transfusion units, Linus Pauling was one of my mother's heroes.

I meet Dorothy Munro who has been most affable trying to fit me into Dr. Pauling's busy schedule of traveling, administering the institute, and thinking and writing, at his ranch in Big Sur. I ask for a recent example of Dr. Pauling's publications and Mrs. Munro gives me: "Icosahedral and decagonal quasicrystals of intermetallic compounds are multiple twins of cubic or ortho-rhombic crystals composed of very large atomic complexes with icosahedral point-group symmetry in cubic close packing or body-centered packing: Structure of decagonal Al_6Pd."

I am saved from comment by the jaunty figure of eighty-nine-year-old Dr. Pauling, six feet tall, carrying a large box in one arm and waving with the other.

We sit beside his large, littered desk, near a wall-sized black-board covered with chemical hieroglyphics. I tell him almost everyone I know in Montreal is taking vitamin C to ward off winter colds. "Yes, even the government says a third of Americans take vitamins regularly and probably a half take vita-min C," he concurs, citing his source, the tenth edition of the RDA (Recommended Dietary Allowance). The day before, in Washington, he tells me, someone congratulated him because progress in the discussion of the role of micronutrients was being made with the people from the National Cancer Institute, the Food and Drug Administration, and the Center for Disease Control, and it wouldn't have been possible if he hadn't been pushing it.

"I have sort of put my reputation on the pan of the balance."

"You've always done that," I say, thinking of the twenties when classical chemists resisted his use of quantum physics in chemistry, and the fifties when he campaigned against weapons testing, and now, when his controversial premise that to be in optimum health we need larger supplements of specific vitamins challenges the RDA set by the National Research Council and the National Academy of Sciences.

I am trying to suss out this ruddy, fit, legendary figure, ready to ask more about vitamins, when Dr. Pauling provides an opening to what will be a much more fascinating conversation.

"I spend quite a lot of my time working on vitamins in rela-tion to disease and things of that sort, although I don't get so much pleasure out of it in an intellectual sort of way as I do from working on a more basic kind of problem.

"What I've enjoyed all my life is discovering things and solv-ing problems. The paper I gave Mrs. Munro, I've been working on several years, trying to solve to my satisfaction a question on the properties of atomic nuclei. There are fifteen hundred different atomic nuclei, not very many considering there are ten million chemical compounds, made up of a hundred and six different elements. A great amount of information has been gathered about the properties of atomic nuclei. In fact, if you take one nucleus, such as uranium 234, and hit it with a fast-moving electron, or something with very high energy, you can excite it to an excited state and there are an infinite number of excited states. There may be thirty, or forty, or fifty low-flying excited states. And they have been classified into bands of excited states that are clearly related to one another. So this paper is about the ground-state bands of the nuclei."

I don't know my ass from an atom but obviously not only the atomic nuclei are excited.

"Why do you want to write this paper?"

"See, all my life I've wanted to understand things," Pauling says. "And when I got old enough I realized that you could do this to discover something new. That's what I like. I enjoy understanding things. I enjoy reading *Nature* and *Science* and *The American Scientists* and *The Physical Review*. I don't read the chemistry literature anymore. Now I read the physics literature and the crystallographic literature."

"Dr. Birren wondered if you find your head works differently at this age than it did in your sixties, or your seventies?"

"I think my retrieval time has lengthened and this shows up in the well-known difficulty that older people have in recalling personal names, although, in general, my recall seems to be pretty good."

"I think he wanted to know if your attack on problems is any different."

"It may be quantitatively but not qualitatively. I was always catholic in my interests, carrying over my knowledge from one field of science to another. All my life I have done this. As time has gone by, my knowledge has deepened and broadened, and I have continued to apply knowledge that I have in one field of science and medicine to another. I think I have always had a sort of gift for coordinating knowledge from different sources and using all of that background of knowledge in attacking problems."

"There's the popular idea that as you get older you're intellectually less capable."

"Well, I think I can move along for two reasons: my background is greater than it ever was before, and I have a good memory. I know a lot and I'm able to make cross-connections perhaps just as well as ever in my life. I've published about nine hundred scientific papers, and except during the Second World War, I just moved along pretty constantly — but going up. I publish about twice as many papers a year now as in my early years.

"And I enjoy, more than anything else now, finding the answer to scientific questions. I enjoy this feeling I remember having in 1931 when I told John Slater [head of the physics department at MIT] how pleased I was that I knew the structure of a particular mineral and nobody else in the world knew what this structure was and they wouldn't know until I told them.

"So, I like to make discoveries. I like to feel that I am adding to the background of knowledge and adding to the amount of understanding of the universe that we have. I feel sorry for people who don't have some background in science because they can't have the pleasure of appreciating the wonder and marvel of the discoveries that the scientists keep making. I keep being astonished at these discoveries and what an astonishing place the universe is."

"Is this what you like best?"

"Yes. I still spend perhaps half my time doing some things as a matter of conscience. But the biochemical and medical stuff bores me. Just reading scientific literature excites me. And when I discover something myself it excites me even more."

Optimal Experience, edited by Mihaly and Isabella Csikszentmihalyi, offers an insight into Dr. Pauling's ongoing mental high. From cross-cultural studies, the authors posit an intrinsically rewarding state of consciousness called "flow." It is characterized by intense involvement, clarity of goals, loss of a sense of time, lack of self-consciousness, transcendence of a sense of self. This is what I experience when I'm writing well. What Japanese motorcycle youths experience during the motorcycle run — *medatsu* — when their motorcycles rumble in unison. What old Korean women report when they read the Bible, knit, or cook an elaborate dinner. "Flow" is a useful concept for the mental exhilaration that keeps the mind alive.

"When you talk about health, you usually talk about vitamins," I say to Dr. Pauling. "But as we speak, it seems clear to me that your curiosity and the fun you have with your work are a basic psychological part of your health."

At first he doesn't know what I mean. He tells me about his revelation that vitamins weren't "just drugs" because they have no toxicity, whereas drugs are given to people in amounts close to the lethal level and too much can kill you. "And I thought if the RDA is the amount that keeps you from dying from scurvy or beriberi, how much does it take to be in the best of health?"

I try again.

"Isn't it possible that someone might take all the vitamins but not have your love of life? Then they might not stay alive. Don't both the mind and the body have an effect on health?"

"Yes. But I wrote to some doctors in Australia who had published a paper on the mortality of surviving spouses — they die faster. And I asked, 'Did you measure the amount of vitamin C in the blood?' because it's known that severe mental stress in humans causes the vitamin C level to drop and that'll kill people."

"Because of who you are, you don't understand that some people don't have a reason to live."

"Yes. Well, I know. If I were a businessman and forced to retire at age sixty-five, or seventy, I don't know what I would do, what interest in life I would have. I know that I'm fortunate in various ways. I'm particularly fortunate in being a theoretical physicist, theoretical chemist, theoretical crystallographer, even in a sense a theoretical biologist and theoretical physician."

And that's as much of a concession as I'll get from Dr. Pauling.

Yet his animated ode to his mental life tells me something new about his remarkable health. Dr. Pauling uses micronutrients, but he also nourishes his mind and his immune system with the joy of scientific work.

"More than anything else," he says, "I enjoy understanding things."

Norman Cousins wrote about the effect of the mind on the body but took vitamin C to cure illness. Laura Huxley works first on her body but suggests children learn to meditate. Dr. Pauling feeds his body and also his mind. Mind/body — it's merely a matter of emphasis.

Back home, I get my thoughts in order and call Ted in L.A. A couple of weeks ago he read me something that made him as happy as scientific work makes Linus Pauling.

"Where was that from, what you read?" I ask.

"You mean," he declaims:

> *O for a Muse of fire, that would ascend*
> *The brightest heaven of invention*
> *A kingdom for a stage, princes to act,*
> *And monarchs to behold the swelling scene!*

He says he thinks it is from the prologue to *Henry V*. I remember other readings, Nabokov's *Lectures on Literature*, I think, and since I am wrapping up with examples of Ted's particular flow state, I ask what other readings inspire him.

"Are you kidding," he rebukes, "you're interviewing me now. It's not a good time. I'm finishing the script for 'Gena' and it's going like a house on fire."

It's time for me to see Lea, a most astounding example of health and vigor who, like Ted, is smack-dab in the world — which many agree is a prime requirement for the prevention of premature aging. At eighty-six, Lea's voice is full to bursting, she walks at a brisk pace, and when she hugs you to her, you feel her taut, wiry strength. When she is not with family, friends, Voice of Women colleagues, union activists, anti-apartheid activists, native women, Latin American women, filmmakers, marchers, writers, I visit her small apartment and she seats me in a stuffed rocking chair and moves her small, straight-backed wood chair into the center of the room, to face me.

In all the years I've known Lea, I've never asked her how she manages to be so vital. Yet, she is my model and knowing her makes aging better. I have seen Lea, arms linked with those of other younger women, march through driving snow at twenty degrees below zero, to protest American cruise missiles in Canada. Last year, when she fell, she held her protruding bone while she phoned the janitor. And four months later we were shopping at an outdoor vegetable market.

Most incredible of all, I have seen Lea recover from the death of loved ones.

How does she do it?

I suspect that if I ask Lea how she *feels*, it will sound like a whine to her. So, I ask her first about the diet she has been following for forty years.

"What do I have in the morning?" she replies. "Three cups: one with prunes, prune juice and hot water; one with boiled water and half a lemon pressed; and a third of plain hot water. After that, I cook cereal — millet, wheat kernels, oatmeal, old-fashioned oatmeal. I get it at the health store, each grain is a grain, and I cook it slowly, sometimes in skim milk, mostly in boiled water. And on top of that, I'll put four heaping spoons of bran and five heaping spoons of wheat germ. Then I'll have skimmed milk — my mother used to call it the *bloyeh millech*, the blue milk — and a bowl of yogurt with banana, cantaloupe, I'll have that. And then I'll have ersatz coffee, which is not coffee, with skim milk in it, and two slices of good whole wheat bread without molasses. And half a grapefruit. This is my breakfast. So, when it comes to lunch time, I'm not hungry. Possibly I'll have some fruit."

"This is a feast."

"And that is why I can go and have this energy. Because it's two-thirds of my meal for the day. If I'm out picketing during the day and it's cold or it's a nasty day, I may have a bowl of soup, my own soup, barley, lentils, potatoes, celery, carrots. I make a good, thick soup."

"What's your stock?"

"Chicken, beef, veal, and a good bone."

"Do you eat meat?"

"I don't go for red meat. I'll eat liver, once a week. I don't eat too much, just a small amount, with vegetables. I have a lot of vegetables. And green pepper and carrots and celery and lettuce and I always have a salad. Always have a salad."

"Are the vegetables fresh?"

"Oh yes. I don't have canned goods here. Never did. Mama didn't either. Just once in a great while she'd be short of something and she'd go to the pantry. But otherwise, I don't. Because when I read what's in it, there's everything in there but dirty socks."

"No red meat, no canned stuff. Chicken?"

"Chicken, and lots of fish. I eat fish. I go to my lovely Greek fish store on Victoria Avenue and I'm very fussy on fresh fish."

"How do you make it?"

"I poach it. I must tell you I had to learn to cook at the age of seventy when Mama died. So I'm not a fancy cook, you should excuse me. Sometimes I just have a salad, because I'm not that hungry, I haven't used up all that energy."

"How about fat?"

"I don't have fat. Take, for example, chicken. I just pull all the skin and fat off before I cook it with the vegetables, so I don't have any of that stuff. Sometimes I'll have butter, I get the unsalted butter, but I don't have much of it. I like my bread, for example, with my yogurt."

"How about sugar?"

"I don't even have it here."

"Jam?"

"No. I don't have jam. I don't feel I need it. I get enough sweets in the fruits, it's there, all the fruits have sweetness in them. So there's salt and sweet in the food one eats."

"Salt?"

"Very seldom. Even when I'm cooking I just use a little bit."

"It's a disciplined diet."

"Well, my dear, it's working for me."

Lea is five feet two inches and about a hundred pounds. Her diet keeps her digestive system uncluttered, her heart and arteries unclogged, and her body well nourished. Like all long-lived people, irrespective of culture or diet, her caloric intake is a maximum of 1,200 to 1,900 calories a day, compared to the average Canadian intake of 2,650 calories a day and the average American intake of 2,800 to 3,000. Judging by her energy, actual physical stamina, and strength, it is certainly working for her.

Lea also exercises every morning — stretching her neck, arms, shoulders, legs, thighs — breathing rhythmically in and out, as she lifts, circles, raises, bends for twenty minutes. She does some of the exercises, such as lifting her legs and the top part of her body, in the bath.

"In a tub of water, it's wonderful. For people unused to exercise, who find it difficult, in the bath, in the water, it's the easiest thing."

One exercise involves circling her arms behind her back as far as they will go. "I used to have bursitis but I don't have bursitis now because I do my exercise."

"So, in effect, you move every joint," I say.

"Oh yes. Especially people of my age, my dear. How are we going to keep our bodies limber? You've got to do this and you've got to walk. Not drag along, that's not walking. Walking means you walk, brisk, your whole body's in movement.

"You've got to be disciplined. Nothing comes easy in life. You've got a choice: to be healthy and *do the things you want to do*, or to be unhealthy and say, 'If only I could . . .' Even up to eighty, I could go full-speed ahead and not have to keep as close touch with myself. After eighty, physically, it's not so easy. But I want to do many of the things I did. And I do. I'm not giving up. If I had to come home and lie down and not feel like anything, well, my God, I'd rather take eight grams of strychnine and be done with it."

I think of my friend's father, Craig, trying to come to terms with a major illness. Craig, eighty-two, has never had a major illness, nor has he ever taken responsibility for his own health. He knows nothing about nutrition, doesn't exercise, and has always followed doctor's orders without understanding what was happening to his body. Now he has symptoms of major disintegration. It is possible that he will never again walk with ease. He has trouble feeding himself. But he has no experience of fighting to make himself feel better. The loss of autonomy makes him feel embarrassed, angry, no good for anything. "No one is helping me," he says. When his son is not there to connect him to the world, he is confused and disoriented. Despairing, he says his life is over.

I think of Ted who has been as sick or sicker but has never *felt* this bad.

While Craig is reeling, Ted, with 40 percent heart capacity, is in New York assisting at rehearsals of his Zen Buddhist Hebrew musical *Chu Chem*, climbing four flights of stairs to his fourth-floor walk-up, blocking out the screaming sirens with his wave machine. He has had an eventful year, meeting with people to produce his plays, writing a four-hour miniseries, fighting to protect his script *Bethune* from "the star trying to hijack the movie." A headline about him reads:

WRITER'S CAREER HITS HIGH NOTE AS FILM WRAPS, MUSICAL OPENS.
Ted Allan, the indefatigable 72-year-old Canadian playwright, novel-

ist, Hollywood screenwriter and official biographer of Dr. Norman Bethune, has been getting his share of good tidings lately . . .

Ted complains that the dancers kiss him like a grandpa but says, "My angina is gone. What everybody with angina needs is a hit play." I try to tease him about being indefatigable but I can't pronounce the word. "Indefuckanikable," he says, "the indefuckanikable Mr. Allan."

Researchers who have studied age and coping mechanisms claim that the decisive factor in coping with stress is the individual's appraisal of the event, rather than any purely objective feature. Kivnick and the Eriksons describe a woman with one leg amputated, confined to a wheelchair, with a chronic heart condition. She has had four major surgeries, is legally blind, her hearing is going, and she may soon lose her second leg to surgery. Although she knows she cannot live on her own, she does not like being dependent, so she does as much herself as possible. She engages her companions in conversation, listens omnivorously to talking books, and acts on impulse in the kitchen. "If I want to bake a cake during the day, I just do it. I get tired, reaching up to the counter from my wheelchair, but I can do it if I take my time and put my mind to it." She carries a portable radio with her at all times. "I try to keep knowing about the world. I try to get as much out of life as I can."

Maggie Kuhn, eighty, leader of the activist Gray Panthers, says, "Even in our weakness and our sickness and disabilities, we have strength." She gives the example of an older woman with lupus, legs bleeding and ulcerated, who testified at the mass transport hearings in Philadelphia. "She came with all her baggage, including a wooden box that was the exact height of the first step on the buses in Philadelphia. And she demonstrated very dramatically how it was impossible, in her condition, to get on the bus. She could not lift her foot to that first step. Nobody forgot that testimony."

I think of Ted, of the blind woman in the wheelchair, of the woman with lupus, of Craig, and it is clear that the degree to which an incapacitated person remains part of the world is not related simply to the degree of incapacity. Even normal aging demands what psychologist Alex Comfort calls "fortitude." Not denial. Or optimistic overcompensation. But the ability to take life by the throat. And an active commitment to staying alive. Ted takes his pills, rubs on his ointment, recovers from a quadruple bypass — "I can't die yet, I haven't finished the rewrite." Barbara Tymbios, weak, too thin, a spot on her lung, says she has to get her health back — "I have my sister Rebecca whom I have to take care of."

Writer Florida Scott-Maxwell, at eighty-two, after a major operation, writes: "The crucial task of age is balance, a veritable tightrope of balance; keeping just well enough, just brave enough, just gay and interested and starkly honest enough to remain a sentient human being."

M.F.K. Fisher sits in her hydraulic chair, recovering from the excruciating displacement of her titanium hip. It dislocated when she bent over and twisted to feed the cats. "I just went up in the air and fell down on the floor. My foot was straight up in the air. It was ghastly. I was appalled at the noise I was making. I was groaning and screaming and I couldn't help it at all." Mary Frances, as she prefers to be called, uses a high-tech pincher to pick up objects — "anything, including pills" — her arthritic fingers can't grasp. Her Stratolounger unfolds her and deposits her, standing, on her feet. A walker or cane supports her. She has a lift on her toilet seat, a bathtub with handles, an electronic pager around her neck, which connects her through the phone line to the hospital. If she beeps five times, the hospital calls back. If there is no response, they send the firemen. Once a week a young man takes her to do her outside chores. Since she can no longer type or write longhand because of the nerve degeneration from Parkinson's, she has made herself learn to dictate and a neighborhood couple serve as her amanuenses. "They say when I speak I'm beginning to sound like me now."

For Mary Frances, aging is "a very painful, terrible process, a physical condition." For over fifty years, she has carried with her the painting of Ursula von Ott used on the cover of *Sister Age*, meditating on it as Buddhists meditate on a tanka. Ursula is her sister and her teacher, representing "the implacable strength of the old." And yet, Mary Frances's company is playful, witty, fun.

"There are many things I don't like about growing older, mostly physical. Mentally, I think it's great. I never thought I'd have as much pure enjoyment of life. Thinking and talking and so on as I do now. Mentally, I've got so much stored up I feel too full. I feel almost fat with all the things I want to say and know I never will. I won't. I feel very fatalistic, you know. What is, is. What will be, will be."

Mary Frances can't read now and has to have an eye operation.

"I can't imagine not being able to read. Yet, of course I probably will be blind if I live long enough. If I live very much longer, the doctors say I have to have an artificial knee in this leg. But I'm going to fool them, I think."

"How?"

"By not living that long or by getting along with what I have."

"How prepared are you to do all these things?"

"I will do anything to live and not suffer. You get used to pain, of course I think if some of the little twinges I have now had happened to me when I was younger, I would have been sure I was dying right then. You just kind of grit your teeth, I think."

"Is there a point where it isn't worth it anymore?"

"I don't think you ever know the threshold of another person's inner anguish that almost any sensitive person feels now and then about life and death. A little itch or burn that suddenly starts hurting and you think, This has got to stop, so you hit it or scratch it or something and it stops. Now I guess some people do that with their lives. I don't think it's a good idea, but sometimes it's better than not."

"It's not something you're going to do?"

"I'm not going to kill myself. But I think I'm strong enough to die very soon anyway if I knew I was going to die a nasty death. I really would prefer to die clearheaded and with all my wits about me. But I'm quite prepared anytime because everything is so unexpected. It is like playing Russian roulette. Will I be alive tomorrow? It's a wonderful feeling."

"What part of it is wonderful?"

"Well, some people like the merry-go-rounds, I guess, and some don't. I find it quite a game, and as you get older you have to have little games, I think."

"You find it exhilarating?"

"Yes, I do. I'm curious. Very curious. I'm curious about what's next."

Florida Scott-Maxwell is one of few very old people to write about the existential challenge of old age. In her eighty-third year, living alone in a London flat, recovering from a serious operation, having seen her much-loved grandchildren leave for Australia, she writes: "We who are old know that age is more than a disability. It is an intense and varied experience, almost beyond our capacity at times, but something to be carried high. If it is a long defeat it is also a victory, meaningful for the initiates of time, if not for those who have come less far."

Mrs. Topham worked hard with her husband Tom when he was sick. And it was very sad for her because she knew he was not going to get better. She dressed him, supported him in and out of bed, put aluminum ladders with boards on the stairs, and held, pushed, hauled his wheelchair up and down. She didn't feel that she was wonderful, as people said, but that "it's Tom keeping going really, he doesn't give up." She felt that when it was over, "I'm going to be here and all right still, but it's Tom is not, he's not going to come out of it okay." So she really tried to do her best for him.

Tom's deterioration continued and was compounded by a lack of oxygen to the brain during a double-amputation operation which "you know, fuzzed him a bit." And then he had a cardiac arrest.

"I took him into the hospital and they put tubes and this and that in him and it was awful. I said to them in the intensive care, I said, 'What are you doing?' And they said, 'Well, we're trying to save his life.' And I said, 'Well, what for?' because it was obviously for nothing and they did save his life and he lived for a year after that. And, Merrily, he was such a man that he read all the time, he wrote, he was interested in everything, and that last year he didn't read a page, he didn't write anything, he just existed, you know, and that was a terrible thing to do to people."

Margaret Laurence, creator of the authoritarian, proud, battling old woman, Hagar, in *The Stone Angel*, first thought the theme of her book was "the nature of freedom" and later realized that this was only partially true. As in the lives of many old people, the nature of freedom is part and parcel of "survival, the attempt of the personality to survive with some dignity . . ."

Mrs. Topham never wants to be put on life support.

Lea, watching her eighty-four-year-old sister, Annie, die painfully of hip cancer, says, "The doctors say she might get some relief if they amputate her leg. Like having a cup of tea. She knows they can't do anything for her, and what she wants them to do, they won't. She's had a wonderful life. She wants them to give her a pill and let her go quietly, with dignity."

Maggie Kuhn has very little time in her busy schedule for reflection. But when she can sit on the back porch or play with the cats, she sometimes thinks about the deterioration of the retina in her eyes and the great difficulty she has at times in seeing. "Now, the deterioration is slow, but if I live and go blind, life will be very different. So, I sometimes think about that and I don't torture myself with it, but I think about it — and what adjustments can I make. But in most instances I will say, well, I think I'll manage to stay alive as long as I have sight. And then take it from there."

"You think life would not be fulfilling enough?"

"Very different without sight. It really would, although the powers of compensation that all of us have are enormous, I've seen that."

"What you're saying is that you reserve the right to end life for yourself if it ceases to fulfill . . ."

"Right. I had some delightful conversations with B.F. Skinner, the psychologist, around the edges of that. He and I both agreed that we want no measures to prolong life. I've signed a living will to that effect. B.F. said, 'I have a bag, and when it's time for me not to go on, I will just put my head in a bag.'"

"There must be a more pleasurable way to end it."

"Well, this is what he thought. It would be simple. He said, 'You can always get hold of a bag.' This is a part of my speech — to thrive and survive. It's not just survival, there has to be a certain amount of joy."

I arrange an interview with George Ignatieff in his chancellery at the University of Toronto. I wear, unusual for me, a skirt, silk blouse, high-heeled shoes. George Ignatieff, tall and stately, comes from behind his desk and ushers me graciously to a chair in the middle of an immense, bright room. I think the floors are marble but that may just be how I feel. I am not sure how to talk to this ex-diplomat, son of a minister to the Czar, Canadian ambassador to Yugoslavia, and Canada's postwar representative to the United Nations. Ignatieff has lived history. I plan to ask him about his postwar role in the UN and about what, after thirty years as a diplomat, he now considers important. I could never have imagined his remarkable candor or foreseen the path the conversation was to follow.

"You wrote about a postwar moment when global, rather than national, security seemed a possibility," I begin. "What happened to that possibility?"

Ignatieff explains that after the Second World War, the Americans pressured their allies in the United Nations to agree to American control of the development of nuclear power. There was serious controversy, but it seemed to Ignatieff, then, that Canadian security was so tied up with American security that on a matter of this importance Canada could not break with the U.S. With hindsight, he thinks he was wrong. He suspects that by backing the U.S., he inadvertently helped thwart what he most desired — an international agreement on nuclear power that might have prevented the postwar arms race.

"But I've always regretted it. And this accounts for the fact that on this hocus-pocus that the Americans are now playing with, Star Wars Defense Initiative, I feel *incensed* and that we really have to part with them. The worst is that they want to shift the human responsibility for initiating a nuclear war onto computers. And I think that any abdication of human responsibility for something which involves our very survival is so fundamentally immoral that this is really the acceptance, by some kind of dulling of one's wits and sense of conscience, of responsibility for mass murder, and it's a horrible, horrible strategy."

"Has this kind of thing changed your worldview?"

"I still believe that the way the human race is likely to survive is that little by little you keep moving toward the respect for human rights and all the things we committed ourselves to under the [United Nations] charter. The alternative, under the rubric of deterrence, or prevention of war by strength, always produces the kind of arms race we are in, always the tit for tat. Now we're faced with state terrorism as the answer to individual terrorism. I think we have to think very seriously whether we're facing a decline of our civilization, because we are losing the sense of community responsibility, that there is such a thing as living according to certain rules. It's happening on a scale which really worries me. So, I haven't changed. I haven't changed."

"Are certain things more important as you grow older?"

"I think that as you grow older your personal relationships take on a greater interest and, also, I think, a sense of satisfaction from the community. You cease to want to climb any ladders. You try to get as much as you can out of the friends you have, out of your neighbors, out of the simple things. Just take life as it is, realizing that you haven't got very much time anyway."

"Do you know yourself better now than you did when you were forty?"

"Oh yes, I think I do. You get to know yourself when your son comes and says to you, 'You know, Dad, you put a higher priority on your career than you did on helping us grow up.' And that really makes you face yourself.

"At forty, for instance, I was at the height of my diplomatic career. And when you're ambition-bound, on the make, you, as it were, massage your image. I see it not only in myself but in politicians that I watch. You're not yourself at all. You act a part. You pay much more attention to image than to reality. You submerge or ignore your weaknesses, you try and justify your insincerities, dull your conscience.

"Now, I find this isn't necessary. Now I try, well, now I do give first and foremost attention to the needs of my family. To know yourself means that you've got to recognize your weaknesses and wrestle with them. You've got to recognize a bad conscience when there is one. You've got to recognize there's something you could do, or could have done, for your neighbor, that there's somebody who is in need of your help, which you could offer. And you do it for the sake of doing it, without any seeking of reward or anything else. And I think that that brings a certain amount of knowing yourself, and by knowing yourself, a certain peace with yourself.

"Which brings me back to your earlier question about the afterlife. I'm quite willing to depart this life tomorrow, but I don't do so with the feeling that it's got to be made any easier by the supposition that I'm going to be wafted into some kind of other world. My son, Michael, has written a very interesting book which includes a dialogue between the philosopher

Hume and biographer Boswell on just what death meant to each of them. Boswell was surprised that Hume should contemplate death with equanimity without a belief in God or an afterlife. Well, I believe in God but I don't believe necessarily in an afterlife."

"And you would still say that you would contemplate death with equanimity."

"Equanimity, yes. And a certain amount of relief. You know, when your physical frame ceases to be equal to the demands that you place on it, that is the time to call it quits. I find I've reached that point. I've reached the point where I find it, in one way and another, a real strain. I tire or I don't feel well. I have pains and aches and all that sort of thing. I know some people are very courageous and feel that somehow or other they must cling to life. I don't feel that way at all."

"Your body is bugging you."

"Bugging me, yes. I'm impatient in that way. I can't say that I don't get fun out of life, but to see all your friends and contemporaries die one after another, and, as I say, you feel that you're not up to the demands that are placed on you. I'd like to do all the things that I'm asked to do. There are a lot of things I don't do. Trent [University] has just made me an honorary member of their community and the students asked me to come and address them and, of course, that was that. But I'm asked to do something every day, in one way or another."

"You said you're not image making, you're doing things for their own sake and that gives you a certain amount of peace. Yet you're saying that this peace doesn't outweigh the pain."

"It doesn't outweigh the feeling of physical degeneration and senility."

"But you don't have senility."

"Well, I do. I can't, you know, words suddenly escape me. I'm all right in a conversation that interests me but I forget names, I suddenly get, you know, blackouts. It's, it's . . . for a person who's been active in his mind, it is a bother. It's frustrating. And I've never been very patient. But the compensations are that I don't have to put on an act and my wants get much more reduced, circumscribed, and therefore they require a little less effort . . . One of the things that does make life both easier and more peaceful is what I believe is really the fundamental relationship of marriage, of friendship, which enables you to live with your wife without having to say very much. You sense when she needs something and she senses when you need something, whether it's cold or pain, or something of the sort. And you help one another and, uh . . . we're going through a difficult time because, as I say, she's got what's called premature senility, you know, what's it called, awful disease . . ."

"Alzheimer's."

"Alzheimer's. Yes. And it's something that one faces. And, you know, you feel, it isn't compassion, it's, it's . . . You feel that this is something you owe one another. I do most of the suffering because she doesn't realize it but we are so close that I think I know what she needs without her saying it."

"That's what's discouraging you too, I'm sure."

"Well, it accounts for what I say because I can't imagine life very much without her. People say that you can switch and start marrying at eighty and enjoying a new relationship but I don't feel that way."

Ignatieff and I fall silent until he extricates himself from the chair and stretches rather painfully to his full height. I stand, too.

"When the book is finished, I hope you will find it worthwhile," I say.

He gives me a long, firm handshake and a flash of a direct, engaging smile.

"I'm sure I will," he says diplomatically.

In the car, I digest what has just transpired between us. Ignatieff, externally the most admirable of human beings, has just told me his life is a strain and he's ready to call it quits. I do not see his suffering as I would in the case of a terminally ill cancer patient, but I know from his tone that the suffering is real. The discussion reminds me that not all people want to remain alive. Then, surprising as it may be for those who have not thought deeply about it, people may want the freedom *not* to live anymore.

Everyone has their own acid test for the quality of life. Children and grandchildren keep many people connected to the world. Writing keeps Mary Frances Fisher going. Maggie Kuhn's productive life is very satisfying, but she does not know if she would want to continue if she were blind. George Ignatieff would greet death with a certain amount of relief. And Ted

Allan dreams that he is flying, soaring, in full flight and then he plunges to the ground and dies. He interprets the dream as meaning that he'd rather be dead than be unable to fly, but then he says as long as he has a tongue and a working brain, he can tell stories and work.

The last time I saw my mother alive was on the Pacific coast in Mexico, twenty years ago. She and my father were on holiday and they took a hotel near the house I had rented with my family. They came over every day and my mother played with the children. Singing songs I remembered, she swished one-year-old Cleo in the water and lay with Kim in her room, reading books and talking. One afternoon after Kim had fallen asleep on the wings of her voice, my mother called me into a private room and closed the door. Out of a plastic bag, she extracted syringes, insulin vials, and a rubber tube and placed them on top of the bureau. Then, she addressed me in her serious voice. "You know I am diabetic," she said. "This is what keeps me alive." I was scared and uncomfortable. I didn't know what to say or what she expected of me. Why was she telling me this? I mumbled something like "But you're okay though, aren't you?" and she assured me she was. I left my mother in the room, with the door closed, putting away her medical paraphernalia. And when she came out, nothing more was said. Soon after, my parents flew back to Montreal. Two months later, my mother got up in the night with angina, went to the living room to sit with her back against the heater to ease the pain, and died two hours later from a heart attack, on a heart badly damaged by sugar diabetes.

I still don't know why my mother broke her private and stoic silence to show me what she needed to do to stay alive. I think now, that it was a matter-of-fact way of informing me about her health and preparing me for heredity and her possible death. I wonder if she remembered how squeamishly phobic I was about needles. Or, perhaps, knowing, she thought, My daughter is a woman now and it is time for her to look life in the face.

Well, I wasn't ready. I'm sorry. But I am ready now.

When I met Mary Frances Fisher, I was so charmed by her openness and readiness to be playful that I settled right in and enjoyed the visit. There was good conversation, peppered by laughter. I felt at home, and if I'd lived closer, I would have come back. So taken was I by the pleasure of her company that it took a while for me to notice the incredible fortitude required for her to be as she is. She introduced me to her survival aids as comfortably as she showed me the Picasso on her bathroom wall. When my mother tried, I wasn't prepared to consider illness or death. But, now, when I hear about dopamine for Parkinson's or the pain Mary Frances went through with her dislocated hip, I don't think about death but about resilience. I am not scared by Mary Frances's disabilities but fascinated by how she remains, as one fan said, "so neat."

At the age of eighty, world-renowned microbiologist René Dubos made this prediction: "The great advances in medicine in the next twenty to twenty-five years will be how the states of mind determine to a large extent how we respond to the limitations of our body."

"René Dubos writes about the resiliency of the human body," I say to Linus Pauling. "Do you feel that the human body is resilient?"

"Well, he's talking about the natural protective mechanism in the human body and, of course, they're genetically controlled and nutritionally controlled, too. So when he says bacteria and viruses aren't the cause of the disease, what he's saying is that people differ from one another in their ability to control disease and the effectiveness of their protective mechanism."

"He also says that shoes will wear out with long-term use, but if you walk barefoot, the skin of your feet grows back, renews itself."

"Yes. That's a morphological example of the body's natural protective mechanisms. But I think you need to expand on that by saying that you can bolster up your protective mechanisms. So don't just rely on the resilience of the human body without doing what you can to make it more resilient."

Dad takes vitamin C, vitamin E, and lecithin. Despite a heart attack thirty years ago, a quadruple bypass eight years ago, and an inherited gene for heart disease, he swims at the Y, hikes and skis with his friend Ralph.

"I never stopped. I always did something. If you reach 68, 70, and you haven't got your health, then no matter how much money you have, it's not going to help you enjoy life. I'm going to be 76 soon. I walk as if I were 20. And that's how I feel. I feel lithe. Exercise requires discipline but it's something you have to do, as important as eating. Even if you are building your career and don't think you have time. It has to be a trade-off."

"Why?"

"To give you a feeling of well-being and prevent you from having a decrepit old age. It's an investment in the future. I see my contemporaries who don't do regular exercise complaining of this and complaining of that. There are things even exercise won't prevent, but it's a preventative and it will help you enjoy everything better and more."

Writer Morley Callaghan knew this too, in a different way.

"The intellect wants to be used. Nature seems to have an attitude about this. If you walked along never using your right arm, your right arm would wither, wouldn't it? And if you walk along never using your imagination, then you end up not having an imagination. Somerset Maugham made an observation when he was in his eighties. He said, 'The imagination is like an elastic band. If you put it on a shelf, it'll rot. If you keep stretching it, it'll far even outlast you if you keep using it.' The capacity is there. The same with the intellect. But if you never meet anyone who says anything slightly stimulating that requires a response from you, then you won't respond."

"People don't realize that their lives are in their hands," warns Lea. "When I watch people in the restaurants — first they take the salt, then the pepper, and they splash the red paint all over. My family laughs at me but I say, 'Here I am, kids.'"

"Old age is a triumph over our own vicissitudes and the vicissitudes of life," says Maggie Kuhn. "To think of the things we have dealt with and survived. The disappointments and failures we've overcome. And think of the triumph — there has to be a good deal of health to have fought off infections. I've had cancer and I have arthritis which is a nuisance. And I have failing eyesight. But these are physiological conditions. They can be overcome with the activity of the mind and a vibrant spirit."

Maintenance for long-term survival is not mechanistic but a complex web of mind, body, and spirit, the added dimensions of which would have thrilled my humanist biochemist mother. It's clear that I have a choice of taking care of myself or hastening the disintegration of my nonrenewable organic resources. What's needed physically and mentally for me to hedge my health bets now seems straightforward and not unduly daunting.

But, as I age, I will have to confront further limitations, both in what society expects of me and in actual physical capacity. I will have to struggle harder to function to capacity and even, perhaps, to stay alive. And I am aware that in good measure whether I do, or not, will be up to me.

I hope I have what it takes to remain independent as long as possible. But, when the going gets tough, will I?

What kind of spirit is needed to stay alive, when staying alive requires daily struggle?

Why do some people carry on and others not?

What will give me the requisite, vibrant spirit?

THREE

Sex/Love

At first, I think what I will need more than anything else to have a vibrant spirit is sex. In my preinterview notes, I write: "Something about the need for sexuality draws people together — hugging, kissing, laughing from the gut, making love — represents the best in people. It contains an impulse for social understanding. And being touched and stroked is an affirmation of one's corporal self, just as conversation is an affirmation that one's mind is indeed working within a human context. Both are pleasurable feedback. They make you stronger."

I know I'm going to want sex when I'm older. But will I be physically able? Will my partner? Will I have a partner? I wonder what sex will be like and then, with an aching anticipation of loss, I wonder how I will survive without it.

Yet, this concern must be socially induced. Because for me, there was never any question about parental or grandparental abstemiousness. My grandfather was a lusty man who married three times after my grandmother died. His children's ribald comments, which I heard as a teenager, were an evocation to their own potential. Mom and Dad were unabashed about their sexuality, and when they returned from a holiday, we saw the afterglow, felt the connection, and were privy to sufficient innuendo to know that Dad was no eunuch and Mom no blushing virgin. They did it, and without rubbing our noses in it, they let us know they liked it.

When Mom died, too young, Dad, who had never loved another woman, began to date for the first time in forty years and I, at twenty-six, was his confidante. My mother, knowing her prognosis was not good, had prepared us, saying, "Daddy has a lot of love in him and if I die, he should marry again." We were all set up, guilt-free, to help Dad get on with his life.

It was the 1960s. Despite his earthy humor, Dad's sexual mores were post-Victorian and he carried within him a love for my mother that I am only now beginning to fathom. I was a freethinker, lacking in experience of real intimacy, but a comparative authority on contemporary sexuality. We muddled through. I encouraged, pushed, insisted it was acceptable to kiss someone, even more than once, without proposing marriage. He confessed that the dating scene made him uncomfortable. He was fifty-six, a young man with a strong life urge and a sense of responsibility to all who were still alive. I took him to a Club Med.

This was his first time away without Mom. And he tried. He swam and he danced and the women liked him. But it was not Sue or even Vivienne who turned my father around. It was Mr. Stern, a sixty-five-year-old widower, on his tenth year of committed and devoted mourning. With his wiry beard incongruously overflowing his gray, dry face, Mr. Stern pulled Dad to him like a sponge. He invited his confidences, he consoled his grief. My dad talked to him. But something was not right. It was Mr. Stern's ten years of gloom. To my father, if truth be told, it seemed self-indulgent and unfair to others. He resolved that he would *not* be like Mr. Stern. He would "get better" and be something for his friends and his kids.

From that moment on, Dad's love of life took over. The sadness was there and is, still, after twenty years. But he has married again. His wife ruffles his hair. He is jokingly proprietary of her well-formed body. They, too, glow after vacations, and since he now works only three days a week they also glow in between. I don't know if he thinks his sexuality has changed. The jokes and earthy comments are the same, but I sense a hesitation there somewhere. When his children were young and had problems, he used to tell us to wash our faces in cold water and take a brisk walk. I think he's realized that not all angst is solved that way. And, as he has survived by rolling with the punches, I sense that sexuality now, for him, requires adaptation. It is not what it used to be, not what the boys where he grew up on de Bullion Street, yelling "Church on fire" and seeing who could piss furthest, had it cracked up to be. Sexuality is not simply shtupping. It has become something else. And what sexuality *becomes* is central to my concerns. I haven't talked to my father yet. But I will — after I see what others have said.

It's raining when I get to Dr. Mary Calderone's elegant, old Fifth Avenue apartment in New York. The doorman ushers me into a black and white marble foyer, opening through french doors into a walled-in garden. A tree is covered in pink blossoms. The walls are covered in vines.

Mary Calderone, eighty-two, preeminent sexologist, humanist, and author, welcomes me warmly into her comfortable apartment. She is tall, slender, her carriage graceful and erect.

"That's the kind of posture I was born into," she responds to my compliment. "Women didn't get the other thing. They were just always erect. Ladies are erect."

And, she adds, she's been on estrogen for twenty years: "Estrogen, calcium, and vitamins, that cuts out osteoporosis."

We make ourselves comfortable on the couch. She takes off her Birkenstock sandals and lounges.

Unimaginative admirers have called Dr. Calderone "the grandmother of sex," and similarly bereft detractors have called her "an aging libertine." When she was young, her mother called her vile and dirty and made her wear aluminum mitts at night so she wouldn't masturbate. When she was ten, she moved into the freer orbit of her father, the photographer Edward Steichen.

These days her special interest is the sexuality of the fetus, infant, and preschool child. And she is "on to something great." Indicating "the tiny little penis between the two thighs," she shows me an ultrasound picture of a fetal erection taken at twenty-nine weeks. But, she points out, fetal erections are observed as early as seventeen weeks, "and he does it every ninety minutes, just like adult males sleeping in sleep laboratories."

The fetal ultrasound confirms Dr. Calderone's theory that the sexual response system "purrs along quietly for a long time without interference from us, rather than being something that has to wait for a stimulus." It is useful data to give parents when she explains, "Your child is born sexual, not reproductive, but sexual." And when they, defensive, respond, "My child is not sexual, my child is innocent," Dr. Calderone answers, "Your child is innocent in its sexuality. You can't say your child is naughty because he urinates in the uterus or gets an erection every ninety minutes, because that's the way it is."

Dr. Calderone thinks children should grow up knowing they are sexual and having the fact accepted. Being silent and over-protective creates "sexual cripples, stammerers, and stutterers, and that's why we have Dr. Ruth." Through original research and thinking, she has freed herself from her mother's repressive legacy and even confronted society's taboos about child sexuality. For Dr. Calderone, "sexuality is a major and God-given part of our human nature."

I want to know what sexuality means to her now, at eighty-two.

"Sex has always been something in which I participated with somebody I cared very deeply about and who cared very deeply about me. And that's been the story of a relatively constricted heterosexual life. I've had two husbands and two very long-standing relationships, one was fifteen years, another was eight years, which pretty well covers the territory. And if I don't have it, I may say to myself, 'I'm lonely. I wish there was somebody around.' But I don't go out and drag somebody in from somewhere just to have it. For me, sexuality is an expression of me, my feelings toward another person, so I couldn't just have it with anybody. Now I don't think that everybody's that way at all. I'm sure they're not."

I ask Dr. Calderone if she finds that age has affected her sexuality.

"No," she says, "totally not. Different people age at different rates and about different things. And I would say that probably sexually I'm more powerful than I ever have been in my life."

This is totally unexpected. I am prepared to nod understandingly about losses and changes and she is ready for the next question. I get my mind around what she has in fact said, and ask what she means by "powerful."

"Well, I mean in the sense of no inhibitions and very easy arousability, intense arousability. And in the last ten years I've probably just finally shoved aside my difficulties that my mother laid on me."

I am not sure what to say. I am too shy, or taken aback, to try to explore what Dr. Calderone means by "no inhibitions" and "intense arousability." I expected an enlightened discussion of physical difficulties, especially the problem of vaginal dryness. If impotency is the fear for older men, "drying up" is the fear for older women.

"Isn't there a problem with vaginal lubrication?" I ask, retreating to my original agenda.

"Well, I've been on estrogen for twenty years. I have no problems. I had a hysterectomy when I was forty-nine, so I never had to worry [about the possibility of estrogen increasing the risk of uterine cancer]. So I'm a really good living example of having perfectly normal genitalia and no problems of lubrication or thinning of the walls or anything like that because I was able to keep up the estrogen. The trick is to find a doctor who isn't so scared of it. A medical advisor."

"Who, in fact, gives you permission to continue to have sex? . . ."

"Who gives you encouragement."

I balance Dr. Calderone's experience against the following confidence, passed on by an older relative as an inevitable law of nature: "As a woman gets older, her hormones react differently in her. It can be very painful for her. And although we try to put on a good act, it still is painful. And if it's painful, it's not enjoyable. But of course, we don't tell our mates this, you know. It's just the process of drying up, internally. And it's very painful."

Since we often study what we are afraid of, I want to make sure I understand to what extent changes in vaginal lubrication will affect my sexuality as I get older. What happens? And what do women do about it, including those who, unlike Dr. Calderone, have an intact uterus?

I go to see biologist and sexologist Dr. Ruth Weg in her office in the Andrus Center of Geronotology, in California. Five feet two, silver hair swept back, dark eyes artistically highlighted, Dr. Weg wears shiny silver jewelry and a loose mauve top, over an ample bosom. When people learn she is sixty-five years old, they ask, "Why don't you say sixty-five years young; you don't look your age." And she says, "You have a screwy image of what it means to look sixty-five. That's the kind of flattery that is almost an insult. What I'd like you to say is, Gee, you're very effective, you're great to listen to, you're energetic — those are compliments. But 'You don't look your age . . .' My face *is* expressive, but it's not young."

I ask Ruth Weg whether the phenomena of women "drying up" is a myth or a reality.

"Drying up in what way?"

"In terms of vaginal lubrication."

"The term 'drying up' is an unfortunate term. The vaginal canal does change as we grow older, but that change doesn't begin at menopause, it's been changing all along. With the decrease in estrogen as we approach menopause, and without estrogen, five to ten years postmenopause, you do find that lubrication upon stimulation takes a longer time, maybe five minutes, instead of fifteen seconds.

"*If* needed, we can maintain lubrication by hormonal replacement. But if a woman has an intact uterus, she needs estrogen *and* progestin, not just estrogen alone. Because, if a woman has an intact uterus, there is an increased risk of uterine cancer with long-term intake of estrogen replacement alone."

Dr. Weg, who has had a hysterectomy, finds that hormonal replacement maintains the genital tissue, has a salutary effect on protein synthesis, on the salt-and-water balance, on the immune system, and on her entire "health profile."

But I wonder about alternatives. *Ourselves, Growing Older* cautions readers to be careful about hormone treatment since "the effects of long-term use of progesterone are not known," and "estrogen is a powerful drug which should not be taken without first considering all of its potential effects." Instead, the book suggests women take more time to become aroused, include more caresses, and encourage oral sex "which provides its own lubrication." Mary Calderone mentions "excellent products that give wonderful lubrication and can be gotten at the pleasure shops, or whatever they're called."

Dr. Weg did say hormones "if needed." I decide that if lubrication depends on five minutes of stimulation instead of fifteen seconds, I'll spare the time.

But I'm still left with the larger question: "How does sexuality change when we are old?"

"The years have very little to do with libido and with the capacity to function as a sexual partner," Dr. Weg answers. "There are changes. We're not the same as we were at twenty. It takes longer for men and women to reach a level of excitement. And the libido is perhaps not as powerful. But all this is very gradual. It still is as pleasurable, as much of a connection with life and the celebration of life as it ever was."

And, then, inadvertently, she gives me the information I need to understand how Mary Calderone can be sexually more powerful at eighty-two than ever before.

"If we've been orgasmic easily as young women, by the time we get older, we will be even more so because we've increased the circulation to that whole pelvic area. Those muscles are better able to handle what they're doing. We are more receptive, better experienced, no longer worried about pregnancy and therefore don't have to prepare in any way with birth control devices. There is a sense of abandon that many older women feel for the first time."

I register this information with some credulity, thank Dr. Weg for her knowledge, and gather up my things.

"Enjoy," she says, as she ushers me out.

Now I have it from two older women that "drying up" need not be a deterrent to sexuality. And in *Ourselves, Growing Older*, I read, "Masters and Johnson confirmed what many women have discovered for themselves: that there is no time limit on women's sexual capacity. Although our [women's] responses may slow down, we can continue to enjoy sex and orgasm throughout our lives."

Still, I wonder if there are any hidden problems that I have overlooked.

"What I don't hear much in the new wave of positive gerontological thinking," I say to Dr. Weg, "are hard facts about the physical changes we have to deal with."

"There *are* physical changes," she agrees, "but the physical changes in the capacity for physical sexual expression are *not* the major changes."

The story is told that when my friend Ted Allan regained consciousness after his quadruple bypass operation, he grabbed a nurse. Only then did he know he was alive. In the frank Consumers Union report, *Love, Sex, and Aging*, a minister describes sitting by an old woman's death bed:

> She was approaching death from old age. In fact, she opened her eyes only long enough to see who I was. Her limbs were already

stiff — but she reached out a hand, took mine in hers, and pressing it against her chest, firmly pushed it toward her [genitals].

When their interlocked hands reached the dying woman's navel, the minister "panicked" and took his hand away. He recoiled, but at least he recorded it. Two days later, the woman was dead.

I tell this story to Terri Allister, a buxom woman in her thirties. And Terri nods knowingly. The other day, she says, she went to visit her ninety-eight-year-old grandmother who was in bed with a cold, fast asleep. Terri sat by the bed and leaned over, close to her grandmother's face. "Baba, Baba, I'm here," she whispered. Her grandmother wrestled open her eyes, level with Terri's bosom. She gathered the full round breasts to her and burrowed in, nuzzling side to side. "So nice, so nice," she murmured.

"What did you do?" I asked Terri.

"I gave them to her," Terri shrugged. "Gradually, she collected herself and remembered who and where she was."

"It's the last thing to go," says my eighty-six-year-old friend Lea when I ask her about sexuality. "The last thing to go," she says, wagging her finger at me.

I arrange to meet Marian Jarvis Lewis who is then ninety-seven years old. Marian is a friend's grandmother and I've been briefed: she kicked her husband out for drunkenness decades ago, worked as a buyer at Eaton's, ran a rooming house in her later years, and always loved men.

There are three immobile old people sitting on a bench in the entrance of the Island Park Lodge, the subsidized old people's high rise in Ottawa where Marian lives. At the arranged time, she comes down to meet me and to get her mail. She feels her way out of the elevator, moving painfully fast for her, to avoid the heavy door. Almost blind, she follows the carpet with her cane, left, to her mailbox. With long, tapered fingers she counts the boxes starting at the top-left corner — over one, two, down one, two, three — to her box. She fumbles the key into the lock and takes out her newspaper.

"There's a bazaar in the foyer," I say after introducing myself.

"What fun, let's go see it."

The large open room is full of old people on padded chairs, behind clothes tables, against the walls. Marian greets everybody. "Hello, dear. Hi, darling. How's your health?" She touches everyone — her little friend Bertie, and even Verle whom no one likes. What she can't see, she asks to have described. "They're marvelous," she says of the hand-embroidery, "very interesting," of some collaged ashtrays. What she wants is a floor-length housecoat, preferably brocade, so she can avoid the gymnastics of wearing stockings. But nothing she can find at the bazaar covers her imposing height. She says her goodbyes. I hold the elevator door so it doesn't get her, and we ride up to her one-room apartment.

"Well, today everyone's talking about identities. That's the big thing, identities. So I've established my identity again," she says, as we settle in. "But time has gone on and I hardly know anyone down there. That little woman selling me the dresses at the bazaar, I kind of pet her because she's such a friendly little thing and no one else gets on with her. Verle, her name is, Verle. I like her, she's quite a little fighter."

"You said hello to another lady, a small lady?"

"Oh, Dalton, Bertie Dalton. She's really gone. She recognizes me but she doesn't recognize anyone else."

"Yet you said women do better in a place like this than the men. Why do you think that is?"

"The men go to pieces much faster than we do. This place is really a return to Amazonian times when women ruled the world. Because the women make these places their homes. And our men were never brought up in the kitchen. We wouldn't let our men in the kitchen. So they weren't brought up to be cooks."

"They can't take care of themselves, then."

"No, they can't. They can't sew and they can't put on buttons. Now some do, you know; there's always exceptions to the rule. But as a rule, they don't. And what's the result? There are three or four bars right across here, and they spend all their time sitting in the bars because they're lonely and they come back home here pretty drunk, you know, terribly unhappy. Because they nearly all have been married and they fear going into a nursing home. And there are not nearly enough nursing homes for us now, you know that, because we aging people, we're going to become more numerous as time goes on."

"Do you still like men?"

"I adore them. They adore me. Men like me, you know. On the elevators they're wanting to know if I'm all right, and pressing the button for me, and making way for me. No wonder the gals downstairs aren't really fond of me," Marian chuckles.

"Did you have relations with men when you were older?"

"Yes, and that's why I'm so well. I had a very active sex life. Very active and a very fulfilling one. I never promoted men to husbands because I didn't think they'd make good stepfathers. You know, I often think back . . . it's amazing. That's why I'm never bored."

"You think back to these men?"

"Mmmm."

"Special ones?"

"No, I was very fortunate. I didn't fall in love with any of them. I never had any heartache over any one of them when our little affair was over. My affairs ran about eight years. And then it seemed we didn't give each other anything. That was the case with five different men who were my lovers. See, sex isn't nearly enough, nice and all as it is."

"Was sexuality good into your eighties?"

"No, I guess until about seventy-five. And then I gave up dear old Pete over the silliest thing. I suddenly grew very modest. I thought, My God, Marian, you must be out of your mind. Here's this poor man, he grew to love me, having a guest house all my life, what I call a revenue-bearing house; it was always very handy because he always lived in the house."

"But it was your house."

"It was my house. And I was charging room rent. You know, when I look back and talking to you like this, it's ridiculous. There was poor Pete, sharing my bed and me demanding my week's rent, and I've never thought about it in that way until now. You know, you're a witch," she laughs, "that's what you are, absolutely."

"You're the witch."

"No," she laughs even more. "My loving never cost me a cent."

"But at seventy-five you got modest?"

"Modest, yes, I thought, oh, this is ridiculous. And I kept drawing away and drawing away from poor old Pete. Of course,

Pete wasn't exactly to the manor born, but he had good bed manners. Very nice. He had nice around manners, you know. And I started not having supper with him. I used to prepare his supper. Charged him a little more for supper and I stopped that. I don't know what excuse I gave for it, but I was bored. And I could see he was bored but he didn't have stamina enough to tell me, and besides, he was comfortable. And men hate change. And I knew I'd have a hard time breaking off the relationship, but we had nothing in common as time went on except this terrific sex drive that I had. I've always been, what'll I say . . ."

"Lustful?"

"A *terrific* sex drive, I've always had it. I have it today. As a matter of fact, I'm a little in love with my doctor. Of course, that's my theory, a doctor is no good to you unless you're in love with him."

"But what do you do about it?"

"Well, it's really very funny. He's a very handsome man, a Hindu, an East Indian, very well educated, very charming person, and he sits there and he uses every excuse in the world to take my hands, you see. And I have what I call a bad toe, and he just loves to fondle my toe. I say, 'What do you think of this toe, is gangrene starting?' And I know damn well it's not. And he has to look at it longingly, and fondle it, and I enjoy it and he enjoys it. Isn't that awful? I really think I'm a bad woman, you know."

"What do you think about when you think about your past sexual relationships?"

"Well, here's a funny part of it, I hallucinate about them. I can create a — what do you call it — you know the word I'm looking for, when it comes to its fulfillment?"

"Orgasm?"

"Yes, I can create an orgasm. And do. I often wonder, you know, I'll get around to it, asking my doctor about it, how harmful masturbation is?"

"Dr. Calderone says it's good for you."

"I agree with her. So I can do without the physical man in the bed. And of course, the poor devils, with insemination we're even pushing them out of their bed, you know. It's a damn shame, soon there'll be no use for them at all. Except we'll have to have the semen, we'll have to have that."

"You know there's a doctor called Wilhelm Reich —"

"I agree with him. I agree with him heartily. And you don't have to go to all the trouble of finding a man. Certainly, it's wonderful. And I remember when sensuality first hit the papers and became topical, I said to this woman — she's a social worker, pretty broad-minded, Catholic girl, shaken off the shackles — I said, 'You know, Louise, I think I'll set up a nice little affair up here.' I said, 'I think a lot of these women are suffering from lack of sexual relationship, that's what's wrong with them, poor miserable creatures. They don't know what's wrong with them and they're not allowed to think what's wrong with them, because they think it's not nice. So I think I'll get a couple of nice males' — she started to laugh — 'and explain to these women that this isn't for pleasure, this is purely therapeutic.' However, it was just a dream, you know."

Bertie arrives with supper just as Marian is showing me the ingenious mechanisms she has set up throughout the apartment to make herself optimally independent. She ticks Bertie off for not telling her about the bazaar. Bertie says she is overloaded with work, Marian raises her voice. The voice has a ring to it. Bertie responds with a loud aggrieved excuse. They both yell — one tired, stocky seventy-year-old, one slightly stooped ninety-seven-year-old. Marian, losing ground, saves face with "Well, in that case, my dear . . ." Bertie gives her the beer they usually share and hurries off.

"Are you tired?" I ask.

"No, I don't feel so tired. I don't know that I ever feel very tired. Of course, I sleep a lot. Probably soon as you leave I'll just put my feet up where you're sitting and have a sleep.

"Often I have a glass of beer with Bertie if she has time to have it with me, but she has a boyfriend who is quite demanding. And she's in the horrible position where she can't help him or criticize him because he designates everything as a nag. She's beginning to call him names and I can see that this affair is beginning to wear thin but he's got a little money and he has a car. And the women around here will do almost anything to get a man with a car. Poor old Bertha. He's an Irishman, very charming, I could go for him myself, although I never particularly liked tall men. I always liked short men. I was just thinking about that the other day. The men that satisfied me the most have always been short men."

"What do you think is the most important thing in lovemaking?"

"I don't know. Like Catherine the Great, I've always been very susceptible to voices. Do you know that story of hers? She was reviewing the troops and they were reporting 'Present,' 'Present,' 'Present.' Then one, in a very low voice, said, 'Present,' at which Catherine commanded, 'Send that man to my boudoir.' I'm like Catherine, very susceptible to voices."

Marian sees me to the door. She is smiling, beaming, and so am I. "It has been such fun, such fun," she says.

Over the years, when Ted Allan came to Montreal to meet the Chinese for his film on Dr. Norman Bethune, or to work on a production of one of his plays, he stayed with me and my family.

I had first interviewed Ted for the Canadian Broadcasting Corporation in London, in 1966; he was my first interview and the first writer I had ever met. He had hit plays in London and Paris, films in Hollywood, short stories in *The New Yorker*. He showed me how to work the tape recorder and suggested questions for me to ask. I followed his career from then on, enjoying the breadth of his creativity and humor, and marveling at how, given the commerce of artistic survival, he continues to augment his profoundly autobiographical body of work.

Women came to visit him at our home and left smiling. He would talk with pleasure about wives, lovers — "girls." Sex was a good-time topic, a polka-dotted life force, surprising and continually fresh. I thought Ted wouldn't mind, might in fact enjoy, talking to me about sex, which would take the edge off talking frankly to an older man. Our initial discussion opened a dialogue which continued over four years.

I began by asking how sex was for him after seventy.

"You remind me of my son, who asked how sex was after sixty, and I said it gets better and better. Better and better and better and better. And I told my son that last week I was in bed with a gorgeous, beautiful woman and it was better than ever. Better than when I was in my teens, in my twenties, in my thirties, in my forties. And then, suddenly, I thought, it could be that I'm suffering from a loss of memory. So I'm not sure. I had one kind of problem when I was in my teens and twenties and I have another kind of problem now."

In his teens, Ted learned to masturbate by watching other boys in the street and his first ejaculation was "just a very strange, frightening experience." Afterwards, he masturbated quite a bit: "I felt that as a result of this masturbation I was going to go mad. I felt that I had no control and that I was totally addicted. I kept thinking hair was going to grow on the palms of my hands and that I would become a mongoloid idiot."

His first intimate experience with a girl was also fraught with conditioning. "I had necked a bit and kissed and touched breasts. I don't think I had been allowed yet to touch below the waist. That was sacrosanct, a dark, mysterious area. So when this woman brought me up to the top of the mountain, took off her dress, and stood there stark naked, I stared at her pubic hair. I had a big erection by then, and she literally placed my penis inside her vagina, the way I later saw men mating a stallion with a mare. And as I started to come, I withdrew because I was afraid I would give her a baby. And she screamed, 'Where are you going?' as I ran down the mountain."

When he was twenty-one, Ted slept with a girl. "And the minute I entered her I came. And she said, 'Oh, you're just a rabbit, aren't you?' and I never forgave her for that. Right through my twenties until an older woman taught me to relax, I came too quickly. And then I read that this was a universal problem because they had words for it — premature ejaculation. So I felt better. Because if you can have scientific-sounding words for a condition, it means that someone besides you has it too.

"When I married, I went through that period of believing what Freud told us — that women who just had clitoral orgasms were immature and had to develop vaginal orgasms. So my poor wife suffered from this. She was having a great time with her clitoral orgasms. She was very happy. And I used to say, 'Well, you're being childish and immature. You have to learn to have a vaginal orgasm.' And she would say, 'I don't think you can *have* a vaginal orgasm.' Obviously, what did she know? I had read what Freud said and Freud knew: she didn't. It was the feminist movement that began to indicate to us brilliant men that clitoral orgasms were probably the only kind of orgasms women could have, although there are some women who tell me there's a mysterious area inside the vagina that helps what are called vaginal orgasms. I really don't know. I don't care anymore. I really don't *care* because I have a lot of fun, and the reason I think I have lot of fun now, at the age of seventy, is because of my heart attack.

"The best thing that ever happened to me sexually was my heart attack. I had a heart attack fucking. I had been fucking this girl and I was having a great time, when suddenly I felt this terrible pain shoot through me. I withdrew, lay back, and said, 'God, I don't feel good.' And she said, 'Oh, don't give me *that.*' She thought I was rejecting her. Or she thought I'd come too quickly. Whatever, she was very pissed off with me. I said, 'I'm not well.' She said, 'Boy!' And she made me drive her home. And I was having this heart attack.

"But that's not the story I wanted to get into. The story I wanted to get to was that after the heart attack where I almost died, I was afraid to be on top after that. And I tried, very tentatively, to have sex with me lying down and the woman sitting on me. It's marvelous. I lie there and I let the woman do the work. I do provide the erection, that's true. But I must tell you that 'I've never enjoyed sex as much in my life as I enjoy it now, lying there. I will touch her breasts, I will fondle her, I will kiss her, but basically she does most of the movement. I move a bit, but my whole attitude is oriental in that I will wait for it to happen. And it's better now as a result, both for me and the women with whom I make love because I've even stopped using the concept of 'I make love *to*' Rather it's 'I make love *with*.' And for me, that's the secret of good sex, of good performance. But we make so much of the business of coming and techniques. I'm surprised that in this day and age there's still so much fetishism. That women's breasts and pubic hairs and vaginas are still apparently considered by the majority of men on this earth to be areas of mystery. The whole thing has been mystified.

"I feel closer to women as people now than I ever have. I find women dear. That's the only way I can describe it. Women are dear to me. And when women make love to me and I make love to a woman there's something very dear about it. It's endearing that we're both pleasuring ourselves, it's very friendly. The whole thing is the epitome of friendship to me. And I never quite had it like this. There was tremendous excitement when I was young and now I'm not excited in that way. I'm getting much more pleasure than the excitement.

"Of course, I always had a love for women, that's not new. I had it since the age of one hour. I think I was born with it. I was born loving the place I came from."

Several years after this conversation, in the spring of Ted's seventieth year, I introduce him to my friend Sandy, a film editor in her early forties, whose kids are grown and who likes to work hard and play hard. Ted and Sandy hit it off and become lovers. So pleased are they both that Sandy offers to take me out to dinner.

"No dinner" — I thank her — "but since my field research is somewhat limited, I would appreciate if you would tell me what it's like to make love to an older man."

Sandy agrees and one fine morning, we breakfast with the tape recorder. I begin with my prejudices in full sail: "Is the reality of older people's lovemaking depressing? Is there a big difference?"

"There's no difference, not mentally. The only difference is physically. And the physical difference has a lot to do with his heart. He can't get on top of me because he can't take that kind of exertion."

"Doesn't it take him longer to have an erection?"

"No."

"Doesn't it take him a long time to come?"

"No."

"I've read that older men take longer and more manual manipulation to get a hard-on."

"Not with him. Well, sometimes, it all depends. I mean, he wakes up with a hard-on in the morning if I'm there, just like any other man I've ever slept with. Sometimes if he's feeling sexy, he'll get a hard-on right away, sometimes not. But it's not different. It's the same."

It dawns on me that Sandy is emphasizing similarities, not differences.

"What do you mean, it's the same mentally?" I ask.

"He has the same interest as a younger man: he *loves* women's bodies, he loves women. If you want to put it in a broader perspective, I think he's been like that and other men aren't always like that and I'm sure aren't at seventy. The only difference is it gets frustrating for him that he wants to be more active than he can and we both have to remember 'Don't get on top, don't do that.' If he does try and get on top, which he does in the throes of, he often loses his hard-on, and I think that's fear from his heart attack. His nose goes blue, you know, his heart starts acting up, and he takes a nitroglycerine pill quick. I know that there's things missing for him. But there's enough passion, there's an edge to it. Obviously, he really wants to make love, so there's that passion."

"He says he feels he doesn't have to prove anything. Is he relaxed in a way that, say, forty-year-old lovers aren't?"

"He doesn't mind if he doesn't come, but I've known younger men who don't mind if they don't come."

"What's the relationship between you that transfers to the lovemaking?"

"We're very relaxed with each other, we laugh a lot. You know, we'll be fucking and he'll say something outrageous. I fell off him one night, right off the bed, because we were laughing so hard."

"And he laughs too?"

"Oh, we were both screaming with laughter."

"What's your attraction? What turns you on about him?"

"I've always been a sucker for anyone who makes me laugh. And he has tremendous insights about people, which I find fascinating, and also his caringness about the world and a lot of political savvy — his whole history. I *love* listening to his stories. I find myself envying him all those years, all those experiences, all those travels, all those things that he's done."

"Nothing in the literature says that this should transmit into sexual desire," I point out.

"Well, I don't know, I've never been attracted physically to men. It's always their minds, for me."

"So, being attracted to his mind would make you like to make love with him."

"Yeah. And there's kind of a sparkle to him too, I don't know."

"Why did you make love with Ted?"

"Ted was coming on to me very hard and I was thinking, This is ridiculous! This man has had a heart attack and he's seventy years old, thirty years older than I and da-da-da. Then I started feeling really patronizing about how dare I pat him on the head and say 'Go home you silly old man, you're past it.' I just felt I couldn't do that to him. At a certain point I thought, How would I feel, being denied adult status in a way. I was starting to treat him like a child. There was the potential for treating him like a child. And somebody with his history and who he is. I think it would have been terrible."

"That's what Morley Callaghan couldn't understand," I tell Sandy, "he said women were being 'kind to him.' But there's a leap from deciding not to treat Ted as a child, to actually enjoying a sexual relationship."

"Yes, well, it was nervous for both of us the first couple of nights. I didn't know what to expect and I'm sure he didn't either. It turned out to be perfectly normal."

"Do you mostly pleasure yourself or does he pleasure you?"

"No, he pleasures me. He makes me come."

"So it's not just his mind."

"I don't know how to explain it, but it's all part of his loving women. His concentration on that makes him sexy."

"How does he make you feel, then, as a woman?"

"Loved and wanted, appreciated."

Three years after his affair with Sandy, and several relationships later, Ted returns to Montreal. It is spring, six months after the quadruple bypass operation that saved his life. His heart works at 40 percent capacity. His energy is unchanged. But two of the pills that he must take to stay alive cause potency problems. Ted tells me he has erections sometimes in the morning and he can masturbate, but "it doesn't get very hard, very erect." This new wrinkle is disturbing.

I tell Dad about Ted's situation on one of our constitutionals. Dad says, "Maybe Ted thinks he has to get laid, and the pressure puts a damper on sexuality." He tells me that when he first met Phyllis, his second wife, he went to bed and "nothing happened. I was very surprised because you know I was after your mother all the time. Phyllis was very good about it. She said, 'Your wife has just died. You've had a very big trauma. You have all the equipment. You'll be okay.' I just slept with her and cuddled and after a while it just happened. She was very good about it. It's something I'll never forget."

I tell Ted what my dad has said. He agrees that to be with an understanding woman would be a good idea. But he's still conditioned by a set of visual stimuli that turn him on. Also, what he wants is a light sexual fling, with no commitment.

In due course, Ted is visited by a young woman of twenty-four whose long model's legs do the trick. Ted takes her out to dinner several times, entertaining her with his stories, giving her books to read, enjoying her beauty, and hoping to get her to bed. One night, she comes home with him and drinks enough vodka to be in the mood. Ted gets into bed. He's best in the morning and this is late at night and after a heavy meal. Through a haze of exhaustion, he sees her coming toward him "as beautiful as a centrespread." She stands by the bed and says, "I have a question." Ted has told her he is fifty. Now, he thinks, she will ask how old I am. "Are these sheets cotton?" she asks. "Yes, yes," Ted says as she gets into bed. Ted is filled with desire but, oh, so tired. He plays with his bedmate but there is no erection. He is so exhausted he seriously feels he might have a heart attack, and to make things worse, he has to pee. He turns on the light. Normally, he has a peacock walk. Now his head lolls, he is stooped, he shuffles to the toilet. When he returns, the young woman asks, "How old are you really?"

He says he was in the Spanish Civil War.

"When was that?" she asks.

"Nineteen thirty-seven."

"How old were you?"

"Twenty."

She is dumbstruck.

"That is so old," she says.

The young woman doesn't see Ted for three weeks. One day she knocks on his door. She tells Ted he is too old and she doesn't think they should have sex anymore. Ted had never felt "old" before. Now, every time he looks in the mirror he sees an old man. Jokingly, he tells me the mistake was getting up: "The varicose veins, the scar." Or, maybe, the mistake was turning on the light. I assure him this twenty-four year old probably knows nothing except the athletic thrust of young sex. What did he expect? But he is shaken. He spends the winter with his daughter and granddaughter in California. On the way back to Canada, he meets "a nice lady," the mother of his granddaughter's boyfriend. They "dig" each other. The granddaughter is embarrassed that Grandpa does more than talk. Ted starts to feel not so old.

When next I speak to Ted on the phone, he is having a series of tests to try to get rid of the two medications that affect his potency.

"Girls want to be licked, sucked, touched, but some of them also want cocks in them," he says. "And me too, I only feel really secure when I'm inside. Then I know everything's going to be okay — the script, the film, the house renovations, everything." We talk some more and I tell Ted I'm glad his work is going well and I'm sorry we're so far apart.

"It's a good thing we're not together," he says, "or I'd want to fuck you with my limp cock."

Several days later, Ted calls for the phone number of my friend urologist Yosh Taguchi. He has found the name of the drugs that are causing problems in Yosh's book *Private Parts*, and he wonders if Yosh has any other suggestions. I get the feeling from Ted that someone close by is hoping the good doctor will say abracadabra. Yosh tells Ted that he must continue to take the offending pills to stay alive. He recommends trying yohimbine, a preparation made from the bark of an African tree.

Several months later, Ted is in Montreal and he goes to see Yosh for further advice. Yosh injects the side of his penis with a very small needle containing prostaglandin-E_1. Ted gets a big erection and walks around the hospital with it for a half hour. Yosh also shows him the Osbon Erect Aid, a plastic suction device that fits over the penis. A vacuum pump on the top sucks the blood into the penis and the erection is held in place by a band, like the cock ring. Ted comes home with a few vials of prostaglandin-E_1 and a $320 erecto kit which he will probably never use. He is rather pleased.

So I don't tell Ted that the next thing conventional medicine has to offer is a surgically implanted penile prosthesis — a Silastic Finney flexi-rod. Since 1973, over 100,000 men in the United States have opted for penile implants, a satisfactory solution for men such as John Buchanan, made impotent by the removal of his prostate gland. "I was always kinda looking out the corner of my eye that people, you know, whether they're kinda sneering at you for being part of a man," he says. "After you have the ability returned, you can — what can I say — you get your self-esteem back. I'm very glad I decided to have it done."

I know penile implants are part of the culture when my dad says, "Moe had cancer in his prostate. So they took his prostate out. But he's not worried. He's going to get a stick in the dick."

Still, penile implants are not something I would personally like to recommend to my friend Ted. Instead, I scour the literature for nonmedical solutions to potency problems.

"Even if erection is lost, my partner can orgasm by rubbing my quite soft penis against her clitoris and I do ejaculate, even though not hard," offers one man.

"If the erection is only partial, I can still achieve insertion by pinching the penis at the base and my wife's hot vagina does the rest — I'm soon fully erect." This man places his hand on his pubic area, squeezes the base of his penis between his forefinger and middle finger, and traps the blood until the penis is firm enough to slide, or "stuff," into his wife's vagina. "If that fails, we have sixty-nine to orgasm. Lack of erection is no sign of disinterest."

No matter how it's done, stuffing seems to trigger erection in many men. Sometimes a lubricant is used for entry. And some men use cock rings to trap the blood in the penis and maintain erection.

But with or without an erection, men can still feel desire and have a sexual life. When I ask Ted about impotency he says, "What man hasn't had a problem with impotency. I've had it intermittently from fatigue, illness, whatever. But after the heart attack, I experienced it much more often. I'm on many toxic drugs and these clearly contribute to its cause."

"But can you make love when you're impotent?" I ask.

Ted laughs. "Of course. Like everything, impotency is a matter of degree — an erection for a very short time, or no erection at all. But I'd like to remind my fellow men that we have other means beside the penis to get and give pleasure. We have our hands and our mouths and tongues. This combination is usually capable of giving pleasure to a woman and bringing her to climax. Being a good lover means just what it says, loving the woman, fondling, caressing, sucking, licking, kissing wherever it gives her pleasure. And something else — if a man's penis cannot become hard, for whatever reason, that doesn't mean he has lost any sensitivity in that area. One can still be pleasured by the woman if one's penis is limp. If two people are happily trying to give each other pleasure, they'll find the means to do so, no matter what degree of impotence the man may have. Let's face it, a man can make love as long as he's alive and wants to."

Confronted by younger men's performance anxiety, Ted develops his most imaginative approach yet. He tells me, "A young man, about forty, asked me if I still have sex. He was very worried. So, I said, 'Sure I have it. When I'm alone, I have it.' He didn't get it. So I said it again, differently. 'I'm tired of so many people. Too many people. So I have it alone.' 'So you *don't* have any problems,' he said. 'No, I don't mind,' I told him, 'I'm very understanding.'"

Now Ted has a new long-legged companion who, he says, is much better for him than Dr. Taguchi's gadgets. When we last speak, he tells me this joke.

"An eighty-year-old man goes to the doctor for his regular checkup. The doctor says, 'How are you, Mr. Stern?'

"Mr. Stern says, 'Fine, fine, I feel great.'

"'And how's your sex life?' the doctor asks.

"'Great, absolutely great,' says Mr. Stern. 'I have sex four, five times a day. It's great.'

"'Four or five times a day,' says the doctor, 'four or five times a day. That's very dangerous. A person could die from that.'

"'So,' says Mr. Stern, 'let her die.'"

Although many men worry about impotence, the reality is that only one out of ten men have continuing or chronic impotence. In general, men do not lose their capacity to have erections and ejaculations as they age. Impotence is not the norm.

Allowing for individual differences, most older men experience a number of gradual and fairly predictable changes in erectile function. It may take an older man minutes, rather than seconds, after sexual stimulation to have an erection. The penis may be less large, straight, and hard, but when fully excited it will be sturdy and reliable, particularly if this was the pattern in earlier life. The need to ejaculate may decrease, which means that older men can enjoy more leisurely lovemaking. My dad says, "It takes longer, but the positive part of it is that you experience that much more pleasure." After orgasm, the interval between erections tends to be longer — from several hours up to several days. So some men have intercourse as frequently as they wish but ejaculate perhaps only once out of every two or three times that they make love. After orgasm, the erection may go down quickly. Orgasm itself sometimes feels a little different and sometimes not: the pre-ejaculation stage may disappear and ejaculation may feel less explosive. According to poet, cartoonist, ex-Fug, Tuli Kupferberg, sixty-five, "The quality of sex changes for men very slowly. The climaxes are not as ecstatic but sometimes they are."

At a geriatric center conference on "Sexuality in Later Years," the speaker distributes a sex questionnaire to the elderly audience. One question asks whether it is true or false that males over the age of sixty-five usually experience a reduction in the intensity of orgasm relative to younger males. The correct answer is "true," but the two old men filling out the questionnaire on the folding chairs next to mine both circle "false."

Potency changes are noticed by different men at different ages, depending, usually, on overall health. Some men notice a significant change at twenty-five and then gradual changes, such as those described above, beginning in their forties. Other men do not notice any changes until much later. Whatever the individual differences, physiological changes in erectile function are normal. They are not signs of emotional or sensual impairment. They need not diminish sexual activity or enjoyment.

But many older men are thrown for a loop by their potency changes because they have accepted two prevalent cultural fallacies: a man has to be able to perform anytime, anywhere; it is normal to become impotent with age. When potency changes occur, men misinterpret the changes as alarming evidence of the onset of impotence, or its future inevitability. They fall into the trap of measuring their manhood by their ability to get and maintain erections. Worrying makes lovemaking difficult, and what might have been accepted as natural often becomes a real problem.

"From a psychosexual point of view," write Masters and Johnson, "the male over age fifty has to contend with one of the great fallacies of our culture. Every man in this age group is arbitrarily identified by both public and professional alike as sexually impaired."

Women, too, are frequently uninformed about male sexual physiology in later years and, therefore, are not as helpful as they might want to be.

"We have to be more active as sexual partners if we seek out men our own age," says Ruth Weg, "because older men need more stimulation to be able to reach the level of excitement to be able to erect. The penis needs direct stroking. And many women of my cohort find that difficult. So, it's something we need to learn. Sexual behavior is learned. It is not instinctive unless we're dogs — and we're not dogs. The fun you share, even the humor, can be part of making love."

In a recent book, written after he was eighty, Morley Callaghan imagined the feelings of an older man who had been a strong confident lover:

> And then one night in the dark, when she was naked on the bed, waiting, he got into bed. She opened her arms and, maybe, taking her in his arms, he couldn't take her. He grew frightened as he lay beside her, the chill of death in him, taking his hand from her shoulder, the hand grown cold. His legs would have grown cold, too, his age catching up to him, afraid to ask his young wife to arouse him, afraid to crawl naked out of bed, and growing frantic, lying silent in the dark, while Cretia waited, wondering.

Some men adapt and enjoy their sexuality. Others, when their body changes, either avoid situations that can lead to lovemaking or contrive to make them less frequent. If they are fearful or uninformed, they often, in their terms, "fail."

Louis Jaques was visiting his daughter, my typist, when Sandy's interview about making love with Ted came off the printer. He started reading and I could hardly get the transcript out of his hands. "You're a good-looking man," I say, looking at his abundant white hair, combed back Gary Grant style, his blue eyes, trim build. "You must have experiences too." I knew that as a professional photographer, on expense-account assignments for a weekend glossy, he'd been around. "No, I don't have experiences. I'm not really interested. You should write more about people who don't have sex," he says, throwing down the gauntlet.

I drive north of Montreal to the village of Ste-Adèle, turn right at the Shell station, past the Alpine Inn, to the Wexford housing development. Retired now, Louis spends half his time in a mobile home in Sarasota and the other half in the Laurentians, near the golf course. He rents a small utilitarian house with a comfortable porch and a spectacular view of rolling mountains and a verdant valley.

Louis warms the teapot with a practiced hand and we sit on the deck in the shade of an old pine tree, listening to the euphonic traffic of purple finches, grosbeaks, and chickadees, to and from the feeders.

"What a lovely place."

"I spend so much of my time out here if the weather's nice."

"On the porch?"

"It's the belvedere, my dear, not the porch," says Louis from his chaise lounge.

He tells me that many of his friends retired "and the rot set in." But he plays nine holes of golf every morning at half past seven, reads omnivorously, tapes music, and has a correspondence with friends from "the paper." He cooks for his brother Ronnie the two months they're together in Florida, and has a very active social life in the Laurentians. His life "couldn't be more agreeable."

For Louis, "sex is not a problem, not at all. Because, as you know, my wife had a rotten time the last three or four years of her life with a brain tumor, and even though I did have sexual urges at that particular time, I didn't find it too difficult not to do anything about it. That was 15, 16 years ago. I'm 81 now, so, I was 62, 63. And after Katy died, I'd been away from it for so long that I became intimidated. Particularly since in that period, sex had become like a trapeze act in the Olympics, you know. So much was expected that I didn't want to go through any of that. I tried a couple of times and I was so goddamn embarrassed about my inabilities to function too well that I just said, 'To hell with this. I don't need this embarrassment.' I don't — it's become a way of life with me. I don't want the hassle. I don't want the intrusion of another external source into the kind of life I live. I like my way of life and I don't want it upset, or changed, or altered. Combined with the fact that right now it's a kind of race against time. I'm racing against inflation. Because I retired sixteen to seventeen years ago and the McDonnell Enterprise, with all their millions, established a pension fund for their employees which really wasn't generous at all. There was no escalated clause built into it. What you got when you retired was what you got for the rest of your life. So I'm in no financial way to entertain anybody or to become involved in any sense and I'm quite happy with the life I've got."

"Is it because of money that you don't get involved?"

"Money's a part of it. Mainly, I like my life. I don't want any intrusions into it."

"You tried a bit with women after your wife died but you were embarrassed. Why were you embarrassed?" I ask.

"Well, I was. I just didn't perform too well. I got carried away. I got too excited . . . I think they call it premature ejaculation, don't they?"

"I wonder if you realized there were things you could have done to make the woman happy, even if you had premature ejaculation."

"But I wasn't concerned with making the woman happy."

"Then why were you embarrassed?"

"Because just as a sexual act, at least, I should have performed well sexually. It's the least I could have done."

"Just to show you could."

"Yeah. I thought I could but I'd been away from it too long."

"But why did you want to perform well sexually?"

"Because it was kind of expected of me, I guess. A man of my years, I'd been around a lot and met a lot of women and had a lot of experiences, and I think they thought, Jesus, this ain't much, is it? And they were people I knew quite well."

"I'm wondering if your giving up sex had to do with a lack of information."

"Oh, I don't know. I guess I went into a shell about sex completely from the time that my wife became so ill. You know, after being sexually active all your life, all of a sudden you just stop completely, four or five years, don't do it anymore . . . I would have needed someone who was going to be around for a while. The two or three occasions I did have sex after my wife died were with close personal friends, but they weren't living where I was living, they were visiting for a couple of days. And, then, I don't know, they seemed so attractive. I was a little alcoholically invigorated, couldn't keep good control of myself, didn't think too smartly and then, of course, it's too late."

"It's not too late."

"It is if they're leaving the next day. Not around the corner either, but the other side of the continent . . . So anyway, though, the hell with this. I don't need this. Too bad."

"You talk about yourself as if that decision is made."

"Oh yeah. I made that decision quite a few years ago. I didn't want to hear about anybody's problems, worry about their moods. I don't need that. I'm happy. I cook well, I keep a clean house, I've got all kinds of friends. I've got all the social life I need, in fact, I turn down a lot of social life."

Louis was going to dinner with a couple that lived nearby. They were going to pick him up so he didn't have to return at night on his "conveyance," a Moped. His friends, he says, are "kind" to him.

"What will you tell them about our conversation?"

"I have told them. The very notion that a man and a woman could sit here talking about this subject makes them aghast, totally aghast. Two of my friends on the golf course said, 'Louis, want to make an extra hundred.'"

"What did they mean?" I ask.

"They were offering me a hundred bucks to let them come and listen."

"Why did you talk to me?"

"I have no sense of embarrassment or personal shame. I think the subject should be opened up and that people should realize they're not out there in left field all by themselves. To my satisfaction, I've resolved it. I'm content with it. I don't want anybody to hug me. I don't want anybody to move in on my life. I don't want to get involved with sex anymore. With this AIDS thing and all the things I read about women's complaints, it doesn't attract me."

For Louis, celibacy is a viable choice.

But for Henry Miller, continued sexuality was vital. Even when he no longer had sexual relations, he sustained himself with their juices. One of the most moving testimonies to the power of desire and fantasy is to be found in the love letters of Henry Miller, written to the actress Brenda Venus.

When he meets Brenda Venus, Miller, eighty-four, is bedridden and almost blind. He has endured a series of debilitating operations, one lasting sixteen hours. His life is on the ebb and he knows it. He describes himself as a "physical ruin." Brenda sends him a picture of her lovely face that begins an "affair of the heart" which, according to long-time friend Lawrence Durrell, was "literally keeping him alive; indeed her generosity and tact allowed him to end his days in a marvellous euphoria of loving attachment." The love letters are an outpouring of what Miller once called his "anatomical style." They include cultural opinions, a two-page erotic fantasy written in French for Brenda, a "most vivid and thrilling" sexual dream, gratitude and praise:

July 15, 1976

I may put your photos under my pillow tonight in order to summon the dreams I desire. Do you mind? Brenda, your letter makes me more and more "delirious" — I think that's the word for it. What erogenous zones I have left are quivering with hopeless anticipation. Nothing in the world would give me a greater thrill than to take you (roundabout expression) or even just feel your secret parts . . .

July 21, 1976

And, as for nudity, don't you go about your own home naked sometimes? Did you know that Benjamin Franklin used to do it and recommended it to all good Americans. It makes one relax, feel free, is good for skin and circulation, and gets one to appreciate one's own body . . .

Do I sound "Hedonistic"? How can I help it with you? You invite romantic dreams, "the skin one loves to touch," nocturnal emissions, and God knows what all . . .

10/7/76

Though I've only known you for a short time, I feel I know you intimately. Not your life but you, your emotions, your dreams, your aspirations. And of course every letter I receive from you confirms this suspicion. So much so that when we meet for just a few minutes — kiss and run — I feel content, satisfied, fulfilled . . .

If we haven't made love here below, we have in dream and reverie. And perhaps those are the best fucks, eh what? . . .

Friday P.M.

I imagine I could fuck you morning, noon, and night, but common sense tells me that's out of the question. But nobody can stop me from fucking your head off — in my imagination. One of the tragedies of old age is that one can be very horny, yet not have an erection . . .

Saturday [10/28/77]

I keep thinking about you as a flower from the deep South, with such a wondrous fragrance, and a seeming fragility. Actually, you are strong as a tiger — and dangerous when angered, I fear. My sight is dimming now. I have been writing without glasses. Hearing from you, I imagine I can do anything.

Yes, dearest, dearest Brenda, it is only because of you that I am alive today. I know it better than anyone . . .

9:00 P.M. Monday [June 25, 1978]

Sometimes I could just undress you and lick you from head to toe. In my sleep I run my hands over the curves in your physique — what a thrill! Like being proficient in runs at the piano . . .

Sept 29, 1980

And now a man of 87, madly in love with a young woman who writes me the most extraordinary letters, who loves me to death, who keeps me alive and in love (a perfect love for the first time), who writes me such profound and touching thoughts that I am joyous and confused as only a teenager could be. But more than that — grateful, thankful, lucky . . . We have been both blessed. We are not of this world. We are the stars and the universe beyond.

Long live Brenda Venus!

God give her joy and fulfillment and love eternal!

HENRY

When sexuality is interrupted by circumstance, it is probably easier for women than men to start again. Women are trained to consider a wider range of exchanges sexual. Their state of arousal does not have such obvious visual manifestations as that of men. And they are not cursed with male expectations of "performance." Mary Frances Fisher was surprised at her own sexual resilience.

"Of course, I'm used to abstaining from sex, because after I divorced Donald Friede [her third husband], I said all I wanted was custody of the two children until they were eighteen. See, I live alone. I have one lover and I like him even though he's everything I detest in a man. He's a top lawyer in the American army and he's a general. And this is awful. I just hate military people and I hate lawyers, although I dearly love my uncle who is a lawyer. He's everything wrong and yet we just are fused when we come together. But I felt kind of silly when he said he'd been in love with me for a long, long time.

"Of course, he's very well married, and has an awfully nice wife so it [his job] doesn't concern me . . . He comes out every six months or something, so, I seem fated to have people like that love me. And I love to be loved by a good man, you know. I really like it. Even now. I was so surprised when about a year ago I just fell into bed with this man and it was great. Fine. And I wasn't out of practice for some reason. I don't know why. As a matter of fact, I'm kind of sorry it happened, in a way, because it was such fun."

"Why should you be sorry?"

"Because it sort of disturbed me for a while, you know."

"Because of who he is?"

"No, no. Just because it interfered with my work. I sound as if all I thought about was work and that's not true at all. But it's the main thing. I would be dead if I didn't write. So, it keeps me alive, not that I want to stay alive particularly, but there's no excuse at all for my breathing if I'm not doing something. If I knew somebody I loved and was really compatible with in other ways than in bed, it would be nice. But I know this man, and when he's being sent to Korea or something he always stops here. And I'm not a Tristan and Isolde type at all. Never see your lover again but you love only him and that sort of thing. I've loved one man [Dillwyn "Timmy" Parrish] and if he hadn't died, I'd be married now, I know, to him. But he did, he died, so there. So I've just made myself get along by myself, you see. Sounds rather revolting, but it's true."

"But what you're saying to me is that your sexuality is still there."

"Oh yes, definitely. I was surprised, you know, I thought it died, maybe. Use it or lose it. Practice, keep practicing. And I thought, well, nobody has made love to me for quite a while, just at my request, because I don't want to get all tangled up for somebody who's going to leave tomorrow, you know. So I thought, I've made it pretty well this far and I'm not going to let it bother me now. And it doesn't bother me a bit about him, this man who's coming out next week. But I don't feel any of the joy of conquest or anything that I used to when I was a little girl."

"What do you feel at his coming?"

"Just a real satisfaction. Pleasure. My vanity is a little pleased that he makes the effort. I really don't see why he does. But he likes me and he's very amusing. He's very pompous in a way, and he's a very well read person, even if he is a soldier. And he didn't want to be a lawyer. He told me that one time he was reading something to me that I didn't want to listen to. I had my eyes closed because I thought at least it's better this way. So he said, 'What's wrong? Are you asleep?' And I said, 'No, I'm not. Do I have to look at you while you read?' Well, he's really quite nice looking and I kinda liked his voice, but I didn't see why I had to look at him all the time while he was reading. But he's very amusing. He's nice to be with and he knows how to behave, you know. He drinks very moderately but well.

But it would be terrible if I really fell in love with him. I think it would, because it would be so frustrating to fall in love and wait six months, eight months before you see him again. Oh, I wouldn't mind falling in love, but I never will now, I know. I was only in love, I mean really, truly, in love, with Timmy. I realized quite a long time ago, but not at the time it happened, that he spent the last three years of his life teaching me how to get along without him."

"Is your friend who visits you your age?"

"No, he's younger than I. You have to get out of the army at a certain age, don't you? Anyway, he's still in it."

"So he keeps in shape?"

"Oh yeah, he's a good-looking man. Nice one to be with. He's got a strange dash to him."

"You said he read your books, then introduced himself by writing to you?"

"Then he started writing more. But he's very religious and he always ends his letter with 'God bless you, I'm praying for you,' or something like that. Oh, blah. But he means it very sincerely. And he quotes things a lot too. He'll say 'You know, as Ruskin said in that essay of his . . .' and suddenly he'll quote a long thing from Ruskin. Well, I never read anything of Ruskin's except when I was a kid. We had a book with a rather fancy William Morris design in gold on leather and it was *Sesame and Lilies* by John Ruskin. I was about eight then. My mother said, 'You can try it.' Well, I thought it was pretty silly. That's all I know about Ruskin, really. This man knows the darnedest things. Suddenly he'll be Nicholas Nickleby or he'll be . . . But he knows and I know that it's just a very physical, good thing between us. It's nice too."

One Way Conversation

There are many men like you, perhaps
most certainly
most

but even though I've had
an itch for the seven-inch
reach   the hard entry
yet
I cannot despise you!

A woman wants above all
to be touched, caressed,
massaged and kissed
and what she carries away
the next day
is pride of flesh
love of link with man
human to human

O do not be distressed
that you cannot create
the great illusion:
thundering gods
at the womb's intrusion . . .
You have a role
valid as sunshine
of speech as equal
of man in parallel
pain . . . joy . . .

partner to woman
You have a role   gently caressing
human to human

Dorothy Livesay, Officer of the Order of Canada and twice win-
ner of the Governor General's Award for poetry, wrote this
poem in her seventies. In it, she voices feelings about sexuality
that I am only now beginning to recognize: "A woman wants
above all/to be touched, caressed,/massaged and kissed . . ."
The act that warms her like sunshine is not a power game but a
link, "human to human."

Now almost eighty, Dorothy Livesay's writing contains a frank
and beautiful record of the evolution of her own sexuality, a life
cycle ode to "the transcendence of the solitary ego through
mutual ecstasy." I admire her for having retained a unique and
poetic vision, even though life is financially hard and society
largely dismissive. And I feel that because she has plumbed her
own continuing passion, it will be easier for me, as I age, to
acknowledge my own.

Dorothy Livesay wrote "The Woman I Am," after the death of
her husband, when she was in her sixties. It declared her dis-
tance from the restrictions of her puritan upbringing. Recently, I
watched her walk resolutely to the front of a junior college class
and say:

The woman I am
is not what you see
I'm not just bones
and crockery

the woman I am
knew love and hate
hating the chains
that parents make

longing that love
might set men free
yet hold them fast
in loyalty

the woman I am
is not what you see
move over love
make room for me

I fly across Canada to Vancouver, take a bus to Tsawwassen, join the orderly crush of backpackers, cars, commuters, cyclists, and board the ferry for Galiano Island, Dorothy's home. The loading dock retracts. The sun warms the kids on the deck. The sea greets the horizon. I stand at the bow, scanning a vast expanse of water as, slowly and magically, like images in a developing bath, Dorothy and the island grow more distinct and take form.

Dorothy's beat-up yellow Toyota winds up and down narrow roads to a small cedar-shingle cottage on the shore of the Georgia Strait. We are talking as we unload. After seven years, Dorothy has just "bedded a man," and the encounter is unpleasantly reminiscent: "We had a nice long kiss and then he said, 'You're *such* a passionate woman.'" This was not a compliment, she explains, but something the man found threatening. "I knew then that I wouldn't be able to move." She mimes lying on her back, arms open in surrender. "But it was too late. I had to go through with it." I am smiling, at the same time trying to understand how this affects Dorothy, when a car with three women pulls up.

Teatime intervenes.

When the visitors go, I ask if I may tape. Dorothy protests that she has said it all before. She would like to walk. I may tape, as we walk, on Bluff Ridge.

A solitary tourist stands at the lookout by the sea where the rocky footpath begins. Dorothy scrambles down but she has forgotten her walking stick. I break and clean a dead branch, hoping it is sturdy enough.

"I think it'll help me just to have the feel of it in my hand. It will encourage me to think I'm getting help."

"Mind over matter."

"That's one of the hardest things to have if you're in pain — mind over matter. You know, I try to live a mantra, and the pain keeps poking in."

"Have you had much pain?"

"I had cancer of the lung. I had one lobe taken out."

"Still, you've written poems about the freedom of getting older," I remind her.

"About not having to look after anything, anybody. But someone said I choose birds to feed. The towhees call me in the morning and I can't resist them. And this woman who's renting my house has cats and my birds will be horrified, they'll get killed. I thought she might bell her cat, but, of course, many of the things one thinks would be pleasant for someone to do, it turns out they get offended. That's the trouble with having been a teacher, I think. You get into the habit of telling people the things they could do to improve something or themselves in some way. And this has been my trouble. I come on too strong. Well, that's what puts men off, obviously."

I wonder if this is what happened with the man Dorothy bedded.

"You think men are scared when a woman makes the first move?" I suggest.

"If, as they find out, or believe, or are told, the woman is a *passionate* woman, they think, Oh God, what am I getting into?"

"What does that mean to them?" I ask.

"Do you think we have to figure out what we think they think?"

"If it means you can't move when you're making love, then, perhaps, yes."

Dorothy tells me that even her husband was "very much a puritan," with a constrained idea of how women should behave sexually.

"When we were first getting together, we were out on an overnight hike, in something like this country here, sleeping on the rocks. And when I woke up in the dawn, with the sun coming up, I moved over and lay on top of him. And he was just sort of sleepy and didn't, you know, pay much attention. Then I had an orgasm. And he said, 'Hey, what's going on here?' It never occurred to him that a woman would make any responses like that."

I ask how she survived the repressive expectations.

"I decided, you see, even though I gave in a few months ago, I've decided I will never find a man with whom to sleep, with whom to fuck, if you like, I never will. I'm seventy-seven. For the last seven years, certainly, I've thought there's no use sleeping with a man. Because they're afraid I'll put them in a poem. So I decided, since I do have these horny times, I decided I would give in to a woman who was courting me, and it worked."

"What do you mean, 'It worked'?"

"Well the difference is, we know how to touch, what gives us most happiness in the way of touch. You know what is needed, from your beloved, what men don't know."

Even so, I wonder if it is hard for her to retain a sexual image of herself as she gets older.

"Indeed it is, because you just look in the mirror and you think, Oh my God, who would be the least bit interested in me? Well, that's another very uncomfortable thing — the fact that some women have their faces blown up."

"Lifted," I correct.

And then, I laugh, and laugh. Too long, maybe, my laughter. But it seems hilarious. Dorothy is a poet. She chooses her words as others choose jewels — "blown up." It is a release from a conversation I know to be difficult for Dorothy and difficult for me too.

"Now I need your hand, I've thrown away my stick. To the birds."

I reach out to help Dorothy negotiate the rocks. Society has always snapped at her heels but with an iron will she has kept her passionate spirit alive. As a girl she was a romantic, but when she married she became "a wife." She was expected to stop dreaming, stay at home, and "handle" her husband. She hated dishonest "maneuvering" and instead fought for what she believed. She was condemned for precipitating domestic confrontations and for having a career. After years of marriage, in London, England, on a teaching internship, she received a telegram advising her of her husband's death. Today she can hardly believe it, but she ran down the street near the university shouting "I'm free, I'm free, I'm free!"

In her sixties, she fell in love with a younger man, beginning a five-year love affair and writing remarkable poems of sensual joy.

Let your hand play first
fanning small fires
over the arms, the breasts
catching responses all along the spine

until the whole body flowering
's enveloped in one flame
that shudders wildly out
to meet your thrust —

Then burn, my fire
burn with a flame so tall
it can unshape the shaping clouds
unearthly move the sphere

When we are on flatter terrain, I remind Dorothy that much of her early sensual poetry accepts what many women are trained to accept — a focus of sexuality on the penis. I ask her if she still feels that way.

"Yes, I'm not a lesbian who really resents and hates men."

"Isn't that different than having your sexuality focused on the penis?"

"Yes, I see . . . that you can only feel sexual if you know a penis is coming. Well, I have a poem that's called 'Widow.' Even the lesbians say that it's the first poem they'd ever read about masturbation. So I don't require the entry. But when it's good and it can last a while, it's great."

"Do you find you can say what you want more fully now than you could when you were thirty or forty?"

"Yes, I have written love poems to a woman and I couldn't have done that before. And it is only because the woman loves them and loves to share them."

Dawnings

I
When the moon stops by
with his bag of silver
I'll not give him
a look-in

I'll wait for the tender fingers
of the woman sun
slipping through the window
sliding like love
into my skin

II

We rise later and later
now that the day's eyes
are laggard

our eyelids flutter open
rubbing away cloud

III

You must let your mouth go
you must drown in me.

You are fresh and sweet-smelling
as apple blossom
but the tree is there:
rough bark gnarled bough

I am that part of you —
let go let go

Bliss me with your mouth

IV

In bed alone
I'm just a bundle of aching bones
with an overhang of belly.
In such disrepute with self
how dare I remember
passion?

For the fire has flown —
Instead: a well of clear water
awaits me
where you let me come
holding a small cup

Dorothy and I leave Bluff Ridge. We drive to Arbutus Park, a retreat of tall arbutus trees, their bark as sensuous and smooth as a peeled green branch. "Touch them," Dorothy offers.

At home, she stretches out on a couch in a small room with a wood-burning fireplace and the family's old butternut drawers and carved wooden chair. Poppies frame the window.

"I need something under my knees."

"I'll get it," I say.

"You treat me like an invalid, you know."

"Do you find that?" I am embarrassed. "I'm just trying to be friendly."

"I couldn't take it all day long. I know you are, but I have to be able to do things for myself."

It is late afternoon and the ferry leaves soon. I find myself being both solicitous and ruthless. I know Dorothy is tired but I want to ask yet another question. I want to know if Dorothy thinks that at a certain age my capacity to attract men will end?

"Yes. You have to accept that about yourself when you're about sixty. You must accept that."

"Accept what exactly?"

"Accept the fact that you will not be attractive and, therefore, you must simply decide to be good friends with someone. I guess I've been lucky having a friendship with Alan and, here, for the last three or four years, a friendship with Tony. Because he helps me out with all kinds of thing that he does that I can't do, like fixing the stove."

"Will I still have the same sexual feelings that I have now when I'm sixty?" I ask. "Because if I have any mystical feeling, it's about sexuality, like what you've written about transcendence through mutual ecstasy."

"I went through a very hale and hearty period in my sixties in which I wanted sex a lot. And I became a bit promiscuous. If a man was at a party and we both drank wine, it could end up in bed. I did that sort of thing for a while. Then one man, an older working man I had several beddings with, said, 'I didn't know you needed it so bad,' and, well, I got through that and that's when I moved into the area of women. She was very much in love with me, and I found I could have sexual satisfaction. So that's when I moved over and, also, as the poem says, I masturbated, which does relax one very much, you can go to sleep after that. They say that if you continue to have sex right through without a break, it'll last much longer into your eighties and nineties."

I sit vulturelike on a chair beside the couch, microphone poised. I am totally engrossed, framing another question, when I hear Dorothy say quietly, "I'm trembling now. I'm not used to talking so much about myself."

I look at her and it's true: she is trembling.

I call Dorothy when I return to Montreal.

"We talked a lot," I say.

"Yeah. Double-talk," she retorts.

A week later I receive a letter referring to our "delightful day," informing me she is going to a writers' conference in Jerusalem.

Several months later, there is a letter from Dorothy, addressed "To all my interviewers":

> Please understand how I must make it clear that just because there are three or four poems which may lead you to think that I am a lesbian, this is not the case. I have great sympathy with lesbians but I am constructed in such a way that I am bisexual and the greater part of my life has been in relationships with men. I am sympathetic, however, to women who have been unable to connect with men and who feel drawn to be close to another woman. "Honi soit qui mal y pense," I am not thinking of injuring anyone.
>
> au revoir

Women live seven to eight years longer on average than men. If you don't count gay men or gay women (10 percent of women) or women already in couples, there are five women over fifty for every available man. The longevity gap relates in part to genetic differences, but these are smaller than we think. Dr. Ruth Weg says that the real killer is stress. Traditionally, men are socialized to support the family, to make the decisions, and to work outside the home in competitive, hierarchical environments. The unabated stress they endure damages organ systems which they don't realize are already less efficient in middle age.

Margaret Day, seventy-seven, notices that it is the men in her circle of friends who are dying off first. She has always felt sorry for the men of her generation because they worked so hard and felt so responsible for their families, "far more than they ought to have. And there wasn't much freedom for them." The women set their own clock somewhat, and "given the nature of women's work they've always been more creative and many-sided because they had to do so many things at one time, keep many balls in the air at the same time. Whereas men led much more single-minded lives." In most cases, Margaret's female contemporaries are more adaptable than the men. More resilient, more curious, and closer to other people.

Often, they continue to play the major nurturing role in the family. If stroking an animal lowers blood pressure, it seems safe to assume that rocking a healthy baby would too. In "Project Caress," seniors rock, feed, and cuddle infants. "Seated on eight wooden rockers in the hospital conference room," reports a hospital newsletter, "the grandmothers lulled themselves and the infants to sleep." In her celebratory "Thoughts on Becoming a Grandmother," Betty Friedan says her hunch is that "the very embrace of changing, evolving life that makes women relish even becoming grandmothers is what helps keep women alive longer then men."

There are fewer women than men like the one Mrs. Topham, sixty-eight, visits — "a very sad eighty-year-old man who is all alone and doesn't do anything with his life. He never did anything except work."

Work alone does not provide the skills and interests we need in old age. Dr. James Birren supervises a research project to help retired older people learn how to make friends. Many are *unused* to a style of conversation that builds an attachment to another person. They are in the habit of making information statements that don't involve an interaction.

> FIRST PERSON: The weather's cold.
> SECOND PERSON: Yup, it's been a long winter.
> FIRST PERSON: The newspaper says we can expect another week.
> SECOND PERSON: That's Canada for you.
> FIRST PERSON: Last year it snowed in April.

This parallel talk — the norm in an active work life — could go on till next winter without any crossover or interaction. Like a game of verbal Ping-Pong. But, to form a friendship, a person needs to ask open-ended questions and, then, follow up on the answers:

> How was your son's visit?
> Oh, do you think there is anything you should do?
> Would that make you feel better?

Birren's studies of attachment behavior show the value of conversation that can build friendships.

"I have one graduate student who is looking at what we call 'the confidant relationship,' that very selective relationship with another person with whom you share intimate details of your life. Apparently, those people who have a confidant relationship prosper better. When unfortunate events occur, people go through the consequences of those events better if they have a confidant. People who don't have any emotional attachments are vulnerable. I think you have to be attached, you have to have emotional attachments to others that are non-exchangeable, special."

For all the put-down of "women's talk" in traditional literary and intellectual circles, its form and subject matter are more conducive to creating intimate relationships than is outer-directed "men's talk." Women, therefore, are more able to buttress themselves emotionally — another factor, perhaps, in a consideration of their comparative longevity.

Twenty-five years ago, large numbers of women started becoming workers outside the home. They also became heavier smokers. As a result, women are beginning to have disorders similar to those of men, such as coronaries and arteriosclerosis. Lung cancer is now more common than breast cancer. And women are getting these disorders earlier than they did before. "Women are losing the *rate* of their longevity advantage," says Dr. Ruth Weg. "We are dwindling our advantage by being foolish and imitating men. It is ironic that women, while reaching for full personhood, are reaching for an early death."

But, for now, there are still more older women than men. If the constraint for one out of ten older men who want to make love is impotence, the constraint for four out of five heterosexual older women is available men. And of those men who are available, a large percentage react to the weighted numbers in a curious manner.

One man says, "We feel chased because we have a few dollars." Another, a member of a widowers' support group in Lincoln, Nebraska, says enigmatically, "Some members don't want to mix with members of the female sex. Those gals are out looking for men and want to grab them for more reasons than one probably."

Dr. Gustave Gingras admits he has no desire to be exposed to "the details that had become reflexes, accepted between me and my wife." He lives alone, consults medically, has a collection of organ music, and eighty feet of operating train track with hand-made mountains, tunnels, and houses. When he listens to the *Messiah*, he stands to conduct. Given the women around, he is amply fed and entertained.

Many older women are treated like my friend Dez was by her ex-courtier, Edward. Dez, sixty-five, and I are at her home in London, England, dancing to Nina Simone and Tracy Chapman records. Dez stomps out the beat. I jump around and twirl. During a breather, I tell her of Dorothy Livesay's experience with a woman, and she tells me about Edward. When she was sixty, he asked her to marry him. She liked his mind and erudition but he was abusive when he drank and had a breast-grabbing-upon-hello kind of "vulgar sexuality." When Dez graciously declined, Edward was extremely upset. "You know," he said, his voice taut, "after sixty-five you won't be attractive to me anymore. This is really your last chance to get married."

What I see, but many men don't yet understand, is that older women have lived complex lives and come through more them-selves than when they started. They may miss male company but they are not going to become pushovers to get it. Dez decides on Edward according to her own values, not out of fear. Mary Calderone, at eighty-two, breaks off a long-term relation-ship because "I don't want to cope with the difficulties. The point is, I don't *need* that kind of relationship. The price I would pay, let's say, for continuing the relationship in time and energy and disturbance, would not be worth the sex."

"So what are all the single older women to do about sexuali-ty?" I ask Mary Calderone.

"I don't think there's anything to be done. You just can't cre-ate fucking machines, you know what I mean? And that is a pretty distasteful thought anyway. It's an interpersonal thing. So I think what you have to do is help people understand that sex is natural, that masturbation is a very good outlet, and fantasy is good, and if you don't have a partner, you just go back and you relive your good times."

Margaret Day says, "I'm not saying I don't miss sexuality because I do. If someone came along, I might live with him, but I would never give up my freedom."

Professor Carolyn Heilbrun suggests it is perhaps only in old age, certainly past fifty, that women can stop being "female impersonators." She quotes an Isak Dinesen character: "Women, when they are old enough to have done with the business of being women, and can let loose their strength, must be the most powerful creatures in the world."

Gerontologist David Gutmann quotes Ernest Hemingway on the same theme: "At a certain age the men writers turn into Old Mother Hubbard. The women writers become Joan of Arc without fighting." According to Gutmann, in later years, women become more like men and men become more like women. In Italy, America, Japan, everywhere he and his colleagues studied, male aggression declines in later years, beginning at about fifty-five, and decreases in old age below the average level of female aggression. Men move away from warlike, predatory, or entrepreneurial roles in the external social world. They become more interested in hearth and home and "a previously undeveloped eros: a hidden capacity for cherishing, appreciating, and bringing together." In Gutmann's words, this is "the necessary prelude to an advance toward new satisfactions."

At the same time, similarly across cultures and with age, women seem to become "more authoritative, more effective, and less willing to trade submission for security."

A Japanese study which tested men and women on an "introversion-extroversion" scale, found men more extroverted than women until age sixty, when a decline in this variable puts their scores below those of women.

An Italian study in an old-age home reports that women seventy and older work more than men, show higher intellectual efficiency, and are more self-directing than men.

In his examination of American postretirement couples, Robert Atchley perceived "a kind of role reversal from the presumed model husband-and-wife relationship in our society . . ."

In institutions and senior citizens' centers, Pauling and McGee found women holding leadership positions and serving as the most influential outside volunteers. "Across cultures," says Gutmann, "depth-psychological measures are unanimous in demonstrating the surgent virility [sic] of the older woman."

Gutmann calls the tendency of older men and women to resemble each other psychologically the "androgyny of later life."

In my interviews, I notice older women in couples are speaking up. Lora and Millie, retired farm women, describe the interpersonal changes that occur in many long-term relationships.

"My husband's tolerance for new things was very short-fused," says Millie. "I hung in there but now I'm yelling back like anything."

Lora says, "At first, my husband complained, 'You never spoke like that before.' And I said, 'You know why? Because I took it all. Now I'm giving it back. So you listen to *me* now.' And he did."

"I'm glad I tolerated it and all that and now it seems that everything is gelling the way I want it to be," Millie says.

"They have mellowed. I haven't mellowed. My guy has mellowed," Lora concludes.

Dr. Birren says, "Late in life what you place value on is the companionship in the relationship."

Irwin Smalley, seventy-seven, and "the widow down the road" spend time together and go on cruises. "Heck, we've been through the Panama Canal a couple of times and a couple of places in South America, all the islands, even Grenada, before we went in there with the marines." Jan Lithwitz, the widow, sixty-six, says she's "too spoiled" to get married again. "I'm used to having my own way. If I were married, I'd probably have to prepare meals and do laundry and all that stuff. I mean, if I want to stay up till two o'clock and read or watch TV I can do that. If I want to get in the car and go someplace, I go." Unmarried, she gets her husband's company pension without the obligation she felt with her husband "to kind of do what the man wants to do." She doesn't let Irwin get away with being bossy: "I don't have to make an account of myself to anyone."

"What do you accept as an obligation to Irwin?" I ask her.

"I'm company, I'm good for him too. I'm company to him."

Joan and Erik Erikson say, "With aging, men and women in many ways become less differentiated in their masculine and feminine predilections. This in no way suggests a loss of sexual drive and interest between the sexes. Men, it seems, become more capable of accepting the interdependence that women have more easily practiced."

I ask Millie and Lora if the changes in their relationships affect sexual love.

Lora replies: "To us, this is the truth, there is ample sexuality. But many a time, it's just holding, touching, and we're satisfied. Snuggling. There's plenty of it. It doesn't have to be the whole act every time. It's the warmthness [sic]. To know that you're there when I need you. To hold you. My guy loves to be near me. He's got to be close to me all the time."

Erik Erikson suggests that the final psychosexual state is a "*generalization of sensual modes* that can foster an enriched bodily and mental experience even as part functions weaken and genital energy diminishes." He seems to be commenting on heterosexual sex, but his statement and Gutmann's findings on the "androgyny" of later life have relevance to older women who become bisexual. Dez's best friend, who is gay, thinks loving other women is the answer to the lack of men: "What's so special about heterosexuality? When you are older you can enjoy sex in a wide range of ways." Dez finds that "with men, once a woman is sixty-five or seventy, she's relegated to the dust bin, but with gay women, age is no barrier to attraction." Sixty-five-year-old Jeanne Adelman's description of her first night with a new love is an ode to the generalization of sensual modes:

> I find myself surpassingly excited by her body, unprecedentedly thrilled by our skin-to-skin-all-over closeness. Our freshness. The differences in our bodies, the similarities in our bodies. Kissing, caressing, kissing, clinging, riding, plunging, biting, kissing, kissing — I feel wild, passionately out of control, then I feel strong, in charge, then swept away, swept, away, swept, away. Feels like vertigo I experience when looking down from great heights: my thighs tremble, my legs seem to melt. Feels wonderful, feels frightening. Like flying and falling, but oh, such a soft warm tired spent landing.

From what older people tell me, *touch* becomes more and more important as a medium of sensual, sexual exchange. Ted Allan mentions "touch" nine times in one interview about sex. Marian Lewis relishes the doctor "fondling" her foot. Dorothy Livesay and her lover "know how to touch." Lora's husband wants to be "close." And Esther Gerstenfeld, seventy-six, has regular massage: "I feel good that someone is stroking me. It's good. When you live alone, you want that." As parents, we recognize instinctively, as Joan Erikson says, that "perhaps the most important sensory apparatus to be aware of is the human infant's dependence on and constant need for intimate closeness, for touching." As a society, we forget that how we are touched and held by another human being remains of special significance throughout our lives. The skin remains "our most consistently active and informing organ of sense." It is a way of getting us "in touch" with ourselves and others.

"I'm baffled by all the talk that goes on about, you know, sex is still important and all that," says Mike Zimring. "Why do they have to talk about it? I don't understand that at all. I mean, to me, when you get older, sex is many things. Sometimes, holding hands is a better feeling than the sex. There are other things — holding each other and just being with each other. Touching is as important as sex really. I don't know why they . . . I keep thinking it's because it sells — they keep talking about it."

Actor Vincent Price, seventy-seven, describes his feelings for his wife, Coral: "There's still the wonderful thing of being *terribly* fond of each other that is very sexual, *very* sexual, really more so than sex. To be really fond of someone, to touch them, to feel them, is wonderful, is something that lasts forever."

"Is that not sex," I wonder.

"Yes, it is sex," he laughs, "but it's not the common definition of sex as being carnal."

I listen to sex therapist Judith Segal, Ph.D., half psychologist, half stand-up comic, talking to a group of older people. She is addressing the problems caused by two common sexual realities: the change in penile function and the lack of a partner. "Down there" is not all there is to sex, she tells them, there are many ways to be erotic.

"If I say that sex is intercourse, what does that to to my partner? That's an awful lot of pressure on the performance of the penis. What happens if my partner, for some reason, doesn't get erections? Do I throw out the person and say, 'You aren't sexy because that one moving part doesn't work'? Sexual activity can be hugging, it can be touching, it can be sitting with, holding hands, having a good laugh. It can be massage, it can be stroking. It's very affirming when I can do that for you and I feel affirmed when you do that for me. And how nice to know that I can do that for myself. And we know that people feel better, they feel more relaxed, they can use it to feel more in control. And a lot of institutions say, 'If we let them alone, they'd masturbate all the time.' Well, why should they make baskets all the time? If I had a choice of making baskets or masturbating, I'll let you know where to find me and it won't be at a table with raffia reeds."

The roomful of older people laughs. They don't ask any questions, but each time Judith Segal uses sexual innuendo, they laugh.

More and more single older people are dating, sleeping together, entering into relationships. When they fall in love they may experience the same emotional somersaults as one seventy-five-year-old man, who says, "Love is when you look across the room and your heart goes pitty-pat."

But older people play fewer power games when they date, and one study (average age sixty-eight) found they more varied dating activities than younger people: camping trips, opera, outings. And they don't play head games. For most, sexuality developed rapidly and was an important part of the relationship. Sexuality included intercourse but the stronger emphasis was on the "nuances" of sexual behavior, such as hugging, kissing, and touching. People said that sexual intimacy contributed to their self-esteem by making them feel needed and desired. One seventy-seven-year-old woman said, "Sex isn't as important when you're older, but in a way you need it more."

My friend's mother, a statuesque blond woman of sixty-seven, has been a widow for several decades. Since I have never seen her with a man, I am a little surprised when her daughter suggests I talk to her about sex. She comes to the interview attractively made up, in a crisp, white sweater and red skirt, nails polished, the picture of poise and country-club class. If I hadn't seen her breathing deeply, inhaling and exhaling with conscious attention, as she entered, I would never have known she was nervous. She agrees to be totally frank, if I give her a pseudonym. "Jane Austen would be fine."

Jane is a Catholic, as was her husband. On their marriage night, he read a sex manual and she downed straight scotch. She was numb soon after, which was just as well since that night set the pattern for all others. Her husband got on top, thumped away briefly, and went to sleep. Married sex left her pacing and unable to sleep. Crying, she confided her frustration to the family priest, who advised her husband to "kiss Jane between the legs." He was shocked, "I could never do that. I respect Jane too much." In the final years of her married life, Jane, with six children, was tired. She had no interest in conjugal sex and the couple didn't have any.

When her husband died, Jane was celibate for years until she rediscovered a boyfriend she'd had when she was a teenager. He was married but showed up at her hotel room when she traveled. They read sex books, tried new positions, discovered oral sex. Released from the fear of having another child, Jane and her partner made love without inhibition. "It was fun," she said. "We felt like kids." She was in her sixties and beginning to really like sex, especially oral sex. The kissing and sucking was "fun." In bed with her lover, she giggled in his ear, "I'm glad I lived long enough to know about this." "Me too," he answered.

When her lover died, Jane was celibate again for several years. In her late sixties, she had a lover of fifty who was "not very considerate" and whom she had to admonish to lie with her after he reached orgasm. She liked the physical contact more than she liked him, and even though she dreaded being alone she broke it off.

Now, Jane has a married lover in his mid-sixties who appears at her door for afternoon trysts. "He's pulling off his clothes before he gets in the door." He has an erection immediately and, despite the textbooks, often has another twenty minutes later. An establishment lawyer in a tight social milieu, he welcomes the respite, grateful to be so virile. Jane doesn't really know him well, but the sex is "great, great. I really like it. I feel so free." She likes walking around naked. She likes her body. She likes being admired. She likes feeling the balls and penis, being touched, touching. "I feel good. It makes me feel good for days." And when she wants more caressing, she takes her daughter's lead and tells her lover, "I thought this was a twosi, not a onesi."

Still, her lover's sexuality is focused on his penis and on his orgasm. Because of time, they are always "watching the clock," and because they both come from the tradition where the missionary position was normal, all else perversion, Jane is still learning what she likes. She tells me that her excitation builds to a peak but she is not sure she has an orgasm. "What does an orgasm feel like?" I tell her I feel contractions in the vaginal wall and show her, with my hands on hers, how I think it feels on a man's penis. "Oh," she says.

Later, I learn that orgasm may feel different for older women. Clitoral response is similar in every way to that of a younger woman but, between ages fifty to seventy, there may be a gradual reduction in the duration of orgasm and the force of uterine and vaginal contractions. Knowing this, I'm not sure what Jane's experience of orgasm would be. I squeezed her hand when I should have asked her how it felt to her.

Yet, orgasm or not, there is no question that Jane enjoys sex. When she talks about it, her face is animated. She stretches like a stroked cat, laughs like a kid with a kite. She doesn't feel "prissy," she feels "free." Her current lover is not available to her, but she feels emotionally responsive and sexually alive. She thinks it likely that she will meet someone else.

Jane's sexuality might be negligible on medical bar charts that measure frequency and intensity of orgasmic response. There is no ascending or descending scale for increased well-being. Nothing for length of glow. No relaxation or looseness quotient. Feeling comfortable and companionable leads to sensual feelings, but this is not a familiar thought. It's not on television or in the literature. "We don't yet have a language for this kind of thing," as Dr. Birren says. Like most people in our culture, I am trained to think of sexuality as physical attraction culminating in sexual intercourse. I am having trouble conceiving of a sexuality that arises from companionship and culminates, perhaps, in touch.

I go see my Aunt Sue, sixty-eight and Uncle Joe, seventy-one, who have been the love of each other's lives since they were thirteen. After a lifetime of work — Joe as an electrician at Radio City Music Hall and Sue as a forelady at Alexanders department store — they winter in Florida and maintain a home, near me, in the Laurentians. Because of physical problems they have cut back on sexual intercourse, yet they love each other deeply. "You mature and you more or less meld into each other. And it's like we can look at each other and know what we're thinking," says Aunt Sue.

Still, having been conditioned to think of intercourse as an integral part of sexuality, I want to know more about how sexuality without intercourse is expressed.

Aunt Sue tells me "there's fondling, there's hugging, and touching."

"What might stimulate you to want to do things with Joe?"

"I think it's just because I'm comfortable with him, because I know he's there for me all the time."

"And that's a sexual turn-on?"

"Yes. I feel I can just sit down and he'll put his arm around me. I feel comfortable with him. And maybe this is what leads to our sexual relationship at this point. Where he'll hug me or how he'll try to make me feel young like I used to be."

"How?"

"Well, he'll hug me and he'll pat me and he'll touch me and this is what we used to do. "We fool around that way. Whether we think about it sexually or not, it's just the idea of wanting to feel that, we can still just fool around. It's really a great comfort to me when I'm feeling low and he puts his arm around me and, you know, tells me not to worry about it."

"What do you mean, 'fool around'?"

"We snuggle or . . . we have a saying that if we hug eight times a day, it's going to make us feel happy and contented. Have you ever heard of that? You hug your partner or your hubby or whatever eight times a day. And really, it makes you feel very tranquil, like you haven't got a worry in the world. And it makes you feel very close. And so that's what we do."

"Did you develop that, the eight times a day, or did you hear about it?" I ask.

"We heard it down in the park. Isn't that something? It's silly for senior citizens to walk around . . . but whenever, if he's got his arm around me, just gives me a little hug, I mean it makes me feel good, it makes me feel that I'm still wanted and I'm still desired, which is important. Without even the actual act of anything, it just makes me feel good."

"Do you love Joe in a way that you didn't love him before?"

"Of course. We've gone through a lifetime together, it means a long, long story, you know. We've gone over a lot of hurdles."

"What does it mean to you when you say you love Joe?"

"Well, to me, I consider his feelings. I try to be patient with him. Just being near him will make me feel good. And so when I say I can't think of being without him, it's because I want to be near him. And sex really doesn't come into my mind now because, not that it's not important, but I have to push it away, I have to block it out. I mean not that we haven't had sex, don't get me wrong, but it's not, of course, it's not as often, which is going to happen anyway, you know."

After I speak to Sue, I speak to Uncle Joe.

"You've loved Sue a long time."

"All my life, it sounds like to me, it seems like."

"And you know her from when she was a young girl. How does she look to you?"

"I don't go by her appearance anymore, 'cause that has changed. You know, her inner self is what I go by. She's still the same person, she's very good. That's the whole thing."

"I'm trying to figure out how people stay loving each other. What do you love?"

"The appeal stays. I find its hard to explain, I've never analyzed it. I just take everything for granted."

"But, you say, 'I've always loved her.' How has that love changed?"

"It hasn't changed as far as I'm concerned. I would have been long gone if it had. My affection for her has remained the same since she was thirteen years old."

"If the affection is not in the looks, is it in something else?"

"It can't be the appearance, her physical features alone, she's changed completely. I see pictures, I take a look and she's completely different."

"In what way?"

"Her appearance has changed. She's aged."

"But you still love her . . ."

"Absolutely."

"It's something else . . ."

"How do you explain it?" Uncle Joe asks me.

"I don't know," I laugh. "I'm asking you."

Joe chuckles. "How do you explain it? I don't know, it's just that — maybe we're used to each other, that's part to do with it . . ."

"Maybe."

"She knows me, she knows my character, my nutty things, my eccentricities, and I know hers, and then we tend to overlook all these crazy things and keep going. We had a lot of ups and downs when we were young. It was never easy. But we managed . . . I don't know. This is an answer I do not have. Maybe you would just take it for granted at this stage in life."

I give it one last try.

"What makes you want to make love to Auntie Sue," I ask him. "Does she do something? Does she remind you of something?"

"She reminds me of her youth," says Uncle Joe.

It sounds like poetry. And it stays and gathers meaning. Sue reminds Joe of her youth and she reminds him of *his* youth too. In Joe's memory, Sue is everything she was and is to him sexually and he is everything he was and is to her. I think of the feeling of being with a lover I knew when I was young. Of experiences with my companion, that I replay. Joe's thought is a new one to me and very sexy.

Joan Erikson, eighty-six, and Erik Erikson, eighty-seven, have been married fifty-seven years. Joan says, "You have to live intimacy out over many years, with all the complications of a long-range relationship, really to understand it. Anyone can flirt around with many relationships, but commitment is crucial to intimacy. Loving better is what comes from understanding the complications of a long-term intimate bond." Erik says, "There emerges also a different, a timeless love for those few 'Others' who have become the main counterplayers in life's most significant contexts. For individual life is the coincidence of but one life cycle with but one segment of history . . ." And Joan adds, "You put such stress on passion when you're young. You learn about the value of tenderness when you grow old. You also learn in late life not to hold, to give without hanging on, to love freely in the sense of wanting nothing in return."

"It's definitely a stronger love," says Joe Kuhl, married forty-five years. "You get to depend, more so, on the love."

"The jealousy gets less," says Gertrude Kuhl. "You accept the person more and more and more. You overlook a lot and you don't dwell on things like when you were younger, things that would bother you, things like you can't do this without me . . . just let that person go their way, you go your way. How would you say, Joe?"

"I think the love turns stronger maybe in a different way," Joe answers. "You don't see pettin' and so forth like that, but you will see on occasion older people hand in hand and so forth, and that's the kind of love I think we have. That type of love."

Yet, firsthand accounts from older men of their actual sexual experiences are as erotic as anything I have ever read about male sexuality. It's as if the physical changes stimulate men to be more sexually inventive than before. And, having accepted interdependence as a way of life, they are free to engage in mutual sexual exploration.

"As I have become older," writes an eighty-year-old man, "there have been some interesting changes. My enjoyment of sex is certainly no less (probably more), and the amount of time we spend making love is much greater since we both retired thirteen years ago. We seem to have become *more and more* uninhibited and free with each other — although we were anything but inhibited. For example: during the day, every now and then, we take a notion to sit on the sofa and open my fly so she can fondle my penis, while I reach inside her panties and stimulate her."

A seventy-one-year-old widower, with a partner he met through "an old folks' correspondence course," says: "As neither of us had ever had a sex relation outside of marriage, we have explored various sex activities with the enthusiasm of teenagers — and [we] both find oral sex to be ideal. We find in it a close relationship far superior to 'normal' sex. Also far less exhausting — and always successful, so there is no frustration."

Another older man says, "My wife and I have found that long-continued, deep soul kisses while masturbating each other, or just lying facing each other, are a very satisfying alternative to genital penetration."

Tuli Kupferberg says, "For me, attraction is not the age per se but how vital a person looks. I know from experience that sex with older people is good. The resiliency quotient of flesh is not what makes good sex. What is good is sex with a nice person. Someone who cares about you and you care for and, as far as physical pleasure goes, is willing to help you, is interested in your particular sexual needs. That's what makes good sex. With older people there is less embarrassment asking for what you like."

There is a sensitivity to the way older men describe their feelings for their long-term mates that I have rarely heard from younger men. From what they say, it seems the sensual feelings of older men, like those traditionally associated with women, can be stimulated by profound appreciation of the other person and of the intimate bond they share.

"What initiates a sexual feeling?" I ask Kalmen Kaplansky, seventy-four, a labor executive and human rights activist, married over forty years.

"Sometimes a gesture, a smile, an expression."

Willie Allister, seventy, can't put into words his love for his wife. "It's too personal, too deep." What he does know clearly is that "when we battle, life has no meaning."

Giff Gifford, sixty-seven, an ex-bomber pilot and now antinuclear activist, found a new love in his late fifties. They have been together for over ten years and "it gets deeper and deeper between Sylvia and myself." Gifford feels that "sexuality is too limited a word" for what they share. "Our physical sexuality, I suppose, is not as passionate as it was seven or eight years ago, but the depth of the relationship and the completeness of it seems to keep on growing, which is a continual astonishment, a constant, quiet wonder."

"Do you still love your wife?" I ask Mike Zimring, married almost forty years.

"Oh yeah! Listen, marriage can be the best of times and the worst of times. But when it's good, it only gets better as time goes on. I mean, there's complete trust. I guess my wife and I we feel we're just like one person now."

I have a question I've saved for him: "A forty-five-year-old friend said he and his male friends are scared they won't be turned on by their spouses when they are old. They married them when they were young, beautiful women 'with perfect parts.' They're worried they won't want to touch them."

"Oh . . . I don't know how to explain this. You're not even aware that she is getting older and may not be as attractive.

They're just as attractive to you as they were before. They're not, we know that age after all . . . But I don't see that at all."

"In what way is the person still attractive?"

"I don't even think about it. I'm not conscious of the way she looks and I think she feels that way about me."

"What are you conscious of?"

"Of her — herself," Zimring says.

"Which is what to you?"

"Well, she's everything, really. All I'd want, you know. I think this forty-five-year-old person you're talking about, he must put a very high premium on what people look like."

The love affair of Louis Gottlieb, eighty-five, and Reva Shrader, eighty-four, seen in the Academy Award-winning documentary *Young At Heart*, provides a portrait of how love and sexuality might be expressed in old age.

Louis and Reva, both fine painters, meet on a painting tour to the south of England. During the flight, "We talked and talked and talked and we were just so compatible we just didn't think we were on a plane," Reva recalls. Once in England, Reva moves in with Louis because he has a beautiful hotel room and hers is a closet. "He didn't object at all. So then we became very friendly." Louis adds, "From then on it was Reva and I."

Little by little, Louis moves into Reva's house, and after several years of living together they marry. During the ceremony, Louis carries himself with dignity and solemnity. Reva is so happy she cries. She answers, "I do, I do, I do," before the rabbi finishes his questions. Louis has trouble sliding the ring over her gnarled finger and she says, "It's enough already," and gets it on herself. Louis dabs her eyes with a handkerchief, bemused, moved. When they hug, Reva strokes and pats Louis's back. They hold each other tight.

After her son dies, Louis paints a portrait of Reva and, later, decides to do another larger portrait to "paint the gracious lady with large charm and life. At eighty-four, she's full of life. It's unusual. And I want to capture that." In the portrait session, Louis cocks his head to take Reva's measure. He smiles and cajoles so she will hold the pose a little longer. He is charm incarnate. "I love her simplicity, her sense of humor and her artistic nature. We have lots of joy being together."

"We touch and we hold hands and we kiss all the time," Reva says. "When you're 80, you're not physically attuned like you are when you're 30 or 40 but that isn't important anymore. It's stronger than just physical love. I think it's nice when you're in bed to have someone to kinda hug to and keep warm with. That's what it's all about."

In 1984, Consumers Union published their *Love, Sex, and Aging* study based on a detailed questionnaire answered by respondents between 50 and 93, the largest sampling of older Americans ever assembled for sex research. Those who filled in the questionnaire are not what scientists call a random sample. Most were married for over 30 years and most to the same spouse. And they voluntarily mailed in the long report. Nevertheless, the study is fascinating.

Almost all the respondents reported rising sexual response thresholds and physiological changes due to health problems and aging. Some have lapsed into inactivity but most remain sexually active. The majority use a wide array of measures to counter any problems. Physiological approaches include: manual and oral stimulation, use of a vibrator, anal stimulation, lubricants. Others use psychological approaches: sexually explicit or pornographic materials, use of fantasy, a new partner. Quite a few use both approaches to maintain and enhance sexual enjoyment. At the end of the chapter on "How Our Respondents Compensate for Sexual Change" the editors concluded: "The broad range of these approaches [summarized above] repeatedly astonished us as we read one questionnaire return after another — 4,246 of them in all."

One example stays with me: A 74-year-old swinger who has been "partying" with his 50-year-old wife for over 30 years, sings the praises of swinging — adventure, newness — then offers this rather unexpected geriatric sexual advice: "The main thing is," he says, "Do not split into separate rooms — stay together!"

Although I was surprised by the indomitable nature of the sexual spirit, "like lemmings to each other," as one man said, I am not surprised at the continuum of sexuality. Both Kinsey and Masters and Johnson found that women and men continue their accustomed sexual patterns throughout their lives. A study of homosexual men over 65 reports that most have satisfactory social and sex lives. A study of gay women finds that lesbians over sixty have sex as often as or more frequently than lesbian couples of any age. The Starr-Weiner Report, which probes the lifestyles of 800 people between the ages of 60 and 91, finds that 97 percent of older people like sex; 75 percent think sex now feels as good or better than it did when they were young; and 80 percent think sex is good for their health. In the Consumer Union study, persons who remain sexually active in their fifties, sixties, and seventies report a higher level of life enjoyment than those who are sexually inactive.

What I didn't know was how necessary it is to open up our standard definition of sexuality and love. Those who live together into old age "love" in a way that has little to do with Hollywood movies, romance literature, or advertising seduction. I remember my mother in the years before she died. Her activity was limited by a heart condition. She could not exercise, so she was over-weight. She needed insulin injections to stay alive. To me, as a teenager, she was woefully unglamorous. But my father was in love. "When I married your mother she was a very beautiful woman. And as the years went by and she changed and gained weight and had three kids and had a cesarean and developed a stomach, I really didn't notice these things. She was always beautiful to me. Her face didn't change. And her eyes didn't change. And when I looked at her, I looked right in her eyes. And that retained the same beauty that it always had."

"You found her sexy."

"Yes. And when I held her in my arms, I didn't think I needed somebody who was slimmer or with longer legs. For me, she was perfect as she was."

As he says this, that which my father loved is evoked between us. Not my mother, overweight and bespeckled as I saw her then, but Annette, in all the beauty of her bright and generous being. For the first time, I understand how my father could chase after my mother and pull her to him saying, "What a sexy little creature you are."

When you get right down to it, there is no standard turn-on. Sexuality expresses itself in many ways, some of which we might not consider erotic or sexual if we didn't see the gleam, pleasure, comfort they create.

It's time to speak to my father, as I said I would when I began. I've done my homework and he's just had his seventy-fifth birthday, so we're both, in a sense, ready. "Can we talk?"

"Sure."

We sit at my table. No one else home. The tape recorder between us.

"What would initiate an actual sexual desire in you?" I ask. "A gesture, a smile, some kind of come on . . ."

"Three days."

"What do you mean three days."

"After three days, it becomes a little urgent. Three days, four days."

"What?"

"Okay. Five days."

"Do you find any sadness in the change in your sexuality?"

"No, no. Not at all. It's also true that at my age, sometimes, you don't have the erection when you want to, and if you're smart, you say to yourself, 'No, not tonight.' And you roll over and go to sleep. If you worry about it, you're dead. A lot of guys when they can't perform, it does them in. I don't worry about it and it helps to have an understanding partner. If it happens, it happens. If not, I think to myself, Too bad, I would have liked it, but if not tonight, tomorrow morning. And if not tomorrow morning, tomorrow night. It's not the end of the world. It's there."

"When you think about sex, what behavior do you include in that? What do you think of as sex?"

"Well, I enjoy the end of the day, getting in bed with my wife, curling around her, and going to sleep. And I don't know if you can say that that's sexy, but it is. It's warm and it's comforting. It's nice to get up in the morning and wrap yourself around someone you love and who loves you. It's important and I'm really sorry for people who don't have that. And it doesn't necessarily mean that you have to have intercourse to complete this. It can be very fulfilling just to hold one another for ten, fifteen minutes, and then get up."

"And how is that different from holding your grandchildren?"

"Well, this is sexual. The way I feel about her is that she's soft, her skin is smooth. There are all sorts of sensitive things that happen to you when you're touching somebody else like that."

"If I had told you when you were twenty or thirty that what you just described is sex, what would you have said?"

"If I were twenty or thirty, holding a beautiful woman in my arms would certainly not be enough. Absolutely not. All it would do is get me all stirred up and I'd probably end up with sore balls. Only petting would have been totally unsatisfactory."

"But now you can be satisfied with just petting?"

"Yes. There may even be times when I feel I would like to have intercourse and for some reason we can't and it doesn't bother me. If it's *nisht*, it's *nisht*. One of the partners might be ill or one may have to go off skiing. So it's *nisht*, it's *nisht*. Maybe as you get older that's the way things work out. At age twenty, I would have been very happy to forgo the skiing. But not now. Skiing you only have four months a year."

Dad is the coda for what I have been hearing from others. Older people feel their sexuality as deeply as anyone else, but with some perspective. If Ted is rejected, he feels sad. "I feel the rejection any man would feel." But it doesn't demolish him or stop him from working. "Being rejected is not cheerful but it's not fatal." On the other hand, good sexuality makes people feel good. As Dr. Gustave Gingras says, "Sex stimulates the cardiovascular system, liberates the spirit, and predisposes one to a peaceful sleep. It is better and certainly more agreeable than jogging." In France, doctors consider sex the most powerful of antidepressants. "Good sex makes you happy," says Sophie Van Bourg. "It puts you, as the Chinese say, in balance."

Listening and learning, I readjust my concept of sexuality to include a wide range of mutual exchanges. I feel I've come as far as I can without getting there myself when, unexpectedly, I experience, firsthand, the gracious warmth of an older person's sexuality.

Norman Corwin, humanist, creator of populist radio epics, and beacon of Jeffersonian values, is, for me, the embodiment of the American democratic spirit. The scores of national radio broadcasts he wrote between 1938 and 1955 include: "We Hold These Truths," a Bill of Rights special, and "Word from the People," a pro-peace response to the founding conference of the United Nations. Corwin produced "Ballad for Americans," sung by Paul Robeson, and "The Lonesome Train," an evocation of America seen from Lincoln's funeral train. Hoping to meet him, I write a fan letter and call when I get to L.A.

Corwin answers. He is overloaded — writing, teaching, serving on academies, committees, guilds — trying to assuage his "perpetual fever of indignation." He knows he has to put on the brakes. Politely, but firmly, he says he is too busy for the interview. I suggest every possible time slot: dawn, dusk, between the elevator and the car, after class. Finally, I say, "Look, you must take time to do household chores — laundry, vacuuming, shopping. I'll do that for you and you'll have extra time." This is greeted by a brief silence. Then, the deep, modulated voice says, "Oh, come on over."

A tall, slender man, with a pencil-thin mustache welcomes me into a high rise, off Santa Monica Boulevard. I follow a brown corduroy jacket, black tie, colored shirt into the book-lined living room and we settle, side by side, on the couch. Corwin talks about peace being the first value and the damage caused by the social Darwinesque concept of dog-eat-dog. He is writing about numbing, illiterate television and the trivialization of American culture. What saves him is "the conspiracy of good people and the contagion of good works."

I wonder what it is that gives him joy and his response is vintage Corwin:

> I feel good when there is something that expresses fulfilment in others. I feel good when a student does a good job and shows promise and I have helped to put that young man or young woman on a path that will bring them happiness and fulfilment. I feel good when I play a string quartet by Schubert. I feel good when I see a great movie. I feel good when I meet a person whom I like. I feel good when I am able to give love and love is returned. I feel good in the presence of beauty. I feel good in an art museum. I feel good when I read a good book. I doubt if Emily Dickinson ever knew the touch of a man on her breast. Yet I love Emily Dickinson so much in her poems that if I ever met her it would be like John Gielgud and that lovely French actress at the end of that glorious French film on the war, racing toward each other over some fields in France and embracing very warmly. I have a physical feeling toward her, because to me intelligence and beauty are aphrodisiacs. And how can one not feel good

about a fine day? There was a simple little lyric in one of the Broadway shows, probably the peak of Oscar Hammerstein's art, "Oh what a beautiful morning, Oh what a beautiful day, I have a wonderful feeling everything's coming my way." How wonderful! How cheering! A lovely, simple little thing. So, a beautiful morning is something that is cheering. A beautiful evening. Rain. Rain in Spain. Or rain in Beverly Hills. Rain in Glendale.

We talk, then, about love, and Corwin says many men give up on love. I say that's the stereotype and he replies that it's been stereotyped with a good deal of support from the Kinseys. "That is to say that if you look at the statistical breakdown of the answers to certain key questions, you'll find that there is a good deal of resignation in later years." I remind him that Kinsey based his results on the sexual histories of only eighty-seven older men and counter Kinsey with the newer, geometrically larger Consumers Union study.

"Isn't the desire still there?" I ask.

"You know, I meet and am attracted to women as though I were nineteen. But from the beginning I have had a great romantic feeling about women. About love. About physical love, about the beautiful qualities of a woman expressed obliquely in what I said about Emily Dickinson. That little sweet — have you ever seen a picture of her? Yet, you know, you want to love her, you want to hug her . . . ."

Later, I continue the discussion and Norman mentions a young admirer who knocked on his door at midnight and "wanted to go to bed with me." He embraced her and, trying to make his rejection as kind as possible, said, "Look at these wrinkles."

"Maybe you should have let her in. It might have been a pleasant initiation."

"I would have felt guilty about exploiting her enthusiasm."

I make more of a case for having invited the young woman in.

"I would have felt like a dirty old man."

"Would you do it now?"

"After you've given me permission?"

"Would you?"

"No, I don't think so. There's too much programming."

Lovemaking, he thinks, is like playing an instrument, "playing in the playground of the senses." On the bookshelf he finds

Overkill and Megalove, which he wrote over twenty years ago. He reads with oratorical fullness:

> *Look out over the city from the high escarpment of your brow,*
>   *and what do you see?*
> *A mesa of stone, pincushion of steel, a grill of avenues.*
> *The census of last count swore so and so many millions live*
>   *therein, gave the numbers of each gender, and the percentage*
>   *of TV sets.*
> *Well and good, but still unmustered are the figures on moist*
>   *lips and searching hands,*
> *The declivities of bosoms, lusher than Kashmir's vale,*
> *The caressing of waists incurved like the bouts of sensual cellos,*
> *The games in the playgrounds of the senses:*
> *Rooms lighting up in the mansions of the body;*
> *And sighs, soft voices, let's not forget soft voices.*
>
> *And the imagery in each head, the coinage of the heart*
> *Whether love be to Her a wind on the water, a meteor shower,*
>   *a beating wing, a hectic hour, a hornet sting*
> *To Him the mane of a lion, a tiger's pride, high as Orion and*
>   *twice the world wide*

As he reads, the chords of my being respond. I have always thought that good lovers are maestros and I, potentially, the Stradivarius of violins. He is, I think, courageous to read this to me and I am uncomfortably moved. I rise to go. His bow, at my compliment on the writing, is courtly. I stand on my toes to kiss him goodbye. He hugs me. And I hug him. He kisses the sides of my lips. Touches my hair. Looks into my eyes, kisses the side of my face. "I like it that you don't wear lipstick. It gets between the lips." He embraces me again, still wearing his reading glasses, and takes them off in mid-embrace, "I don't want my reading glasses to get first billing."

"This is silly," say I.

"This is what is wonderful about life. Even if it is a fleeting moment."

He hugs me again.

"You ask such good questions."

Norman Corwin walks me to the elevator and accompanies me to the front door. I am aroused, in a tizz, and laughing inside all at the same time. Interviewing intelligently and attentively is a subtle form of protracted flattery, and if often creates the illusion of intimacy. I am prepared for its repercussions. What I am not prepared for is me. I am standing on the street, with the equivalent of my balls in an uproar, trying to remember if I had a car . . . It serves me right.

My interviews confirm that desire and sexuality are lifelong attributes which, if nurtured, contribute to the enjoyment of life. Yet the taboos against sexuality in old age are obvious and insidious. Norman Corwin doesn't make love with a willing young woman because the programming is too great. And older women, even given the opening, don't come on to younger men. It is a conditioning even the great activist leader Maggie Kuhn cannot break.

I contact her at 8:00 A.M. at the Airport Park Hotel, in L.A. She has come to receive the keys to the city and send off the Great Peace March.

"Have I awakened you?" I ask after four rings.

"No, I'm rushing out. What do you want?"

I ask for an interview.

"Every moment is accounted for. You should have done this earlier."

She invites me to a Gray Panther meeting in the afternoon. And I go back to sleep, as eighty-year-old Maggie Kuhn rushes out the door.

When "our own Maggie Kuhn" mounts the podium, it is obvious she has been touring for days. She stands at the mike and I wish she'd sit down. Her face is chalk-white except for the orange blush below her cheekbones. Her skin looks translucent. Then she speaks — eloquently, intelligently. Her speech ends with the communal ritual of the Gray Panther growl:

> Stand as tall as you can. Raise your hands. Lift. Lift them. Reach.
> Reach. Reach. We're reaching toward a new society, to the goal
> of a just and peaceful world, we're working toward it, but it's not
> within our grasp. Reach. Reach . . . Now put your hands down.
> Relax. Next reach toward your neighbor. Now you can touch the
> neighbors in this room. But as you are touching the neighbors in

this room, envisage with your whole psyche the neighbors around the world. The neighbors in South Africa, the neighbors in El Salvador, Angola, Lebanon, the Soviet Union, people who may be considered in the worldview as the enemy. They are our neighbors and they too seek peace and justice for all. And we are a community, so we reach toward each other now, with love and forgiveness and hope that we can together be equal to the task. We can't do this alone. We can't be human alone. We have to be part of a loving community. We are building a loving community. And while you're reaching you open your mouth to cry out in outrage at what needs to be complained against and spoken out against and you open your eyes as wide as you can to see the whole world, and you stick out your tongue as far as you can, in derision, way, way out. Just like that. You can do better than that. Way, way out. Try it. It's good. Try it. Now with your tongue out, your eyes wide open, your hands outstretched — growl. Three times. Right from the belly. Growl.

And, with that, Maggie growls. And all the people around me growl — GRRR, GRRRR, GRRRRR — belly-curdling growls to make the walls fall down.

"That's the real thing," says the tweed-suited lady beside me.

Finally, Maggie Kuhn sits. She holds out her hand as people come toward her. They touch her hand, shake it, cradle it. A gray-haired black man says, "I am the first Nicaraguan to hear you." He is shy, charming. Another man trips over his feet, "You don't know me but . . ." Another man just holds her hand, thanking her. At one point, the admiring men surround her, like groupies. She is warm and gracious. There is a twinkle in her eye, or is it only in mine?

Two months later I am at Maggie Kuhn's shared intergenerational home in Philadelphia. Her assistant installs us on a couch and both my tape recorder and theirs are going. After a wide-ranging social discussion I raise the subject of Maggie's intellectual groupies.

"They were men who admired you so much that they loved you as a woman. And they weren't seeing you as an eighty-whatever-old lady."

"That's right."

"Have you noticed that?"

"Yes. And I'm very proud and pleased and very, very gratified. I think it's the discovery and the excitement that is generated and the affirmation that comes when you are exploring new and creative ideas."

"It also says something about what sexuality is."

"Yes, and it's more than the sex act. That's just a tiny part of it, really, of the way in which we relate to each other. Sexuality takes many forms. And sexuality can be expressed, as you have observed, in an intellectual exchange. And a mutual exploration of new ideas can be really sexy."

"From my point of view, it was wonderful to see you being full and powerful in that way, enough so that a kind of sexual energy came toward you. You must have felt it."

"Yes, yes. But I'm interested that you observed it too. This is very interesting. There is a young man, a very skilled and creative architect, who started an architect's workshop which gives time free to community groups. He's a lovely man, just an absolutely delightful man, and we've been together on many occasions where we were looking at housing and thinking about neighborhoods, and he told our editor, 'You know that Maggie Kuhn,' he said, 'I really feel a great sexual attraction for her.' And [when she told me this] I said, 'Did he say that?' And she said, 'Yes, he did.' And I said, 'Well, I'm not surprised because I feel a great sexual attraction for him.' It was just lovely."

Given the natural reticence of people about sexual matters, it is generous of Maggie to tell me this story, acknowledging, despite age, the natural attraction of two vibrant, compatible energies. But the avowals of attraction had been made through a third person, not face-to-face. It is clear that even Maggie was stymied. I put it to her.

"The Gray Panthers and others will succeed in breaking down many ageist taboos, but to break down the taboo that separates you from this young architect is going to be a quantum leap, don't you think?"

"I think it is, I think it is. And you're very perceptive to observe it. I think it is."

I am no longer afraid of "drying up" or impotence because old people say that a wide range of sexual exchange is pleasurable and possible within the bounds of normal health. I know that I will always have a need for sensual human contact and that other older people will have that need too. I can only hope that when I am old, North American society will have loosened up enough to let me have a twirl — out in the open, under the stars, in front of the grandchildren — with whatever consenting adult I wish. Because I have no doubt that it will always be as it is now — that a pat on the bum, a big hug, a special word, will bring color to my cheeks and a lilt to my walk.

FOUR

Confluence

Ten days have passed since I wrote the last few pages. Family matters have commanded my attention and I am trying to rev up to writing again. There are few distractions and I have no excuses. My youngest daughter and my companion have exempted me from the annual September migration back to Montreal and I am alone in a self-imposed exile in the house in the country. It is mid-February. There are ten inches of snow on the ground. On good days, when I get up, I begin my prewriting ritual. I put on long underwear, two layers of cotton tops, socks. If my bedroom is warm enough, I lie on the Tibetan rug, looking out at the bare maples and white birch and do the back exercises effectively prescribed by my dad — press the hollow of the back against the floor, hands to bent knees, knees to forehead. Then, I squeeze three oranges, and mix the juice with one teaspoon of vitamin C crystals: cheers to Linus Pauling. I put on more socks, a wool sweater, thermal boots, scarf, hat, down jacket, Inuit gloves, and walk briskly for twenty minutes, in any kind of weather, à la Lea and Dad. As I walk, the crisp air clears my head and lungs. I open my eyes wide, à la Maggie Kuhn, and molecules of cool air refresh my sleepy eyes.

When I come home, I go straight to the word processor and turn it on. If all goes well, the hours pass surprisingly quickly and at 5:00 P.M. I will have eaten two or three very light meals and have written three, maybe four, new pages. I drive to the closest village, St. Jerome, and swim a half hour in the school swimming pool. Then I read and prepare for the next day.

For me, now, this is the only way to write this book. I am set up here and minimally distracted. When it works, it works.

But I am often alone. I know from my research that people need other people, and I miss people. I miss caring for my daughter, the humor of my companion, the conversation of my friends. I am torn by the contradiction between what I know is a well-balanced life and what I'm doing. And, meanwhile, I deal every day with the experience of aging. I see that old age has inevitable and realistic reasons for despair — physical pain, loss, inescapable death. I also see that the work of old age is to get a whole life together in some way. I am beginning to see that lifelong relationships are more important than career goals. New values can emerge. We may feel we have the time to scatter and splurt, but old people have to make sense of their lives.

I hear about a Ph.D. student studying older people's coping strategies who quit, unable to face the challenge even second-hand. I understand. Many middle-aged people of my generation are only just emerging from an extended adolescence. Our concept of self is out of sync with dying parents, growing children, our own aging.

When I began this book, I had a mechanistic approach to the advent of old age. Just give me the vitamins, the swimming pool, and the secret and I'd crash my magic amulets through the shadowy obstacles. What I am realizing is that a complicated domain of mind and spirit informs the health of every older individual. Not only nutritious food and regular exercise, but a matrix of thought, curiosity, and connectedness is necessary to support and sustain life. It is hard to get a fix on these intangibles. Harder still to feel I can do it too.

Insofar as there is an element of faith to our existence, we seem to have to win it back all over again.

I read Hugh MacLennan's memories of his loves and realize we have only *one* personal life history. I feel that I should have chosen my lovers more carefully, so as to have *loved*, to have and to hold. I prepare for old age, drinking in the beauty of the trail between the spruce trees, of the chaotic snowflakes in the eye of the headlights. I treasure my senses against the day they will lessen. I know more than a person my age should know. Or do I?

The morning mail brings notes on the "Sex/Love" chapter from a writer friend, a man who says I have let my father "off the hook." He says I set up this interview about my dad's sexuality at the beginning of the chapter and it doesn't pay off.

I'm not sure what's lacking but I call my dad, who is coughing again after being briefly cured by a course of antibiotics. I joke that at least this time I'm not shouting questions at him through the bathroom door, like I did for my last book. We arrange a time when he will be alone.

I read from the manuscript and tell him about my forty-five-year-old friend who can't accept what he's said. I ask why he doesn't worry when he doesn't have an erection.

"Because it's just temporary," he says, as if it's obvious.

"But why aren't you worried that it's temporary?"

"It can be that I'm tired, or had a few drinks." He's trying to help me. "What I do know — it's not me permanently. It corrects itself. There'll be another time when we'll be able to do it. It's just something physiological that isn't working at the moment."

I suggest that maybe this is not most men's idea of masculinity.

Dad wonders what masculinity is, what we mean by it. He guesses that with some men being able to perform on demand is a sign of masculinity. But he doesn't have to prove anything anymore. At this point the sex act is not the most important part of being loved. He says, "The body behaves in mysterious ways and we have to learn to accept it. Right now, I'm more worried about keeping my spirits up with this cough."

I call my friend and read what Dad has said. I finish and he says, "And then what did you say?"

"Nothing else." His silence makes me laugh. "That's it." I say, "This is what there is. We'd better just accept it."

"Right" he says. "Intellectually I accept it, but then the 'male' part of me says, 'Aw, come on . . .' It's one thing to recognize that I can be impotent if that's the way it's going, and even recognize that as a sign of intelligence at times. But I have a real horror of total impotence — fear of death works in a peculiar way."

I point out that he has linked impotence with death.

"True," he realizes, "it's part of the whole thing. I don't have the assurance that I will feel like your father at seventy-five. I don't have any way of getting there. I'm afraid of the weakness, the slowdown of the intervening years. I'm experiencing the first instances of real exhaustion. I don't know if I have the jam to get there. It needs a totally different kind of stamina."

I think of Lea, her cancer operation, her broken wrist, sick for months in the dead of winter, deciding at eighty-six she's not ready to go out in a box.

Lea doesn't give up and she doesn't give in to despair. Not even this year when her beloved younger brother Leo died, when I know she struggled and hurt terribly.

She is not introspective but I am her friend, and I know it will help me very much as I grow older to know how she survives. I have asked her about diet, exercise, the nuts and bolts of her incredible vitality. But I still can't comprehend her passion for life — her outrage, for example, at apartheid, "the sons of whores with their fuckin' lousy attitude toward people because their skins are black." Or her joy at being alive. Finally, I tell Lea that even with all she's said, I still don't understand how she is like she is. There's got to be more to it than diet and exercise — a spirit, an approach to life — that keeps her trucking.

And, at that, Lea talks.

"No, it's not only food. Most people don't like to know themselves. I know myself very well, I know my good points and I know my lousy points and nobody, *nobody*, can tell me that I don't know myself. All right, I'm not *le bon Dieu* and I'm not a miracle maker, but I feel we're all worthy. I feel very badly with historians who do not write about the people who make up the people. These people don't get their worth. They're not with themselves.

"There was a little woman where I got my papers, a very nice person, but she was afraid to complain too much, in case the boss wouldn't like her.

"'What do you care?' I said to her. 'You don't have to jump into bed with him. He owes you this and you've got to get it.'

"'Ya, I know, but, maybe . . .,' she replied.

"You know this 'maybe,' *efsher*. Well, this little woman worked at Cantor's for a while and somebody else bought the place and, if you please, she wasn't fancy pants enough and that nasty creature threw her out because she was a *nebach mensch* [good-natured sad sack]. All her life she got her ass kicked and never kicked back. And now she says, 'I'm glad now, I'm very glad now I don't have to go to work.'

"'It's good,' I say, 'that's the attitude.' But there she was, her dignity, you know, she didn't have the opportunity for dignity."

"Lea, did you tell me this story because you think that having dignity is a necessary part of staying healthy?"

"Yes, my dear, it's all part. It isn't just one thing. It isn't just food, it isn't just having a nice apartment or anything. It's all that makes up life. An attitude, an appreciation . . ."

"Your brother Leo called you every morning, understood you, loved you. How did you come back after Leo died?" I ask.

"Oh, my dear, well, I want to tell you that it hasn't been easy. When my mother died it wasn't easy, and when my brother Michael, and my dear precious sister Rose, and all of my loved ones . . . Life teaches us. And I've found if I say to myself, well, what am I going to do? I can't get Leo back. But if I will dwell on the wonderful things — I have books there, all of them inscribed '*à nôtre chère*, Lea,' and so on. All the love is there. So, what I feel which has helped me is that he's not coming back, but he's left me a wealth of memories, just as Michael left me lots of beautiful memories, and all my loved ones. I have packages and packages of letters and poetry, poems that they wrote and so on. These are my crutches. I'm being very honest. These are my crutches.

"My sister says, 'Well, if you didn't live in a place like this and you lived in a nicer place, you would perhaps not be out so much.' I say, 'I don't give a hoot about this stuff. A table is handy, I can put things on it and I can eat there. The rocking chair is handy because I can relax in it. The telephone I need there, the desk, I put my papers there. All these things are useful things, so that's part of my needs. But I don't need all the tra-la-la with the crystal chandeliers and all that kind of stuff. I need something else.

"I need, first of all, to talk to myself. And that's what I have done, and I say to myself, Just you listen to me, Lea Roback, this is the situation. There's absolutely nothing you can do but face up to it and do the best you can. So, to add to my crutch, I go out. I go out every day even if it's raining. I've got heavy boots, a raincoat, even if it's just an hour. And the moment I'm out, I am, in the spring, especially, when it's so beautiful, I am happy. I have a poor little tree here right near the balcony, makes me think of *A Tree Grows in Brooklyn*, that little tree in six years I don't know how it grew, *nebach*, in asphalt, at the backside of McDonald's. And yet it grew, my dear, beautiful green leaves, and then the birds come and they eat, I give them stuff. And that's it. I go out on the street, I go to the art galleries, I love that, and I see things, I speak to people, and I can get all of the pains, aches, and heartaches out of my mind."

Paula Altrovitch, on the other hand, has nothing to raise her spirits if such, in her horrendous situation, is possible. She shares a room in the chronic care ward of a Montreal hospital and eats in the hall. Each day, she gets a lot of pills, "The pills make me sicker." At eighty, she can't see from her left eye, her stomach is swollen, legs hurt, hands hurt, "I'm in pain." Her daily routine is, "Nothing, I just sit here." There's a constant moan in the corridor and someone screams, "Eeech, eech, help, help." Paula hasn't been out of the hospital for six months. It's early afternoon and she's waiting to be put to bed. She's cold. "They forget about me. I can't stand it." Finally, the nurse lifts Paula onto her bed. Gently this time, not like the orderly who picked her up by the ribs and threw her. The nurse, the bed-pan, the waiting, the pain, the feeling of being "not good any-more," of getting sicker every day, this is Paula's world.

No hopes, "nothing to live for."

The bogeywoman.

When we are old, what gives life meaning?

When staying alive becomes more and more demanding, why do we live?

What pumps up, flows into, and tickles the spirit so that it can light up the implacable face of age?

I go back to see Lea.

Whether or not she can tell me how she does it, she is coura-geous, a survivor, alive to passion and joy.

"Last year I wasn't well," Lea says. "I didn't accept that my sis-ter was going, my sister Rebecca, who is so precious. She suf-fered, suffered greatly, lingering and lingering and there was always the hope that maybe they'd find something and that's the hardest thing. And my nephew, who was at the Jewish Hospital, he said, 'Aunty Lea, I think you should see a psychia-trist. There's a lovely woman there.' And I said, 'Oh, darling Edgar, not Aunty Lea.' And so that gave me the ramrod I needed for my spine. So I said, 'Okay, let me just talk to myself a bit more and it will be all right.' And that was it . . . And this year we lost Leo. He went just like that. So I say it's so important, oh, I find we don't know ourselves enough, we don't know our strengths. This is the thing: we don't know our strengths."

"What do you mean by that? What are your strengths?"

"My strengths are your strengths, everybody's strengths. When I came home and my nephew and my niece sat here, I knew there was something wrong. But not Leo. I just — the world just caved in, just like that. I said, My God, I can't live like that. Leo isn't here. My nine o'clock phone call. And Leo — always concerned, the hug and the kiss — he could have been my lover, he could have been my husband, he was my brother but he was all these things. And all of a sudden I felt robbed. I felt really, how could a thing like that happen? Well, it's not even a year yet and I've got all kinds of things. Leo is just floating all around here because there are books and there are papers and letters and postcards from when he'd go on trips. As I say, my strength is what? I feel everyone has a *peckle* and that I learned from my mother."

"What's a *peckle*?"

"A *peckle* is a pack on your shoulder that everyone has to carry. We all have problems. We all have difficulties. Some people can't cope. They never learned to cope, you see? So I feel children must learn to cope. We learned to cope."

"So part of learning to cope is saying that everybody has problems."

"My dear, but this is it: you cannot constantly dwell upon yourself."

"But what is the obverse? You don't dwell on yourself and you notice a tree that grows in asphalt. What else keeps your spirit up?"

"People — I love people. I've *always* loved people. I love children, and I love to feel the pulse of people, that's why I like to talk to them, on buses or on the street. And I do that all the time. I'm very fond of kids and here on Côte des Neiges, a mother and her kid got on the bus after work and the kid was singing, he's going 'Da, da, da, dada, hey maman, *on a chante ça aujourd'hui*,' and this lovely kid was just full of beans, and she says, '*Oui, oui, oui, pas aussi fort.*' And I just said, 'Let the kid sing it as loud as he wants!' And these are — it's all little things. It's all little things."

Once, in a restaurant, I offered Lea wine. "No," she said, "what do I have to raise and lower my blood pressure for?" Lea knows what she wants. She wants to be alive: "To be able to be there on the question of peace and on the question of social justice. I cannot sit back. I haven't got the energy I had when I was twenty but I try. Younger people feel good when they have an older person marching with them. And it gives me the mental health that makes living so much easier."

When we finish our long, sometimes difficult conversation, I thank Lea. I know it is not her style to "contemplate her navel."

"Thanks for talking to me," I say.

And Lea shrugs, "If not you, *maidela*, then who?"

The wisdom of the sage, elder, prophet is traditionally thought of as practical wisdom, given to others. But Lea can't codify her wisdom. She might tell people to act and get together with others. But the wisdom she has developed from the struggle with what Simone de Beauvoir called, "the almost metaphysical fact of old age and death" is more elusive to grasp and to transmit. Yet this is the wisdom that gets each person through.

The first step, philosophically, seems to be to know who you are.

Betty Friedan learned this after she turned 65. At 60 she began to identify with the sociological problems of aging, but 65 was her own coming of age.

"When my friends had a surprise party for my sixtieth birthday, I had a fit. Who needed it? Who needed to be reminded? But when they had this huge bash for me in New York, celebrating my sixty-fifth birthday, in the Palladium, this 'in' place that used to be an old movie theater and was made into a big disco, they thought I'd object. But I didn't object. I thought, That's nice. For this one, I'd come across the great divide and it was fine, a wonderful life-affirming party. It was just beautiful. Everybody whose life had ever touched mine — my kids, my friends, my men, my sisters-in-arms. They did a musical comedy. It was the best week of my life."

"What can we hope for as we get older?" I ask.

"I think that if you are free, you can finally become yourself. Fully, truly, yourself. And take risks you never took before . . .

We are just sure in some way. You know what's important and what isn't. You're not bothered as you used to be about what other people think.

"That's one kind of aging. That's the kind that nobody knows about."

Working part-time, post retirement, in the accounting firm he co-founded, my dad gets a call berating him for having missed an arcane tax loophole. As the irate client raves, Dad lifts his binoculars to his eyes, looks out over the St. Lawrence River, and thinks, I don't need this. It gives me the shits.

Mitch Van Bourg, recently retired, says with relief, "I used to do things for appearances. I just shed it all. I don't have to sell myself anymore."

"The different selves are now fitting together like spokes of a wheel, whereas they used to be sticking out all over the place," says Dorothy Livesay.

And, in her journal *At Seventy*, May Sarton notes "the muse literally opens the inner space, just as November light opens the outer space . . . I am more myself than I have ever been."

Malcolm Cowley says the first step in finding a shape in one's life is "simple remembering." To explore this thought, I go to see Hugh MacLennan. I am fascinated by his novel *Voices in Time*, and by the mind and memories of the main character, John Wellfleet, an old man who has survived the Smiling Bureaucracy, the Destructions, and the Great Fear. Cast off into nowhere, with a routine as deadly as a prison term, Wellfleet is discarded as "inoperative." He protects himself by shutting off his emotions, "as though his soul had arthritis." If he still feels a part of humanity, it is the life of his mind that keeps him so.

Hugh MacLennan greets me in his new office at Concordia University, where books and boxes lie stacked on the floor. McGill, the university where he taught for over thirty years, has just kicked him out of his office. "Stephen Leacock was kicked out of his office at sixty-five. If you have compulsory retirement at sixty-five, you are making people inoperative often when they are at the very height of their powers."

He maneuvers around boxes and shakes my hand, a tall, gaunt man with chiseled features and gray hair long enough to curl. It is January, the second month of a cold six-month Canadian winter, and for MacLennan it has been "a very frustrating year." His wife, an invalid, can't go out alone for fear of falling and will no longer go to the country because of the stairs. He's "very sad" to lose going to the country. And it's "too bad" what's happened to his naturally joyous wife: "But that's the trouble when you get old and infirm, you get frightened and helpless. It's a matter of feeling helpless." People are always telling MacLennan he is famous but he thinks he lives a quieter life than anyone else he knows. His socializing is curtailed because of his wife's illness and the severed connection to the company and conversation at the McGill Faculty Club. What he'd like, really, is "a bit more society."

MacLennan wrote *Voices in Time* over a thirteen-year period, during his sixties and his seventies. He says the character Wellfleet is *not* modeled on himself. Yet, like Wellfleet, MacLennan has been declared inoperative. And, like Wellfleet, he has an internal life that helps him transcend external circumstances.

MacLennan remembers patches of poetry that stir his soul. He discovered Shakespeare, at fifteen, when he picked up *Othello*: "Oh God, that suddenly got a hold of me as if I could practically see the heavens open — 'Like to the Pontick sea,/Whose icy current and compulsive course / Ne'er feels retiring ebb, but keeps due on . . .'" When he went up to Oxford in 1929, the chancellor, Lord Grey, then almost blind, made a short speech: "I've got only one piece of advice to say to you young men. When you are young, read all the poetry you can and listen to all the music that you can and then it will be with you all your life."

Even when he is most isolated, MacLennan's character Wellfleet falls into reverie and remembers passages of poetry and surges of music. The scent of the lilac in bloom is "so intoxicating" it brings mist to his eyes.

Yet, it is of the dreams connecting Wellfleet to those he has loved that MacLennan writes most passionately. For love dreams have their own beauty and MacLennan thinks remembering them is something that happens more and more as we get older. Wellfleet dreams of Joanne:

> Once more he was a man in his prime, for in a long dream
> Joanne had returned to him in the full reality of the living flesh

and spirit . . . Only those who had been truly loved by her had discovered how rarely beautiful she was, for only they had seen the wonder of her love-smile. He lay still. She had returned to him with uncanny accuracy — her eyes when she loved, her lips when she loved, the body of a profound human being as supple as the muscles of sea tides when all of her moved and rippled in a whiteness of love — where was she now? *What* was she now? Her body had been dust for years but she had never been more real than she had been a few minutes ago.

For MacLennan, those we have loved "so vastly" are "translated into the memory cells and the mystery of our minds," and after they have been dead long enough we can recover them only when we are asleep.

For writer Eudora Welty, eighty, past and present combine in a *waking* inward journey. The journey takes her through time, "forward or back, seldom in a straight line, most often spiraling." Memory and present experience feed each other. She glimpses her whole family life as if it were "freed of that clock time which spaces us apart so inhibitingly, divides young and old, keeps us living through the same experience at separate distances." She discovers connections and meeting points between people, for which she uses "the wonderful word *confluence.*" Her autobigraphy ends with a meditation on memory.

> Of course the greatest confluence of all is that which makes up the human memory — the individual human memory. My own is the treasure most dearly regarded by me in my life and my work as a writer. Here time, also, is subject to confluence. The memory is a living thing — it too is in transit. But during its moment, all that is remembered joins, and lives — the old and the young, the past and the present, the living and the dead.

Malcolm Cowley, writing about his fellow "octos" under nursing care, says, "They can be rejoiced by visits and meetings, but they also have company inside their heads. Some of them are busiest when their hands are still. What passes through the minds of many is a stream of persons, images, phrases, and familiar tunes. For some, that stream has continued since childhood, but now it is deeper; it is their present and their past combined."

Visitors expect Auntie Katie will be afraid to sleep alone in her parental summer home, but she says, "I have lots of company in that house. I'm eighty now. I first came when I was twenty-eight. The house was one room and my papa said, 'Next summer, *klenela*, there will be a new house for you.' And next summer when I came back, Papa and my brother had built three new rooms. It was beautiful, like a dollhouse. The room I sleep in now had my baby's crib in it. Memories are company. They're nice memories to remember."

At seventy-eight, George Bernard Shaw decided it would be impossible to remain chairman of the BBC's Advisory Committee on Spoken English because he was beginning to forget people's names. In his letter explaining his difficulty, he wrote: "At Emerson's funeral, Longfellow, who was overwhelmed with grief, said to the man next to him, 'Sir: will you be so good as to remind me of the name of that dear friend of ours whose loss we are now lamenting.' It will come to that with me presently."

And yet, when he was ninety-one, Shaw wrote endorsing a plaquette with his name on Torca Cottage where he lived from ages ten to fourteen: "I owe more than I can express to the natural beauty of that enchanting situation commanding the two great bays between Howth and Bray Head and its canopied skies such as I have never seen elsewhere in the world. They are as present to me now as they were eighty years ago." Shaw counted that scenery as a factor of the first importance in his real education, "which was essentially aesthetic." And he never forgot it.

Writing in her journal, Margaret Randall discovers she spends more and more time trying to understand the many moments or passages she once let pass her by in relative abandon. "As I grow older my memory changes. It is too easy to say 'it gets worse.' I forget a great deal, it is true, but I also remember things I was not capable of remembering before. My reasons for remembering have changed as well."

Memory is a way of actively administering one's own reality. It can integrate, validate, be joyful. Too little is written about what writer Meridel Le Sueur calls "the bursting flowers of memory."

Winter iron bough
　　unseen my buds,
Hanging close I live in the beloved bone
Speaking in the marrow
　　alive in green memory.

Katherine Smith, eighty-five, talking about names, blurts out that she and her twelve-year-old cousin used to call each other "Stink Eye" and "Puke Bill."

"What a relief it is to remember that," she says through waves of giggles.

"Why a relief?" I wonder aloud.

"Because we were so crazy. We did such crazy things. We had such fun," and she giggles again.

Lawrence Durrell, sixty-five, writes to his long-time friend Henry Miller after Anaïs Nin's death from cancer has severed their last link with the long-ago Paris of the Villa Seurat: "It will please you to know that the Cacharel scent named after Anaïs [Anaïs-Anaïs] is a great success and when I last had the luck to take a youngling to bed in Paris that was what she smelt of. I lay there in the dark smelling it and thinking and never saying a word."

Lying close to a youngling who smells of his past life, Durrell experiences what Eudora Welty calls confluence. He writes to Miller, knowing the moment will be appreciated since it, most fully, makes him what he is.

Sometimes in remembering, even the detritus may be more revealing than suspected.

"Right now, while I'm talking with you and thinking about you and myself, what you ask me and stuff, I'm also getting a thing I have to write for the North Point Press autobiography of Marcel Pagnol," says Mary Frances Fisher. "Part of me is going on doing that. And I'm also thinking about everything you've said which has evoked something else that I would either have said or not said. I'm thinking about Anne [her sister] and Mary Kennedy [her daughter] and Grandfather and Grandmother and Neddy and Grandmother Holbrook and stuff."

I ask if a spiritual belief sustains her, and Mary Frances says she's always been terribly confused about why the world was in such a mess and she is even more confused now.

"But have you figured out anything for yourself?"

And she launches into a story about herself and her sister, how they were taken for twins, how they never fought, how she couldn't live her sister's hardworking, "drunk as skunk on Sunday" lifestyle, how as they grew older they were poles apart ethically and morally, how she didn't really like her sister but she loved her — "I would have given my life for her."

Something I have said (Have you figured out anything for yourself?) has evoked a seemingly unrelated digression. But when I listen to the interview again, I hear Mary Frances saying, "Everything you've said has evoked something else that I would have said or not said." Her complex, lifelong relationship with her sister is something she thinks about but normally wouldn't discuss. It may seem out of context in a linear conversation but she has tapped into an ongoing, if unspoken, existential process. In a real way, it is an answer to the question of what she has figured out for herself.

The "globe of memory . . . in free spin, with no obscure side."

I do not mean to imply that old people do or should live only in their minds. Nonstop remembering is exhausting, not revitalizing, as Ronald Blythe pointed out when he quoted the old lady who longed for a visitor to "stop my thoughts of life going around and around and wearing my [sic] out."

In MacLennan's final novel, Wellfleet's rebirth is due to André, a young man, who discovers archives from the past and wants to learn about them from Wellfleet. For Wellfleet, "talking to someone real is like eating after you've been nearly starved to death." Beauty returns to him in waves. His health is better than it has been for years.

When Wellfleet finishes writing his book, he realizes "with some incredulity" that he is, as MacLennan was on the publication of *Voices in Time*, in his seventy-ninth year. He spends much of his last summer sitting in the sun and listening to the birds singing. When he dies, André is sure that "in this last instant of his life he was remembering someone he had loved."

"It's a nice way to die," I say to MacLennan.

"Very nice," MacLennan says softly.

In the beginning, suggests poet Stanley Kunitz, eighty-four, our choices are infinite. Then, as we make choices or they are made for us, we reduce our choices exponentially until finally we face the fact that "the only choice that matters is living and dying, that that's the one important, unresolved act of a life . . .

"So there is a need, I think, to deal with essences. Gradually I'm changing to a word. That's the new manifestation of the self. One has become one's language, one has become one's poetry."

"I feel I am wiser not because I am older, but because I was almost dead," says Ted Allan emphatically. "Since the heart attack, my whole concept of time has changed. Now, when I hear my children or grandchildren or my friends tell me in deep agony about some lover's quarrel, a jealousy, cancer, or even the threat of death, I cannot get myself excited about it. I no longer see things in terms of this year or even this lifetime anymore. For I see this lifetime in connection with thousands of lifetimes before and, possibly, if we don't destroy ourselves, thousands more. I see everyone and everything and even what we're saying now as a sort of, almost a — I don't want to be vulgar but" — he gestures grandly — "a fart in the wind of time, a breath, a belch, or, to get a better metaphor, a whiff.

"I'm saying if there is any wisdom in what I've developed, it is that I feel closer to what is really going on in the universe than I ever have before. I am more conscious that I am a combination of chemicals, minerals . . . whatever is out there, I am too. It's all connected in a way I never saw it so connected before."

He's sitting at the kitchen table, hair disheveled, nose a little blue, a born-again Buddha in a Chinese kimono and fine English leather slippers. I ask him how this feeling has affected him.

"So much makes me laugh," he laughs, overlaying Buddha with the Ted I know, "because we take it all so *seriously*, instead of chuckling and giggling and being happy at the miracle it all is. It makes me laugh, and at the same time I'm sorry in an even deeper way than I ever have been that most of humanity is still laboring under the need to get enough food.

"Also it makes me calmer. Situations that used to get me hysterical or in a panic don't upset me like they used to. I've lost what I call my ambition. I can handle problems more easily and don't have as many as I used to. And when I see my friends suffering with their children, their careers, their relationships, I try to give them love. Because no one can take advice. All you can do for someone who is in a state of hysteria is attempt to show them you love them and hug them and that may help calm them down.

"Of course, my physical limitations are a pain in the ass. I don't like that. Neither would any man who is partly crippled like it. I *am* partly crippled as a result of my heart attack and it frustrates me a little, but it's not a big thing in my life. It doesn't make me unhappy. I wake up every morning and my first thought is, Wooo! Another day! I'm going to maybe have a whole day! Well, in that day that I'm going to have, I want to have as much joy and pleasure as possible. And, for that, one would think, well, leave me alone. But that is not so. I'm more concerned now with others, particularly my children, than I was when I was younger. I am a better father now than I ever was, a better grandfather, a better friend. I don't know if I'm wiser but I'm happier."

I think of the many older people who have *come to their senses* and see, touch, hear, smell, and taste the flow of life. Malcolm Cowley described the pleasure of "simply sitting still, like a snake on a sun-warmed stone, with a delicious sense of indolence that was seldom attained in earlier years. A leaf flutters down; a cloud moved by inches across the horizon. At such moments the older person, completely relaxed, has become a part of nature — and a living part, with blood coursing through his veins."

George Bernard Shaw, at ninety, replies to the persistent Sydney C. Cockerell, sounding him out on funeral possibilities:

> My ghost would be bored by big buildings like the Abbey or St. Patrick's Cathedral in Dublin. I need seasons: trees and birds. What I would really like would be a beautifully designed urn on a little pedestal in the garden here at Ayot with Charlotte [his late wife] and myself inside listening for the first cuckoo and the nightingale and scenting the big cherry tree.

And on the weekend, Ted Allan visits me and we walk along the country road. The dead are speaking to him lately — his grandfather, mother, sister, brother. And, as he walks, he lingers near birch and maple trees.

"When I was four, I had a total affinity for all that is. I loved trees, flowers, grass, sky, birds — but especially trees. I used to hug trees, put my face against the bark as if they had life. I felt a communion with trees. And I'm getting that back again, that's coming back."

In an interview given several years before her death, Marguerite Yourcenar warned: "He who does not feel deeply does not think. I am almost tempted to say that a kind of specialization has taken place in man: just as certain insects have transformed their bodies into useful tools, we have tended to transform a considerable part of our sensory and affective capacities into a kind of computer, which is what the brain is for us. If by so doing we have lost the almost visceral sympathy with which we were born, nothing has been gained."

I know, as Joan Erikson says, that all knowledge begins with sensory experience, and that what we have that is genuinely our own is our personal accrued store of sense data. I understand Ted Allan and Marguerite Yourcenar. But many of the interviews describe a further spiritual development that leaves me feeling like a researcher in a foreign culture.

"Our spirit never dies, you know," says Indian elder Andy Commodore, eighty, of the Soowahlie Reserve in British Columbia.

"I think we're plowed under, recycled," echoes actor Vincent Price. "My daughter's very like my mother who died long before she was born. There's some part of some of them who are dead still here."

And Dr. Mary Calderone describes the vision of eternal time she has had ever since that bad summer following the "crucifying" death, from pneumonia, of her eight-year-old daughter.

"I remember one morning when it began to stop unraveling and began raveling again. And I suddenly got an image of myself at a point in eternal time and I thought, If I reach out my hand back here and reach out my hand to here, two mothers who had lost their children will hold my hand. I'm just one in a long, long, long chain. And, then I felt a part of the cosmic process, and I started battling and beating my breast, for myself — because I could roll with it, I could deal with it. Others had, see. And from then on, I was all right."

And this is why Dr. Calderone loves nature films so much: "The whole panorama of the nine billion years of this earth . . .

I sit there mesmerized. And I get that sense of being part of that stream. You see, here we go again, your hands back and forward again, I'm part of the next generation and part of the last, of the others too. And it doesn't bother me to know I'm going to stop."

My skeptic reader goes through these quotes and scribbles "goofy, bordering on silliness" in the margin of the manuscript. And I understand his problem. I can imagine the kind of sexuality described by older people but I can't really imagine *having* these spiritual, philosophical feelings. Yet, so common among older people is the feeling eighty-year-old Edith Wallace described as being "in life but not of life" that Joan and Erik Erikson tentatively call it "age-specific spiritual readiness." Given the present demographic revolution, they are considering adding a ninth stage to the eight currently described in their model of the life cycle. This final stage would include "some sense or premonition of immortality."

I think about this as I walk with my dad the mile through the woods, to the lake. We sit on the rocks and I ask what is important to him.

"My family . . . my friends . . . keeping my health up . . ."

I nod but he is not satisfied.

"When you mother was alive, we walked here to the lake in the woods. We sat on these rocks and looked at the lake, at the trees. It was very, very quiet. And she said, 'It is wonderful to think that our children and our grandchildren and their grandchildren will be here looking at this same beautiful view.' I often remember that."

I remember it too. He's told me this story before. And he's told my brother and my daughter Kim. The memory connects him to my mother, to the children, and to the generations to come. It is his very own intimation of immortality.

I begin to understand. It is not yet the kind of preoccupation I need to live fully. But, for Edith Wallace, and my father, "facing the other shore" is a needed and rewarding preoccupation. It is a vital part of the discourse necessary to make sense of it all.

Reverend Gordon Nakayama, eighty-six, stands in the doorway of his white frame house on Semlin Drive in East Vancouver, a small man with an unlined, round face. He ushers me in and takes his place beside his pale, slender wife, patiently upright with her cane. He cradles one arm around her and talks directly into her ear, referring to me. She nods and smiles. Nods and smiles. "She can't hear, can't see," he tells me. We sit a while in a comfortable, cluttered living room and then move to the dining room. Rev. Nakayama leads his wife by the hand to the table. He guides her and helps her sit. And his murmured words sound like a lullaby.

Rev. Nakayama was the Anglican chaplain of the Japanese Canadians during their internment in the Second World War. He is the author of *Issei*, brief biographies of Canada's earliest Japanese immigrants, and the father of Joy Kogawa, poet, and author of *Obasan*, a beautifully written novel about a Japanese-Canadian family during the internment.

On the bus from the Vancouver radio station where I have recorded my weekly film review, I prepared questions about formal religion which I planned to ask Rev. Gordon Nakayama as another take on "age-specific spiritual readiness."

Now, all I see is the exquisite gentleness with which Rev. Nakayama treats his wife. It is heartrending. All the more so for me because I have just done a radio review of *Cobra*, Sylvester Stallone's violent ode to vigilante terrorism. After that screeching, brutal terror, this household is almost unbelievable. How, after that, can this love and care exist so gracefully and cheerfully? As Rev. Nakayama and I talk, his wife eats noisily. Sometimes she smiles at me, sometimes she laughs to herself. He touches her delicately. Talks in her ear. Attends, even as he talks.

"In my case, wife is older than I am, and wife is not strong, now, she is weak, and I'm well enough to be able to help her, and it's my great joy. I do things for her with real respect and love.

"Wife was so faithful to me, so good to me, really, for fifty years I was in the ministry, always willing to help me. And I was rather weak physically, heart trouble many years, but she didn't have any illness at all, and so she took care of me very, very well, very kindly. Now, she's old age [*sic*], she can't hear very well and she can't see very well and her walking abilities are remitted and she falls down sometimes. And I get better. I am strong, so it's my turn to repay the service she rendered to me, so many years, and I'm very lucky to be able to do that. It's not burden, not doing for duty. It's one of the joys of living old age — without saying anything, you know each other.

"To me, to give to my wife is joy, happiness, and she depends on me so much, and I feel I should be with her.

"She depends on me so much. I feel I'm worth living.

"When I was sixty-nine, I had wonderful experience of spiritual insight. I was up in the Rocky Mountains, early, watching the sun going up from east. And the sun hit the top of the snow-capped mountain, and the color of the white snow changed to almost purple. And watching that mountain, I felt something strange, and I said, 'God is wonderful! God created these wonderful mountains! God created the universe, the whole, wonderful, wonderful universe!' And then suddenly I felt that God created *me, myself*! And so even though so weak and so small, compared with all this universe I am nothing, yet God created me. And I had heart attack and I died once, but I'm living here now. So I dug into my life, deep, deep, deep into my life, in thought, you know, and I found something inside of me, some spot, some beautiful bright spot inside of me, and I felt, Oh God, you are living in me! I didn't realize. I thought I was living by myself, all alone. But I am not alone, you are in me. Ever since, I began to realize that the most valuable thing in life is your own life.

"If each individual could wake up and realize this is God's part in each person and understand the value of each person's life and help each other, I think we can overcome the atom bomb, power, you know. Make peace, make real peace, peaceful life. And sometime I discuss this matter with my daughter, Joy, and Joy says, 'I am lucky to have you. So I can rest in peace because I don't worry about you. You are a strong man.'

"From the youth up to middle age, and old age, each time, a different time. In the past when I was active in the ministry, I was thinking more of other people, trying to help others. Now, at this moment, I more or less concentrate on the deep spiritual matters, more I think of future, eternal life, and so forth. Still, I try to help others as best as I can, but not so active way, more quiet way. Because I can't go out, you see. My wife is like this, I have to be with her all the time. Instead of going out and preach in the churches and so forth, I stay home, send out, every day, five, six letters. And then I use telephone, and I make tape to send out, and every day there are people who need my prayers, so I say prayers, five hundred prayers every morning. And every day, one poem.

In the shade of a rock
High in the mountains
A flower
Even without name
Shedding lovely fragrance
Nobody noticed it
Perhaps an angel
Is watching
And smiling

"That is the wife's life. Wife is so gentle and so quiet. She doesn't say anything. Nobody noticed her. And yet she is so helpful to others and nobody praised her. But, for me, I thought the angels were watching her and enjoyed her, my wife.

"So just living here, helping my wife, that's enough. That's missionary work."

We sit in the living room awhile and I sign Rev. Nakayama's visitor's book. If I had to do my review of *Cobra* now, I'd do more than make glib, disapproving chatter. I'd say *Cobra* is destruction. The lifelines that connect Rev. and Mrs. Nakayama are our survival.

They are standing beside each others as I leave, holding hands.

I see Rev. Nakayama holding on to his wife's hand and I see my Aunt Sue wanting "to be like a kid again," tied to her children but trying to stand up for her fledgling self. I see that and no more. I am stuck. Bucking. It is spring again. The snow is melting, the water rushing down the road, the sap running. My sap, too. It's hard to sit here. I am a mass of conflicting emotions that I don't understand. The computer hurts my eyes and I know it is not good for me. I am only glad that I have had my children and, whatever else it does, I don't have to worry about my fertility. I find the light in the house beautiful and I soak up the sun on the porch like a dry, dormant bulb. I feel good. I feel bad. I wake up and stretch. I wake up and cry. Juices are running, churning. It snows again and they are leaden. I want to fly the coop. I want to write what I know. No one has read the pages. I have no idea if anybody cares or, worse, how I ever presumed to write on such a complex subject. I remind myself that the book is based on hundreds of interviews and years of observations — not only my own. It is certainly not only me. And then, because there has to be a reason to continue, I tell myself that the questions I ask and the answers I'm looking for begin where the Baltimore Longitudinal Study left off: "How do we cope, adjust, adapt, or defend so as to preserve our essential characteristics unchanged in the face of all the vicissitudes and transitions of adulthood and old age?"

How? And why?

Scientists have studied blood chemistry, cell culture, epidermal hydration, mood states, reaction time, testosterone, time perception, and psychomotor function. What I am after is something they can't measure. And every time I think there is an answer, there is, of course, an addendum, a caveat, a parenthesis, another question. There is no straight line. I am Möbius-tripping through many life experiences, letting them wash over me like waves, coming up and saying "ah ha," just as another hits me, a lapper or a breaker, and I go under, hoping to come up again.

I think of Marguerite Yourcenar, at sixty, hoping to "die a little less besotted" than when she was born, wondering if the broad outline of her life will become clearer when "the day's warm fog gives way to dusk's sharp outlines."

And I remember Mary Frances Fisher's description of Grandfather Kennedy, an enormous old man, with streaming hair and beard, tall and gaunt as an Old Testament prophet: "Grandmother Kennedy died. And Grandfather Kennedy died two weeks after she did. In a rage. He had believed in God since he was forty. God and Jesus, the Devil and Hell and all that. But he had made a pact with Mary Louella, his wife, my grandmother, that she would die the last of the two because he did not care to grieve. And so she'd have to grieve for him and he'd be spared having to grieve for her. But she didn't. She died two weeks before he did. And he was just furious. He'd blaspheme God. He'd say, 'God damn you, God.' And of course he could quote in Hebrew and Latin and Greek, and for the two weeks before he died he was going blathering on."

No one pitched "life review" to Grandfather Kennedy. Or told him to reconnect with deeper levels of psychic organization. Or designated the final period of life as essential to the existential development of all human beings. Grandfather Kennedy did not go gentle into the good night. He did the good old-fashioned "Rage, rage against the dying of the light."

I begin to write dogged by the specter of physical disintegration and death. But as I speak to older people I am less and less spooked. Most do not appear to fear death.

"The only thing I have against dying is the debilitation and pain," says Ted Allan. "Otherwise, it's something I'm accepting as part of the scheme of things. I'm not saying I like it. But just as I had to face the fact that I wasn't Cary Grant, so I accept the fact that I have to die. I don't *like* it, I don't *like* not being Cary Grant. I would have liked to be Cary Grant. Cary Grant and William Shakespeare actually. I would have liked to be William Shakespeare looking like Carry Grant. But I accept the fact that I wasn't either. So too I accept the business of dying. But I *hate* being uncomfortable or in pain, in that sense I don't like being ill."

"How do you feel about death?" I ask Mary Calderone, who is eighty-two, a decade older than Ted.

"I don't feel anything about it at all. You die, you die."

"You're not fearful?"

"I'm curious. It's a strange thing. For the first time, I'm confronting death. Before I thought I was going to go on forever. It never occurred to me I wouldn't. Now, I have a lot to do. My first gesture was to buy in to where I wanted to be buried and take care of all that so the kids wouldn't have to worry about it. And that said, 'My life is finite.' And I felt very good about that. Then the autobiography, and a new computer because this one is an orphan and nobody ever reads what I have in there. And I'm on the list for a Quaker retirement community, not a home but a community, total complete medical care and facilities until you go. And there are many intellectual people, my caliber which is good, I need it. What I'm doing is taking steps to protect me."

"Taking care of all that you can anticipate."

"Yes. I made my will, very carefully and, yes, I have, except for the death."

On May 23, 1948, George Bernard Shaw, almost a decade older than Mary Calderone, writes to the Very Rev. W.R. Inge who is in hospital, recovering from prostate surgery:

> I know that the contingency of death does not trouble you. For you as for me "la morte e nulla." But I am sure that you share my very lively objection to pain, which drives us to the surgeons who, never having been operated on themselves, and associating operations pleasantly with guineas, are apt to promise that they are painless. So it is as well to have lay evidence.
>
> At ninety-two I am very groggy on my legs; but I still have my wits about me, or imagine I have. I sleep well, always in the hope that I may not wake again; but I am not in the least unhappy.
>
> Old age is not unhappy. I have talked to three centurians about it: all three women. One said, "What is it but buttoning and unbuttoning?" and amused herself by arranging her funeral. The second said it is like being a child again: little things amuse you. The third did not discuss it, but chatted normally. Not one of the three was otherwise than cheerful. There were all resigned to live as long as they must, and had given up hoping for death with all the other vanities.

Dr. James Birren tells me young people project a lot of misgivings on to old age. He says they think: I must wall it off, I must deny it, my physical attractiveness is gone, I can't play baseball like I used to, therefore I must feel depressed.

"No," he says, "old people do not feel depressed." Read the empirical data, he suggests. The majority of people over sixty-five are in good health and happy with the quality of their lives. In fact, in thirteen countries of the world where they were surveyed, older people are deriving *more* contentment from their lives than younger people. They are not obsessed with dying. They are, like Malcolm Cowley, thinking about "What to do with those six, seven years, more or less, that the Census Bureau has grudgingly allowed me."

In the afterword to *Sister Age*, Mary Frances Fisher writes:

> We must accept and agree with and then attend to with dispassion such things as arthritis, moles that may be cancerous, constipation that may lead to polyps and hernias, all the boring physi-

cal symptoms of our ultimate disintegration . . . What is important, though, is that our dispassionate acceptance of attrition be
matched by a full use of everything that has ever happened in all
the long wonderful-ghastly years to free a person's mind from his
body . . . to use the experience, both great and evil, so that the
physical annoyances are surmountable in an alert and even mirth-
ful appreciation of life itself.

Mary Frances says we like old people who have aged well
because of what we experience as their "reassuring warmth of
amusement."

And Erik Erikson concurs, "I can't imagine a wise old person
who can't laugh. The world is full of ridiculous dichotomies."

Normally, Mike Zimring would instantly agree. But the first time
we meet is not a normal day. As I walk along El Camino Drive,
to the imposing black glass William Morris Agency and into
Zimring's paneled office, the veteran agent sits in a high-back
swivel chair, surrounded by pictures of his children marrying,
his grandchildren smiling, his wife's red, hey-day hair cascading,
while his contemporaries die "like flies" around him.

"We lost the head of the motion picture department, worked
with him for over thirty years. He died. The chairman of the
board is in a hospice — you know what that is? It's a part of the
hospital where they put people who are going to *die*. And then
the ex-president is very ill too."

That very morning, the man who suggested Mike work with
Orson Welles at the Mercury Theater died.

"He died hard, the man who died this morning. He was rich.
It didn't help him. He didn't even enjoy it very much. He left the
bulk of his money to charity. It was like he didn't even have it."

Zimring, ex-actor, agent, and friend of, among others, Kate
Hepburn, Gore Vidal, Frank Capra, and Jean Renoir, is under
siege. If he had a tribal dance to make the lurking evil spirits go
away, he would leap out of his internal twitch and wail around
his desk. But Zimring's tribal impulse is humor, not dance.

He tells me about a friend who "just expired," while sitting in
his chair, and Frank Capra, eighty-eight, who was taking care of
his invalid wife until his stroke several months ago. Now Capra
can't remember recent events — which reminds Mike . . .

"Do you know what the four stages of senility are? No? Well, first you forget names. Then you forget faces. Then you forget to close your fly . . . Then you forget to open your fly."

Mike's timing is perfect and he likes the story. Capra's problems and his own are momentarily forgotten as he laughs — big, all-encompassing belly laughs that shake off the sticky mental cobwebs and leave him looking and sounding a lot livelier.

"When you're older you learn how to cope and that's what life is all about, isn't it, the need to cope with things. I think the secret to coping is your sense of humor. If you can maintain even a modicum of a sense of humor about things, you can cope with them much better. I was in the theatrical branch in Europe during the war and some of the greatest humor this world has ever seen came out of the war. Being able to laugh made it possible to survive. It was amazing.

"Abe Lasfo, the man who built this company, told me something once that I've never forgotten that sort of makes life easier for me. He said that if he could change something, he worried about it, but if he couldn't change it, he didn't worry about it anymore. That takes care of a lot of things.

"I used to worry about deals. God, I should have done this and I should have done that. Now, once the deal is set, I don't worry about it anymore. If you can't change it, what's the point? I've learned to turn off. I no longer take things home with me. And if I've made an investment that turns out bad, I've become very philosophical about it. Anything that is not a matter of life and death is not important. If it's only money, what's the big deal? I keep saying to myself, If you don't die from it, it's not final.

"I think about quitting but I'm afraid if I don't work, everything will change. It's like the old joke: A guy retires and he's having lunch with his wife one day and she turns to him and says, 'You know, Sam, I know I married you for better or worse, but not for lunch.'"

A surprising number of people I interviewed read the comics in the newspaper. Linus Pauling even has a cartoon collection. And my father and his buddies have a stock of jokes that they update and trade: at dinners, in the Y locker room, on the phone. Since a joke often goes the rounds, there's even a joke about everyone knowing the same joke. This is it: A guy walks into the lobby of an old persons' home where a bunch of old people are sitting around. One of them calls a number and they break into gales of laughter. Another one calls another number and they break into gales of laughter again. The new guy wants to be part of the crowd, so he calls out, "Sixty-three." There's a dead silence. "What's the matter?" he asks the director of the home. And the director says, "It's the way you told it."

Extensive recent experiments show that humor contributes to good health, increasing the number of disease-fighting immune cells and mitigating the ravages of overstress, or distress, a major factor in much modern disease. Dr. Birren refers me to a Harvard longitudinal study that posits a sense of humor as a vital feature in an adjustment to life. "Humor is adaptive, it's tension reducing," he points out. "One might call it [laughter] a luxury reflex." Adds Arthur Koestler, "Its only purpose seems to be to provide release from the stress of purposeful activity."

No one is quite sure exactly how it works but everyone agrees that he who laughs, lasts.

Solly, Gwen, Paul, and Angie are at my dad's house for supper and a joke session called in my honor. These guys know each other's old stories, and by the time I arrive they have traded the new ones. From the vast repertoire that they file, I know not where, I request a sampling of "geriatric jokes" and Solly tells the first story.

"Mrs. Cohen and Mr. Ginsberg went down to Florida. They were both widowed, they liked each other and started dating. Mr. Ginsberg said, 'I don't want to get together unless we get married.' And Mrs. Cohen said, 'Fine, I like that.' So he said, 'Let's see a doctor and make sure we're okay. There's no sense if we're not well.' So they went to see this doctor. And the doctor said, 'Who'll be first? Mrs. Cohen?' And Mrs. Cohen said, 'Sure.' So she goes in and she's with the doctor twenty minutes, a half hour and the doctor says, 'Okay, you can get dressed now. I'll go out and speak to Mr. Ginsberg.' And he goes out and says to Mr. Ginsberg, 'Mr. Ginsberg, I spoke to Mrs. Cohen about what we found out and I think you should know that she has acute angina.' And Mr. Ginsberg says, 'Doctor, you're telling me.'"

When Solly tells the joke, he anticipates the punch line and has the doctor saying, "You should know she has a cute vagina." Everyone laughs just the same. When the laughter subsides my dad says, "Two months later Mrs. Cohen and Mr. Ginsberg go to another doctor, and since Mrs. Cohen doesn't have to stay, she says 'I'll meet you at home.' Mr. Ginsberg goes in and after a while the doctor days, 'You know, you have a venereal disease. You have gonorrhea.' So Mr. Ginsberg says, 'Okay.' He doesn't know what gonorrhea is. He phones Mrs. Cohen and says, 'Look up gonorrhea in the dictionary.' She looks it up and 'Oh,' she says, 'it's a venereal disease but we don't have to worry because it only effects the Gentiles."

Then ensues a discussion of what joke to tell next. They urge Solly on.

"A guy comes to play golf at a new golf course. He says to the starter, 'Can you get me someone to play with?' The starter says. 'Yeah, that old fellow would like to play.'

"'Can he play?'

"'Yeah, he hits a good ball.'

"So the guy goes up to introduce himself. He says, 'Tell me, you hit well or you going to shlep around?'

"'Not to worry,' says the old fellow.

"'Well, I'll tell you. Very, very important. What's your eyesight like?'

"'Perfect.'

"''Cause I'll tell you, one of my problems and the reason I need someone to play with all the time is that I've got cataracts and I really can't see the ball well, so if you don't mind, if you can see well, could you tell me where my ball is?'

"'Sure.'

"So the new guy tees off. 'How was that?'

"'Good. Good shot,' says the old fellow.

"'Did you see where it went?'

"'Sure.'

"So the old guy tees off and they start walking and the new guy says, 'So tell me, where's my ball?'

"And the old guy says, 'You know what, I don't remember.'"

My dad waits a beat and continues Solly's joke.

"So this older gentleman goes to the urologist to have himself examined and the doctor checks him. Then he thinks it's only right that he should ask him about his sex life as well because it's important. So he says, 'Mr. Cohen, how often do you have sex?' And Mr. Cohen says, 'Almost every night.'

"'No,' says the doctor.

"'Yes. Almost every night.'

"'Are you sure?'

"'Yes,' says Mr. Cohen. 'Almost Monday, almost Tuesday, almost Wednesday.'"

"And then," says Solly, "there's the one about the ninety-five-year-old couple who wanted a divorce but were waiting for the children to die." "And," says my dad, "the one about the old man who wants a penile implant because he goes to the *schvitz* [turkish baths] every Friday night and he wants to be a sport." And the one about . . . They branch out from geriatric jokes to a story about a man who gets a wish from a genie and wishes for a longer and longer penis, until finally his penis is trailing on the ground and he has only one more wish, and he wishes for his legs to be four inches longer. And that reminds my dad about the genie who promised a man so many things that the man let him have his wife for one night, and as the genie was making whoopee with his wife, he commented favorably on her husband but asked if she didn't think he was a little old to believe in genies and . . . I left them to it. Their fifteen facial muscles were contracting into a laugh pattern, their breathing was visibly altered, they may or may not have been producing more endorphins or stimulating the thymus gland, no one knows for sure — but whatever was going on, they liked it. They had risen above memory loss, diminishing sexuality, dependent children, doctors, illness, death — bobbing above them on the waves of their altered respiration. They hardly noticed me leave.

Microbiologist René Dubos, eighty, has faith in the "resiliency of human nature" and considers the power of self-renewal "the most important aspect of human life."

"How do we learn to do this?" interviewer Bill Moyers asks Dubos. "Because now it seems like we are self-abusive, it seems we have created an environment which sucks out of us that self-renewal energy."

And Dubos, who has had more reason and taken more time to consider this question, responds to Moyers.

"You know, how we use it, I am afraid I am going to use a word that I shouldn't use in front of you, through faith. And when I use the word faith, I am not using it as applying to a specific religion. Faith in life . . . I believe that in all its phases, in all its aspects, there is in life something very unique, something very different from the rest of inanimate creation — the power of restoring itself. The difference between shoes and the soles of your feet is that if you walk for a long time, the sole of you shoes wear out and you have to discard your shoes. If you walk barefooted, the skin of your feet grows back, renews itself. Your feet are living, the shoe is dead. And somewhere or other there is something very profound there — the power of renewal. I have — this is very deep in me, it's a kind of faith, call it, will you, just faith, if you will."

If old people are more intensely present, more in touch with the essential "self-renewal energy," it is because they are "on" in a profound way.

When Katherine S. White, respected fiction editor of *The New Yorker*, retired, she moved to the country and grew flowers. Her husband, essayist E.B. White, describes her annual bulb-planting ritual in the fall. "As the years went by and age overtook her, there was something comical yet touching in her bedraggled appearance on this awesome occasion — the small, hunched-over figure, her studied absorption in the implausible notion that there would yet be another spring, oblivious to the ending of her own days, which she knew perfectly well was near at hand, sitting there with her detailed chart under those dark skies in the dying October, calmly plotting the resurrection."

I have never been bored interviewing for this book. I came heavy with the compulsions of my age. And soon I laughed, relaxed, and enjoyed gracious company and compelling conversation. René Dubos has faith in life. And I, listening to the elders, have regained my faith in the human spirit. Not a cardboard cutout spirit, but human spirits in real-life struggles.

I recall Giff Gifford's description of his love for his wife as "a constant, quiet wonder." And Mrs. Topham who lives alone saying, "I've got *love*, you see, I have little grandchildren to cuddle and hug, and a baby to goo at."

I see Dorothy Livesay gesturing to the great, large trees at the edge of the ocean and Ted Allan wanting to hug trees. Mary Frances Fisher feels "fat" with all she has stored up to say. And Marian Jarvis Lewis, deaf and almost blind, loves to "partake of life."

I will always remember what Lea told me about how she survived the deaths of her brothers and sisters — how she remembers them alive, even the fights, how she soaks in what they have written her, given her, left her. When I have to live through the death of someone I love, I will think of what she said and the strength it gave her. When I need it, I will have at least that.

I think of Malcolm Cowley, never saccharine, who says, "Old age may have its inner compensations." And Norman Corwin, more exuberant, extemporizing an ode to joy. The muse opens up May Sarton's inner space and my dad finds the eternal at the back lake.

Now as never before, I understand what Maggie Kuhn means when she says, "There needs to be an appreciation of the aspects of life that involve the mind and the spirit. Those are absolutely essential. Absolutely. The body may fall by the wayside, may be in a sense quite useless, but the mind and the spirit have to thrive."

Light in inner space.

Connection to the stream of life.

Mirth.

Older people have more high blood pressure than younger people, but if there were statistics on ecstatic states and age-related insight, they would have more of those too.

And now it is time to ask my dad why he *jumped* onto the table for his quadruple bypass operation.

"There was no doubt in my mind I was going to get better. I had a body that was great except for one part. I figured, I fix that one part, I'd be able to keep going."

"Are you happy you had this operation?"

"Sure. I don't take any pills anymore. At times I forget I've even had this operation." He pulls up his shirt and points to a healed, hairy chest, where once there were black stitches and a lurid red scar.

"What do you like about being alive?"

His answer is quick. "I feel good. I get up every morning — I just feel good. Most of the time I look forward to the day."

"And what's of value to you?"

"The reputation I have as a professional, my friendships, and, of course, my family. Like today, I knocked together a bookcase for Kim, nothing fancy, but she thinks it's gorgeous, beautiful, it made her so happy. And it gives me great joy to be able to do that.

"And my sisters, my brother-in-law Joe. I feel very, very close to the guy. You know, we play together — we go off buying wood together, which we did this morning. I'm going to help him build a bookcase."

"You listen to a lot of music. Why do you do that?"

"Just the sound of the music, the rhythm, the notes, relaxes me. And then it enables my mind to just float free and think of all sorts of things. And I think that helps me get a better grasp on life."

"Do you think it's important to get a grasp on life?"

"I think it's vital because it helps me get a perspective on life, and the thing that maybe bothered me at the moment fades into insignificance when I think how fortunate I am to love and be loved by a lot of people and to have my health. It's sort of retrospective and introspective as well. I just get an overall feeling of goodness listening to music."

"Why do you want to go over your past life?"

"Well, a person is the sum of the things that happen to him in his life, or her life. And I'm sure that most of us who reach this age think about their lives. I think that distinguishes us from the animals."

"What do you think about?"

"All sorts of things go through my mind. I think about your mother. I think about Uncle Nat. And I think of my kids, my grandchildren."

"When you think about Mom, what do you think?"

"I just think of the times we had together. How beautiful she was. I even think back to the times we were in high school together, how we met."

"Uncle Nat?"

"Well, I'm just sorry he's not around. We were close. We were even closer as the years went by. There were four of us in the family. Now we're three. The three of us miss him. We talk about him a great deal . . . But I find it interesting that you haven't asked me about death and dying."

Now, he's thrown me. I haven't asked about death because thinking about my father dying is almost too painful to contemplate. But he's raised it and I am a dutiful journalist.

"Is death something you think about?" I ask my dad.

"Now and then."

"And what do you think?"

"I would like to think that death is something like running a long marathon. And you're tired and you're kind of happy you're coming to the end of it."

His answers have often surprised me. This one sets off upsetting alarms.

"Do you have this feeling yet?" I ask as coolly as I can.

"No. Now and then I think all people my age think to themselves what have they got left to live — another five, six, three years — and then it's ended."

He says this matter-of-factly, but not easily. And now I have to ask him how it feels to think he has so few years left to live.

"I think how you feel depends on what you think of yourself. And I don't mean you've necessarily had to do great things — discover a cure for cancer, or TB — I don't think it's that. I think how you feel about that has to do with your relationships more than anything else. At this stage, when you're seventy-five, you look back and you think to yourself, have you done everything you should have done? Are there other things you should have done? I think I've done what I wanted to do, what I should have done."

I am listening but still dealing with the short lifespan my dad has allocated himself. He, however, has raked that ground before. He's waiting.

"So, how do you feel about death then?" I ask.

"Well, I'd like to postpone it for a good period of time." He smiles at me, considerably more on top of this discussion than I. "I'd like to become a great-grandfather. I'm having fun in life. And while that's continuing, I'd like to be around to enjoy it."

Then, he sits back, looking at me for further questions.

I have none.

Younger generations may anticipate the horrors of old age, but as Edith Wallace says, "When you get there, it isn't like that at all." Listening to my dad, I know this to be true. This knowledge and my trust in what older people tell me, helps calm the fear and guide the way.

I thank Dad formally, as I always do at the end of a session. As he always does, he says it's a pleasure.

Then he stands up, dons his cowboy hat, and goes off to see Uncle Joe.

Notes and Sources

The notes and sources listed below provide additional discussion of specific subjects, as well as references to resource material quoted in the text: books, film, TV, radio.

The interviews done by the author for this book all occurred between 1986 and 1991 and are not referenced below.

* In citing works, short titles have generally been used. For full entry please see the "Bibliography" arranged by the author.

Identity

Page

3. "How does it feel . . . ": Joyce Castiglione interview with Mr. Smith (Montreal, 5 Oct 1985).

4. "critically aware . . . ": Gray Panthers of Greater Boston, "Old Person Stereotypes," Media Watch Project pamphlet, 1985.

4. "Stereotypes encourage . . . ": Ibid.

4. "This indignity works . . . ": Ibid.

5. "I'm so wrinkled . . . ": Phyillis Diller, "Just for Laughs Festival" (Montreal, 21 July 1988).

5. "Older people constitute . . . ": Dychwald and Flower, *Age Wave*, 307.

5. "even when my generation . . . ": Projections based on United Nations. *World Demographic Estimates and Projections, 1950-2025*, 1988, 191, 237.

6. "eighty percent live without . . . ": Marshall, *Silver Threads*, 19

167

8. "Take me . . . ": Copper in *Women and Aging*, 52.

9. "creativity diminishes . . . ": Writers Guild of America, *The Journal*, November 1989.

10. "You begin to resemble . . . ": Farber, *How Does it Feel to be Old?* unpaged.

11. "that virulent stereotype . . . ": Copper in *Women and Aging*, 55.

11. "Unique to our culture . . . ": Comfort, *Practice of Geriatric Psychiatry*, 2.

11. "At any point in time . . . ": Shock et al., *Normal Human Aging*, 136.

11. "It seems disconnected . . . ": Macdonald and Rich, *Look Me in the Eye*, 14.

12. "Without a history . . . ": Ibid., 55.

13. "In this situation . . . ": Cowley, *The View from 80*, 7.

13. "Between 1981 and 1984 . . . ": "Report of the American Society of Plastic and Reproductive Surgeons," *Newsweek*, 27 May 1985, 64.

13. "This situation . . . ": Comfort, *Practice of Geriatric Psychiatry*, 69.

13. "infection and nerve damage . . . ": Cousins, *Head First*, 161/2.

14. "Youthenasia": *Women and Aging*, 34.

16. "our social image . . . ": Comfort, *Practice of Geriatric Psychiatry*, 70.

17. "It is raining . . . ": Macdonald and Rich, *Look Me in the Eye*, 227-229.

26. "a burst of affection . . . ": Cowley, *The View From 80*, xiv, xv.

29. "A revolution is implied . . . ": "Not for Women Only," *Modern Maturity*, April-May 1989, 71.

29. "The title of this . . . ": Le Sueur in *Women and Aging*, 9.

29. "Parts of the aging . . . ": Fisher, *Sister Age*, 237.

30. "I consider myself . . . ": Myerhoff, *Number Our Days*, 19.

Mind/Body

32. "We now know that there is a high correlation between high-fat intake and breast, bladder and colorectal cancer," says Dr. Ruth Weg. "There is also a high correlation between a low intake of vitamins A and C and a high level of certain kinds of cancers. The prudent diet we're talking about with low fat, low salt, low sugar, high complex carbohydrates, raw fruits and vegetables, can do no harm and may do a great deal of good."

32. "Physical exercise has . . . ": M. Gatz and C. Emery. "The Effect of Physical Exercise on Cognitive and Psychological Functioning in Community Aged," *Andrus Annual Report*, 1984-1985.

32. "Physical activity in . . . ": Kaplan et al., *American Journal of Public Health*, 307-312.

32. "people with chronic . . . ": Money et al., *Journal of the American Geriatrics Society*, 348.

32. "Even men and women . . . ": Schwartz, "Benefits of Regular Exercise Even Greater for the Elderly," *The Montreal Gazette*, 19 January 1989, C8.

32. "I went to a doctor . . . ": Le Sueur in *Women and Aging*, 9-10.

33. A phone call to McGill University reveals that medical students take no courses in alternative medicine. They take a total of 24 hours of nutrition, and only 120 hours of pharmacology. Their stock in trade is surgery and drugs. A congressional subcommittee reports that doctors performed 2.4 million unnecessary operations in 1974, which resulted in 11,900 deaths. (*Cousins, Head First*, 160.) Every year unneeded prescription drugs or side effects of such drugs kill or harm 200,000 elderly Canadians. (Nicolas Regush, *The Montreal Gazette*, 4 March 1989, 1.)

According to Alex Comfort, "Social ostracism apart, the most common cause of sudden, unexplained mental illness in the old is medication . . ." (Comfort, *Practice of Geriatric Psychiatry*, 3.) A recent study of American nursing homes, for example, found extensive use of psychotropic and antipsychotic drugs in 20 percent of patients who have not had a mental disorder diagnosed. (Burns, B.J., et al. "Psychotropic Drug Prescriptions for Nursing Home Residents," *Journal of Family Practice*, 26 (1988): 155.) One hint from Cousins that may be relevant to many older people is that sleep patterns in the old differ from those of the young. The typical pattern of intermittent sleep in old age figures widely in hypnotic advertisements under the label "geriatric insomnia" but it is normal and should not be medicated (Comfort, *Practice of Geriatric Psychiatry*, 7), especially by "long half-life tranquilizers" prescribed for 30 percent of geriatric cases, which, among other noxious effects, increase the risk of hip fracture by 70 percent. AARP [American Association of Retired People] Bulletin, March 1990, 31, no. 3: 14.

Many older people practice preventative health care and have developed a healthy scepticism toward traditional medicine. Marian Jarvis Lewis tells me:

"When I use what I call the state facilities, naturally they prescribe medicine and I took a little bit of it last week. They sent me a hundred of those. And they just drove me into a frenzy. God know what they are."

"They're Novagesic Forte," I read on the label. "Forte means strong. What were they supposed to be for?"

"Just for my general health."

"And they made you sick?"

"A terrible experience. Roaring in my head as if my whole blood system was upset. So now I keep them because my nurse is part of the state facility and every little while I take three or four and drop them in the wastepaper basket. Isn't it awful? To live a life of duplicity . . . 'How are you getting along with your medicine, Mrs. Lewis?' Oh, fine."

"Despite everyone," says Eroca Coty, "we are learning how to take care of ourselves."

33. "Each period of stress . . . ": Selye, *Stress Without Distress*, 96.

33. Nobel laureate Linus Pauling wrote: "Every insult to the body, every illness, every stress increases the physiological age of a person and decreases his or her life expectancy . . . This effect has been described by saying that each person is born with a certain amount of vitality, that some vitality is used up by each episode of illness or other cause of stress, and that death comes when the quota of vitality has been exhausted." (Pauling, *How to Live Longer and Feel Better*, 220.)

35. When doctors told Norman Cousins that his excruciatingly painful disease was potentially terminal and there was no medical solution, he thought, "If negative emotions produce negative chemical changes in the body, wouldn't positive emotions produce positive chemical changes?" Using positive emotions, including a systematic humor program, he helped cure himself of two potentially fatal diseases then, in the past decade, coordinated a series of scientific studies on "the biochemistry of the emotions." For the first time, scientists mapped the two-way brain/body communication system, demonstrating that brain cells and immune cells (the cells that fight disease) are physiologically equipped for direct communication with one another.

Cousins' book, *Head First: The Biology of Hope*, contains a wide range of mind/body studies. In Elena Korneva's USSR study, stimulation to the front of the hypothalamus (the part of the brain involved in calming of emotions) *increases* the body's immune capacity, while the back of the hypothalamus (which relates to stress) impairs the performance of the disease-fighting cells in the immune system. (Ibid., 72). An American study observes that depressive behavior in breast cancer patients is associated with diminished natural-killer cell (NK-cell) activity and faster tumor spread. (Ibid., 85) Another study finds that creative imagination exercises are helpful in producing positive immune responses — stimulating lymphocytes, increasing antibodies and interleukin-2 cells, enhancing NK-cell activity, augmenting the effectiveness of the cytotoxic T cells (Ibid., 86) — just as creative sexual imaging might help produce a positive sexual response.

35. "the life-problems . . . ": Huxley, *You Are Not the Target*, xiii.

36. "a diamond . . . ": Ibid., 25.

36. "I have eliminated eggs and milk and that has given me some advantages," says Laura Huxley. "I gave up coffee because my heart was going too fast. And I cannot drink because it gives me a headache right away. I eat a lot of complex carbohydrates, a lot of vegetables, salad, not "la cuisine" as we know it in France or Italy with lots of condiments, just olive oil, lemon, herbs, and garlic which gives a great deal of taste. It seems the simpler the food, the more tasty it is because you feel the natural taste, not the taste we add. It is very satisfactory to me. I eat with pleasure."

38. During exercise a biochemical process occurs that produces endorphins and enkephalins, biochemical substances that have analgesic and pain-inhibiting effects. Some popular writers have likened this chain of biochemical effects to a natural high.

40. Marian Jarvis Lewis says she and her fellow residents like living alone in the subsidized housing development with home care support but they don't like nursing homes "because here we can get up when we like and make our little meals. And we have our maximum amount of privacy. That's what we like."

When Lea returned from several months in the convalescent hospital where she had been recovering from a wrist operation, I invited her to stay with me.

"I can't," she said.

"I'll feed you your kind of food."

"I really can't, Merrily. I need my autonomy back. You understand that."

Ninety-three-year-old George Bernard Shaw wrote to Nancy Astor when he read her injunctions on his life: "You must positively not come . . . If you will not let me manage my work and my household in my own way you must not come at all . . . I write in great haste, and am rather angry with you for forcing me to put my old foot down and make you understand that in this house what I say goes." (Shaw, *Collected Letters, 1926-1950*.)

According to Kivnick and the Eriksons, autonomy keeps disability at bay. "Elders have a responsibility to themselves to maintain their own physical capacities until advanced old age makes them too fragile to exercise the physical autonomy that safeguards independence." (Erikson, Erikson and Kivnick, *Vital Involvement in Old Age*.)

43. Even scientists cautious about vitamin supplementation, such as Ruth Weg, when faced with studies that actually involve elders admit that "older people do suffer from nutritional deficiencies. We probably do need supplements at certain periods in our lives, especially if we're

going to have some stress, whether it's emotional, let's say bereavement, or physical, like we undergo some surgery. Because if we are suffering from malnutrition, we get depressed more easily, we become confused more readily, we lose motivation. The micro-environment of our neurons is very sensitive to vitamin deficiency. The better our nutritional status, the more satisfactory our recovery will be."

Dr. Pauling not only makes me aware of the benefits of nutritional supplements but, much to my regret, he also proves that sugar is as much a culprit in heart disease as fat — fifty pounds of sugar per year is the limit. Sugar contains high concentrations of fructose which studies show to be correlated with an increased incidence of heart disease and increased cholesterol levels. "If I can get malted milk containing maltose, a disaccharide composed of two glucose residues," he says, "this would be acceptable to me. And even corn syrup is acceptable because it is largely a hydrolysis product of starch and would contain essentially glucose."

45. Aging North Americans worry, almost reflexly, about mental disintegration. Yet recent research shows that among people who are generally healthy, the crucial areas of human intelligence do not decline in old age. A study of brain chemistry, at the National Institute of Aging, using a brain scan to assess metabolic activity in men 21 to 83, found that "the healthy aged brain is as active and efficient as the healthy young brain." (*New York Times*, 21 February 1984, C5.) In fact, the ability to use an accumulated body of general information to make judgments and solve problems, what experts call "crystallized intelligence," continues to rise over the life span in healthy, active people, as it does with Dr. Pauling. (Ibid., C1.)

"The belief that if you live long enough you will become senile is just wrong," says psychiatrist Robert Butler, founding director of the National Institute of Aging. "Senility is a sign of disease, not part of normal aging." (Ibid., C5.)

"The healthy nervous system continues to acquire information with age," says Dr. James Birren. "The speed of the intellectual process is reduced. There's nothing like the quickness of a high school student to startle you. They're very, very quick. With age you have more experience and that's the reagent but you have a little less of the catalytic quickness of the young.

"It also depends on the value you place on these things whether you pursue them. Anything can suffer disuse and neglect. Piatigorsky talked about the necessity of keeping his passions alive in his music and Ray Bradbury said his late life novels were derived from the passions of his childhood. That's the energy and spark. Old age can be passionate and that's a quality of creativity."

45. "flow . . . ": Csikszentmihalyi and Selega, *Optimal Experience: Psychological Studies of Flow in Consciousness*, 365.

49. "average Canadian intake . . . ": "Nutritional Quality of the Canadian Diet, 1986," *National Institute of Nutrition Report*, 3, no. 4 (October 1988): 6.

50. "Writer's career . . . ": *The Montreal Gazette*, 2 January 1989, F4.

51. "Kivnick and the Eriksons . . . ": Erikson, Erikson, and Kivnick, *Vital Involvement in Old Age*, 192.

51. "Even in our weakness . . . ": "Gray Panther Power," *Center Magazine*, 25.

51. "fortitude": Comfort, *Practice of Geriatric Psychiatry*, 68.

51. Most older people are not crocks or hypochondriacs. On the contrary, researchers report a longitudinal decline in hypochondriasis. Dr. D. Eckstein, a geriatric physician, reports that, "given the large burden and disabilities the elderly endure . . . the complaints of the elderly are remarkable low-keyed and valid." (D. Eckstein, *Common Complaints of the Elderly*, in W. Reichel, ed., *The Geriatric Patient*, New York: HP Publishing, 1978, 16.) At any age, psychological distress (hostility, depression, anxiety, susceptibility to stress) gives rise to diffuse somatic complaints. But older people, even with all their disabilities, have fewer unwarranted complaints.

52. "I have my sister . . . ": Tymbios, *Long Time Passing: Lives of Older Lesbians*, 207.

52. "The crucial task . . . ": Scott-Maxwell, *The Measure of My Days*, 36.

54. "the nature of freedom . . . ": Laurence, "Ten Years' Sentences," *Canadian Literature*, 41 (1969): 10-16.

59. In a copy of *Network*, the Gray Panther newspaper, I read a cry from a man with a psychological "sickness of the soul" worse, he says, than any physical suffering.

> To the editor:
>
> . . . I am 89 years old, and have seen all kinds of dying and suffering . . .
>
> I lost my wife after 61 years of marriage. Our souls were so intertwined that I suffered and am still suffering more than any imaginable physical sickness. Although I am mentally and physically capable of living independently — doing shopping, cooking and keeping up the house as it was in my wife's time — I would like to die . . .
>
> Hartwig Heymann
> Berkeley, CA

Arthur Koestler committed suicide when he could no longer endure his "pain-racked mortal frame." He had survived Franco's prison camps and fought the Stalinist purges but at the end of his life he fought for a dignified death for "those condemned on mistaken humanitarian principles to a painful and degrading prolongation of life." He was a member of Exit — The Society for The Right to Die with Dignity. His preface to Exit's technical "Guide to Self-Deliverance," available only to individuals who had been members of the Society for at least six months, presaged his own suicide.

"If the agnostics among us could be assured of a gentle and easy way of dying, they would be much less afraid of *being* dead . . . the prospect of falling peacefully, blissfully asleep, is not only soothing but can make it positively desirable to quit this pain-racked mortal frame and become unborn again."

For Koestler, the only thing worse than being chained to an intolerable existence was the nightmare of a botched attempt to end it. "I know that I am speaking in the name of many (some of them personal friends) who tried and failed — or who don't dare to try for fear of failure."

Approximately one sixth of those who die every year in the Netherlands, some 20,000, die from euthanasia. Euthanasia is not legal in Holland but doctors who practice it follow an unofficial code and are not, generally, prosecuted. They make sure the decision is voluntary; the patient well-informed; the pain untreatable; and that money, loneliness or other correctable problems are not the cause of the decision. They then consult one other doctor.

The Dutch experience provides a source of first-hand reports on euthanasia practices.

Mrs. Katerina Reydag, 82, keeps the drink that can end her life in a gray velvet pouch on her bedboard. "Since the time I have the bottle, I'm at ease, I'm peaceful inside. I'm glad to know that when my time has come, I needn't be a burden to everyone who loves me and other people and to be helpless. I don't want to be helpless."

Mrs. Reydag has had to give up knitting and the piano she loved to play. Sometimes, when she is very ill and in excessive pain, she thinks, 'Well, it's enough.' But then she sees the children and the growing grandchildren and she's glad that she's still alive. "But I leave it open. I leave it open. It makes me happy to know the possibility is there."

Still, Mrs. Reydag has never "almost taken" the liquid. The bottle is insurance for a peaceful end, a mental out that gets her through the pain. "I think I love life too much to do it. But I have peace inside. I am very happy with the bottle."

Documentaries on euthanasia in the Netherlands often include scenes of peaceful deaths. A man with painful, terminal lung cancer makes the decision to have active euthanasia and his decision is supported by his wife and children. The man says goodbye to his relatives, they wait outside the sleeping-room, the doctor administers the injections. "Ten minutes later he was dead and everyone was pleased it went in such a smooth way without any suffering anymore," says the doctor.

A mother whose cancer has taken away her ability to function says, "It's enough, this is the moment. I want to die." She holds her daughter's hand as the injection is administered. "She smiled and was very happy," says the daughter. "I would like to have the same right."

Opponents of voluntary euthanasia say that it will eventually lead to involuntary euthanasia. They suspect that the euthanasia movement will pressure people who are very ill or handicapped to do away with themselves. Baba Copper says, "Talking about choice in relation to dying always makes me very nervous . . . we are at the beginning of a world-wide demographic boom of old women. It is easy to predict that our society will soon be subject to all kinds of 'new looks' at death and dying. I read a clipping from a futurist magazine suggesting that a demise pill be available to the elderly (but not the young, of course). The old are seen as half dead already. Old women, like everyone else, buy into the prevailing concepts surrounding both worth and death — we are as easy to brainwash as the next."

61. "The great advances in medicine . . . ": "René Dubos: The Despairing Optimist at 80," *Bill Moyers' Journal*, Show 711.

Sex/Love

69. "After menopause, there is less capacity for the vaginal wall to sweat, or lubricate," Dr. Weg explains. "The lubrication is from the wall, not from the Bartholin glands at the lower opening of the vaginal canal that we used to feel were the major source of lubrication. The main source is actually the mucosal lining itself in the walls of the vaginal canal. We call it sweating in the sense of perspiring, but it is the exudation of this mucous lubrication."

69. "We've know for 25 to 28 years about estrogen and progestin," says Dr. Weg, "and it's only in the last few years that the medical profession has deemed it worthwhile to recognize the fact that if we give both hormones we shed the thickened lining of the endometrium of the uterus, the increased blood vessels, just as if we were still having a menses. But, if you keep supplying just estrogen to a woman with a uterus, you're going to keep building on lining tissue that is already built. Building, building, and no shedding. You need the progestin to have the shedding. And if we can get rid of that extra tissue once every two months, or once a month, the chances are, not only no cancer, but a lower rate of cancer than the population that is not taking anything. That didn't get out to people. The only thing that got

out to most lay people was that estrogen was carcinogenic. But with the 25, 26 years of research that's been done with both hormones, I am confident that they *lower* the risk of cancer rather than raising it."

Dr. Hugh Barber cautions that it is safer to use a natural estrogen than a synthetic estrogen. There are fewer adverse effects. Dr. James Long adds that "synthetics are apparently associated with the thromboembolic phenomena." He calls synthetics "the real culprits in thromboembolic problems." (*Geriatrics*, 64) *Geriatrics*, 44, no. 3, March 1989, has a clear discussion of current medical thinking on estrogen replacement therapy.

Women considering taking hormones should first have a comprehensive medical examination to be certain there are no contraindications. They should ask for the minimum effective dosage. And they should reevaluate treatment and dosage every six months or immediately if there are problems.

70. "the effects of long-term . . . ": Doress and Siegel, *Ourselves, Growing Older*, 269-270.

70. *Ourselves, Growing Older* offers a discussion of external lubricants such as vitamin E oil and Trans-lube or Kama Sutra oils. They report that some authorities recommend only water-based lubricants such as Koromex, K-Y Jelly, and Ortho II which, unlike Vaseline, flush easily out of the system.

71. "Masters and Johnson . . . ": Doress and Siegel, *Ourselves, Growing Older*, 80.

71. "She was approaching . . . ": Brecher, *Love, Sex and Aging: A Consumers Union Report*, 345.

82. The pills are furosemide (Lasix) and digitalis (Lanoxin).

84. Doctors used to say that most impotence is caused by psychological factors but current studies indicate that 50 percent of men's potency problems are medical. These medical problems include impotence caused by: impaired blood flow, hormone deficiency, nerve damage, or impotence related to drugs that affect sexual function, especially those used for heart disease, hypertension, diabetes, or depression.

There are some 200 different medicines that affect sexual function. ACE-inhibitors are among the antihypertensive medications least likely to impair erections; these include captopril, lisonpril, and enalapril maleate. Probably the least problematic betablocker is atenolol. The calcium-channel blockers least likely to cause sexual dysfunction are nifedipine and diltiazem. Some men can associate the beginnings of impotence with the beginning of a new medication and then it is a question of finding out if the medication can be replaced.

Dr. Taguchi uses various tests to determine whether or not the impotence is physical or psychological. The doppler flow study, for example, uses ultrasound waves to record the density of red blood cells in the penis. The pattern derived from the penis is compared to the pattern in a leg or arm. If there are significantly fewer red blood cells in the penis, the potency problem is probably due to impaired blood flow. In the sleep lab study, the man's erections are measured during the night for duration and rigidity and then compared to normal functioning to see whether there is a physical impairment.

84. "Since 1973 . . . ": "Sex and Aging," KUON TV, 1987.

84. "I was always kinda looking . . . ": Ibid.

85. "Even if erection . . . ": Hite, *The Hite Report*, 887.

85. "If the erection . . . ": Ibid., 889.

86. "only one out of ten . . . ": "Sex and Aging," KUON TV, 1987.

86. "Allowing for individual . . . ": Butler and Lewis, *Love and Sex After Sixty*, 19-25.

87. "At a geriatric . . . ": White, *Archives of Sexual Behavior*, 495.

87. "From a psychosexual . . . ": Butler and Lewis, *Love and Sex After Sixty*, 19-20.

88. "And then one night . . . ": Callaghan, *A Wild Old Man on the Road*, 120.

92. "physical ruin . . . ": Miller and Venus, *Dear, Dear Brenda: The Love Letters of Henry Miller to Brenda Venus*, 9.

92. "July 15, 1976.": Ibid., 35.

92. "July 21, 1976.": Ibid., 40.

92. "10/7/76.": Ibid., 64.

93. "Friday P.M.": Ibid., 76.

93. "Saturday, [10/28/77]": Ibid., 123.

93. "9:00 P.M. Monday [June 25, 1978]": Ibid., 139.

93. "Sept. 29, 1980": Ibid., 191.

96. "One Way Conversation": Livesay, *The Self-Completing Tree*, 247.

97. "The Woman I Am": Ibid., 117.

100. "Let your hand play first . . . ": Livesay, *The Phases of Love*.

101. "Dawnings": Ibid.

104. "Women live seven . . . ": "Sex and Aging," KUON TV, 1987.

105. "In 'Project Caress' . . . ": "New Care Service is Launched with a Hug," *Viewpark Community Hospital: In the News*, 27 March 1980, 1.

105. Initiated by Laura Huxley and tried at the Verdugo Vista Convalescent Hospital, at the Viewpark Community Hospital, and at the Foothill Family Service.

105. "the very embrace of . . . ": Friedan, *The Feminine Mystique*, 416.

106. "We feel chased . . . ": Buzz Dewey, "Sex and Aging," KUON TV, 1987.

108. "female impersonators . . . ": Heilbrun, "Women Writers: Coming of Age at 50," *New York Times Book Review*, 4 September, 1988, 23.

108. "At a certain age . . . ": Gutmann, *Reclaimed Powers*, 133.

108. "a previously undeveloped . . . ": Ibid., 98.

108. "the necessary prelude . . . ": Ibid., 99.

108. "across cultures . . . ": Ibid., 133.

108. "introversion-extroversion . . . ": Ibid., 149.

108. "An Italian study . . . ": Ibid., 149.

108. "a kind of role . . . ": Ibid., 158.

108. "In institutions . . . ": Ibid., 158.

108. "Across cultures . . . ": Ibid., 151.

108. "androgyny of later . . . ": Ibid., 135.

109. "With aging . . . ": Erikson, Erikson, and Kivnick, *Vital Involvement in Old Age*, 64.

110. "generalization of sensual modes . . . ": Erikson, *The Life Cycle Completed: A Review*, 135.

110. "androgyny . . . ": Gutmann, *Reclaimed Powers*, 135.

110. "I find myself . . . ": Adelman, *Long Time Passing: Lives of Older Lesbians*, 37.

110. "I feel good . . . ": Esther Gerstenfeld, interview with Phyllis Amber, Montreal, 12 July 1989.

111. "perhaps the most important . . . ": Erikson, *Wisdom and the Senses*, 21, 22.

111. "our most consistently . . . ": Ibid., 21, 22.

111. "Down there . . . ": Judith Segal, Director, Corporate Consulting Services, Pacific Oaks College, Pasadena, California, speaking at the 14th Annual Clinical Day, Maimonaides Hospital, Montreal, 26 October 1983.

112. "But older people . . . ": Bulcroft and O'Conner-Roden, *Psychology Today*, 68.

117. "You have to live . . . ": Goleman, "Erikson, In His Own Old Age, Exands His View of Life," *New York Times*, 14 June 1988, C1.

117. "There emerges a different . . . ": Erikson, *The Life Cycle Completed: A Review*, 65-66.

117. "You put such stress on passion . . . ": Goleman, "Erikson, In His Own Old Age, Expands His View of Life," *New York Times*, 14 June 1988, C1.

118. "As I have become . . . ": Hite, *The Hite Report*, 904.

118. "A seventy-one-year-old widower . . . ": Brecher, *Love, Sex and Aging: A Consumers Union Report*, 362.

118. "My wife and I . . . ": Hite, *The Hite Report*, 912.

120. "We talked and talked . . . ": Marx and Conn, "Young at Heart," 1986.

121. "The broad range . . . ": Brecher, *Love, Sex and Aging: A Consumers Union Report*, 420.

121. "Both Kinsey and . . . ": Doress and Siegel, *Ourselves, Growing Older*, 80.

122. "A study of gay . . . ": Berger, *Gay and Gray*, 15.

122. "The Starr-Weiner Report . . . ": Dychtwald and Flower, *Age Wave*, 44-45.

122. "persons who remain . . . ": Brecher, *Love, Sex and Aging: A Consumers Union Report*, 345.

127. "Look out over the city . . . ": Corwin, *Overkill and Megalove*.

Confluence

138. Paula Altrovitch, interview with Shuyee Lee, Montreal, 7 October 1985.

140. "the almost metaphysical . . . ": Bair, *Simone de Beauvoir*, 540.

141. "the muse literally . . . ": May Sarton in *Women in Aging*, 212.

141. "Simply remembering . . . ": Cowley, *The View From 80*, 72.

141. "as though his soul . . . ": MacLennan, *Voices in Time*, 4-5.

142. "Once more he . . . ": Ibid., 4, 5.

143. "translated in memory . . . ": Ibid., 3.

143. "forward or back . . . ": Welty, *One Writer's Beginnings*, 112.

143. "Of course the greatest . . . ": Ibid., 113-114.

143. "They can be rejoiced . . . ": Cowley, *The View From 80*, 13-14.

144. "At Emerson's funeral . . . ": Shaw, *Collected Letters 1926-1950*, 375.

144. "I owe more than . . . ": Ibid., 794.

144. "which was essentially . . . ": Ibid., 663.

144. Academic researchers and scientists study older people and their memories. However, they are primarily interested in what they can

quantify: short-term memory, long-term memory, working memory and, because it is associated with Alzheimer's disease, memory loss.

"Most older people are worried about their memories," says Dr. James Birren. "The truth of the matter is that the older nervous system continues to acquire information with age. The vocabulary of an older adult is probably twice as big as it was on leaving school. A real loss of information is probably due to some illness. But what we tend to do is confuse loss of information with inability to access or retrieve it. In normal aging, the issue is usually retrieval. When we're in school we learn a lot of mnemonic devices to remember facts because we're tested on examinations. But these fall into disuse. Those older people who have to remember things like surnames begin to use devices to retrieve information. If they've forgotten their keys they think, 'where was I standing, what was I doing, what time of day was it,' and then it begins to come back, indicating the information is in there.

"What we're doing is searching through much more information than the young child. So to find the particular thing means groping around a bit more. This is called benign memory loss. It really doesn't mean that we've lost the information, but it's inaccessible. Malignant memory loss means pathological loss of the information due to illness, stroke or Alzheimer's disease."

"I heard Linus Pauling speak to an audience of hundreds," I report to Dr. Birren, "and in the middle of an intricate rhetorical speech, rich with metaphors and quotations, he couldn't recall Salvador Allende's name. And he said, 'Oh, that's something that happens as you get older, you lose proper names from your brain stem.'

"Two hours later you remember the name. You just can't bring it up at that particular moment. But remember two things: you're searching through a bigger store, and often proper names are the most difficult things to remember because they have no associations. What does the name of the Prime Minister really mean? If his name were Scarecrow, you'd never forget it. But if his name is . . ."

"Mulroney," I admit.

"See, that name has no associations with it. So when the people who are good at this put it into store they try to form a visual image and then it can be retrieved. The technical term for this in psychology is 'mediators.' What you do is put it in store with more mediators. See, my name is Birren and that has no meaning, and people stumble over it. But I say, well, think of it as 'beer in,' think of me standing there with a beer stein and pouring beer in. Once you get that visual image you'll never forget it. It's so simple."

144. "As I grow older . . . ": Randall in *Women and Aging*, 128.

144. "the bursting flowers . . . ": Le Sueur in *Women and Aging*, 10; 12.

145. "It will please you . . . ": MacNiven, *The Durrell-Miller Letters 1935-1980.*

146. "The globe of memory . . . ": Anderson, *Tirra Lirra by the River.*

146. "stop my thoughts . . . ": Erikson, *Wisdom and the Senses*, 44.

146. "talking to someone real . . . ": MacLennan, *Voices in Time*, 11.

146. "with some incredulity:" Ibid., 313.

147. "the only choice that matters . . . ": "Dancing on the Edge of the Road.," *The Power of the Word with Bill Moyers*, 3 October 1989, show 5.

148. "simply sitting still . . . ": Cowley, *The View From 80*, 12.

148. "My ghost would be . . . ": Shaw, *Collected Letters, 1926-1950*, 767.

149. "He who does not feel . . . ": Yourcenar, *With Open Eyes*, 253.

149. "that all knowledge begins . . . ": Erikson, *Wisdom and the Senses*, 23.

150. "age-specific . . . ": Erikson, Erikson, and Kivnick, *Vital Involvement in Old Age*, 226.

154. "How do we cope . . . ": Shock et al., *Normal Human Aging: The Baltimore Longitudinal Study of Aging*, 169.

154. "die a little less . . . ": Yourcenar, *With Open Eyes*, 254.

154. "the day's warm fog . . . ": Ibid., 250.

155. "Rage, rage . . . ": Thomas, *The Poems of Dylan Thomas*, 207.

156. "I know that the contingency . . . ": Shaw, *Collected Letters 1926-1950*, 820.

156. "What to do . . . ": Cowley, *The View From 80*, 29-30.

156. In a major survey of people over 65, it was found that an average of four of five older people look back on their past with satisfaction and three in four feel their present is as interesting as it ever was. (National Council on Aging, Harris and Associates, 1975) In another survey on the quality of life, 85 percent of one thousand 70 year olds indicated that the quality of their lives was "good, very good, or excellent." (Survey by American Institutes of Research, Flanaghan, 1978)

156. "We must accept . . . ": Fisher, *Sister Age*, 236-237.

157. "I can't imagine . . . ": Goleman, "Erikson, In His Own Old Age, Expands His View of Life," *New York Times*, 14 June 1988, C1.

161. "resiliency of human . . . ": "René Dubos: The Despairing Optimist at 80," *Bill Moyers' Journal*, Show 711.

162. "As the years went by . . . ": White, *Onward and Upward in the Garden*, Preface.

163. "Old age may . . . ": Cowley, *The View From 80*, 47.

Biographies

Ted Allan (1916 –   )

Born in Montreal, Canada, Allan's long list of credits includes short stories, radio dramas, teleplays, screenplays, stage plays, and books.

His most recently produced stage play, *Chu Chem, a Zen Buddhist Hebrew Musical*, opened on Broadway in 1989. *Gog and Magog* played for five years in Paris (1960-65). In London, Sean Connery directed *I've Seen Cut Lemons* (1970). In Los Angeles, John Cassavetes directed *The Third Day Comes* (1982) and British critic Bernard Levin called his tragedy *The Secret of the World* "a play to match other plays by."

His most recent screenplay, *Bethune: The Making of a Hero*, had its premiere in 1990. He won an Oscar nomination and a Golden Globe award for his screenplay *Lies My Father Told Me* (1976), and *Love Streams*, written with John Cassavetes, won the Golden Bear, Berlin Film Festival (1984).

Allan's best-selling book, *The Scalpel, the Sword: The Story of Dr. Norman Bethune*, written with Sydney Gordon, was published in nineteen languages, and *Willie, the Squowse*, a children's book, in ten countries. His comic novel, *Love is a Long Shot*, won the Stephen Leacock award for humor (1984).

In 1990, Ted Allan was honored by the Alliance of Canadian Cinema, Television, and Radio Artists (ACTRA) for lifetime achievement in writing.

James E. Birren (1918 –   )

Born in Chicago, Illinois, Birren, Ph.D., D.Sc., is Adjunct Professor of Medicine/Gerontology and Director of the Anna and Harry Borum Center for Gerontological Research, University of California.

He was founding Executive Director of the Ethel Percy Andrus Gerontology Center and Dean of the Leonard Davis School of Gerontology, University of Southern California (1965-86).

Birren has published over 225 articles in academic journals and books and is series editor of *Handbooks on Aging*, recognized as a definitive source of current gerontological thinking.

Acclaimed as a preeminent contemporary psychologist, Dr. Birren explores aspects of human behavior such as perception, memory, intellectual function, creativity and wisdom, in relation to age. He is one of the world's most widely cited psychologists on adult development and aging.

Mary Steichen Calderone (1904 –   )

Born in New York City, Calderone, M.D., M.P.H., has spent much of her career educating the medical profession and the public about human sexuality.

She was Medical Director of the Planned Parenthood Federation of America (1955-64) and cofounder and president (1964-82) of SIECUS (Sex Information Education Council of the U.S.), an organization dedicated to establishing sexuality as an acknowledged aspect of both mental and physical health. She is Adjunct Professor, New York University, Human Sexuality Program.

Calderone is an Honorary Life Member of the American Medical Association, an Honorary Life Member of the American Association of Sex Educators, Counselors and Therapists, a Charter Member of the American College of Sexologists, a Fellow of the Scientific Study of Sex, a member of the Board of Directors of the American Association for World Health and the U.S. Committee for the World Health Organization.

Her many honors include: Humanist of the Year award (1974); one of the fifty most influential women in the United States, Newspaper Enterprises Association (1975); the Edward Browning Award for Prevention of Disease, the American Public Health Association (1980); and more than a dozen honorary degrees.

She is the author of *Release from Sexual Tensions* (1960); editor, *Sexuality and Human Values* (1974); author (with Dr. James W. Ramey), *Talking With Your Child About Sex: Questions and Answers for Children from Birth to Puberty* (1984).

Morley Callaghan (1903 – 1990)

Born in Toronto, Ontario, Callaghan, L.L.B., worked as a reporter on the *Toronto Daily Star* (1926), lived and wrote in Paris (1928-29), and gave up law for writing when his stories found their way, via Ernest Hemingway, into the Paris little magazines, such as Ezra Pound's *Exile*.

In the 30s and 40s, there was no more successful writer of short stories than Morley Callaghan. Of the more than one hundred stories he published, many appeared in *Esquire, Harper's Bazaar, Scribners, The New Yorker* and later in the "big slicks" – *Redbook, Cosmopolitan, The Saturday Evening Post.*

He also published fifteen novels. The first, *Strange Fugitive*, appeared in 1928 and the last, *The Wild Old Man of the Road*, sixty years later.

Of the novels, *They Shall Inherit the Earth* (1935) has been most critically acclaimed; *The Loved and the Lost* won the Governor General's Award, the most prestigious Canadian literary award (1952); and *The Many Coloured Coat* (1960) caused critic Edmund Wilson to call Callaghan "a writer whose work may be mentioned without absurdity in association with Chekhov's and Turgenev's."

Alex Comfort (1920 –   )

Born in London, England, Comfort, M.B., B.Ch., M.A., M.R.C.S., L.R.C.P., D.C.H., Ph.D., D.Sc. was the Nuffield research fellow in gerontology, Department of Zoology, University of London (1952-64); director of the Medical Research Council Group on Aging (1965-73); clinical lecturer, Department of Psychiatry, Stanford University (1974-); Adjunct Professor, University of California, Neuropsychiatric Institute (1979 -).

Twice he was the gold medalist in Classics at Highgate School, and, in 1962, was awarded both the CIBA Foundation Prize for research in gerontology and the Borestone Poetry Award. He is a scientific humanist: a biologist who publishes fiction and poetry, a specialist in the problems of aging as well as in the erotic literature of India.

Comfort has written more than ten books including: *First Year Physiological Technique* (1984), *Sexual Behavior in Society* (1950), *The Biology of Senescence* (1956), *A Practice of Geriatric Psychiatry* (1980).

He is known popularly for his best-selling books on sexuality — *The Joy of Sex: A Gourmet's Guide to Lovemaking* (1972) and *More Joy: A Lovemaking Companion to "The Joy of Sex"* (1974).

His latest book is *Say Yes to Old Age* (1990).

Norman Corwin (1910 –   )

Born in Boston Massachusetts, Corwin made his reputation at CBS as a writer/director/producer in the heyday of radio drama (1938-56).

For CBS, Corwin wrote: "The People, Yes" (with Earl Robinson); "We Hold These Truths"; "The Roosevelt Special"; "Word from The People," a United Nations San Francisco Conference Special. He produced "Lonesome Train," written by Milliard Lampell and Earl Robinson.

He was much acclaimed for his V-E Day radio script, *On a Note of Triumph*, published by Simon and Schuster (1945). Poet Carl Sandburg called it "one of the great all-time American poems" and Robert E. Sherwood thought it a "stirring statement of the lessons that must be learned from war." It had the quality of "universal truth," said the *New York Times Book Review*, and described the style as "an essay in which speech by different speakers is used to give an interplay of ideas — a sort of pageant of voices . . . the sum of his argument is a statement of the people's will for peace."

Corwin has also written, directed and produced for stage, television, film. He was cowinner, first prize, the Metropolitan Opera Award for a new American opera, *The Warriors* (1947); received the Freedom Award for the telecast "Between Americans" (1951); an Oscar nomination for his screenplay *Lust for Life*; and the PEN award for his body of work (1986).

His books include two collections of his radio plays, *The World of Carl Sandburg* (1961), *Overkill and Megalove* (1963), *Greater Than the Bomb* (1981) and *Trivializing America* (1988).

Norman Cousins (1915 – 1990)

Born in Union City, New Jersey, Cousins was editor of the *Saturday Review* for more than 30 years, changing it from a specialized literary publication to a cultural and world-affairs review with a circulation as high as 600,000.

After retiring (1977), he became know for his best-selling book, *Anatomy of an Illness: As Perceived by the Patient* (1979), which presents the argument that a person's attitude can help combat a grave illness.

In the last decade of his life, he was adjunct professor in the School of Medicine, University of California, where he helped create and assemble a body of scientific studies proving that positive attitudes are not just moods but biochemical realities.

Cousins is the author or editor of more than twenty books reflecting his humanitarian, scientific concerns such as *The Good Inheritance: the Democratic Chance* (1942), *Present Tense: an American Editor's Odyssey* (1967), *The Celebration of Life* (1974), *The Healing Heart: Antidotes to Panic and Helplessness* (1983).

Malcolm Cowley (1898 – 1989)

Born in Pittsburgh, Pennsylvania, Cowley, literary critic, historian, editor, poet, and essayist, is one of the twentieth century's most influential critics. He celebrated the so-called Lost Generation in his most famous critical work, *Exile's Return* (1934), and continues his incisive critical and social history of American literature between world wars in *A Second Flowering* (1973) and *The Dream of the Golden Mountain* (1980). In 1984, he wrote *The Flower and the Leaf*, about American writing since 1941.

Cowley was literary editor of *The New Republic* (1929-44) and editor at Viking Press (1948-85). He wrote hundreds of book reviews and literary essays as well as many books, most notably, *Blue Juniata* (1929), a collection of autobiographical verse, *And I Worked at the Writer's Trade* (1978), and *The View From 80* (1980).

Erik H. Erikson (1902 –   )

Born in Frankfurt-am-Main, Germany, of Danish parents, Erikson graduated from the Vienna Psychoanalytic Institute (1933) and, following Hitler's accession to power, emigrated to the U.S. There he began private practice and a series of research appointments: Austen Riggs Center, Stockbridge, Mass.; Harvard Medical School; University of California; the Yale School of Medicine; University of Pittsburgh School of Medicine. He is presently Professor Emeritus of Human Development, Harvard University.

Over the years, Erikson developed a theory of the wholeness of the human life cycle in which he describes the development of basic strengths in successive stages of our psychosexual growth: hope, will, purpose, competence, fidelity, love, care, wisdom.

His books include: *Childhood and Society* (1950), *Young Man Luther* (1958), *Identity and the Life Cycle* (1959), *Gandhi's Truth* (National Book Award, 1970, Pulitzer Prize, 1970), *Identity and the Life Cycle* (1980), *The Life Cycle Completed* (1982), *Vital Involvement in Old Age*, with Joan Erikson and Helen Q. Kivnick (1986).

Joan Mowat Erikson (1902 –   )

Born in Canada, Erikson, dancer, psychologist, craftswoman, married Erik H. Erikson in Vienna (1930) and worked with him on a psychosocial model of development through the life cycle. In their mid-80s, the Eriksons have addressed the question of how the lessons of the early stages of life can, in old age, ripen into wisdom, which they see as "the strength and goal of old age."

Joan Erikson is author of: *Mata Ni Pachedi: The Temple Cloth of the Mother Goddess*; *The Universal Bead*, *Saint Francis and His Four Ladies*; *Activity, Recovery, Growth: The Communal Role of Planned Activities* with David and Joan Loveless; *Vital Involvement in Old Age* with Erik H. Erikson and Helen Q. Kivnick.

In 1988, she published *Wisdom and the Senses* which hypothesizes that "creative expression demands of us only that which is genuinely our own

. . . our personal accrued store of sense data." The book offers readers parallels between the creation of art and the creation of the self, as sources of human growth and vitality.

Mary Frances Kennedy Fisher (1908 –   )

Born in Albion, Michigan, Fisher is best known for her gastronomical classics — *Serve It Forth* (1937), *Consider the Oyster* (1941), *How to Cook a Wolf* (1942) — and her ability to write not only about food but about food and people. W.H. Auden wrote, "Mary Frances has known her guests, not as eaters only, but also as friends, lovers, husbands, so that she has been able to see their gastronomical habits in relation to the rest of their personality."

Mary Frances Fisher has written 18 books including: *A Considerable Town* (1978), celebrating Marseilles; *Among Friends* (1983), about growing up in Whittier, California; *As They Were* (1983), a book of reflections; *Sister Age* (1983), fifteen stories about living and dying; *Long Ago in France, The Years in Dijon* (1991), a gastronomical and womanly coming of age as a student in Dijon.

M.F.K. Fisher is renowned as a prose stylist. W.H. Auden dubbed her "the best prose writer in America."

Betty Friedan (1921 –   )

Born in Peoria, Illinois, educated at Smith College; the University of California, Berkeley; University of Iowa; and the Esalen Institute, Friedan became a respected leader of the American women's movement with the publication of her best-selling feminist classic *The Feminine Mystique* (1963). "For sheer impact on the lives of American women," observed Jean Sprain Wilson, "no book written in the sixties compares with Betty Friedan's *The Feminine Mystique*, sometimes called the *Uncle Tom's Cabin* of the women's liberation movement."

Betty Friedan was the founding president (1966-70) of NOW, the largest (160,000 members), most visible feminist organization in the U.S., and has lectured and taught at more than fifty universities, institutes and professional associations worldwide.

She contributed to *Voices of the New Feminism* (1970) and is author of *It Changed My Life: Writings on the Women's Movement* (1976) and *The Second Stage* (1981).

Laura Archera Huxley (1911 –   )

Born in Turin, Italy, Huxley studied violin in Berlin and Paris and came to the United States to make her debut as a concert violinist at Carnegie Hall.

She was a student at the Curtis Institute, in Philadelphia, when WWII began, making her return to Italy dangerous and difficult.

Prevented by U.S. wartime regulations from pursuing her concert career, Laura Archera produced films, played in a symphony orchestra and began her lifelong study of health, nutrition, and psychology.

In 1956 she married writer Aldous Huxley and together they explored ways of opening the mind to new levels of consciousness.

She is the author of: *You Are Not the Target* (1963, reprint 1986) and *The Timeless Moment: A Personal View of Aldous Huxley* (1968).

In her sixties, she undertook to raise an infant daughter. This inspired the books *Oneadayreason to Be Happy* (1986) and *The Child of Your Dreams*, with Piero Ferrucci (1987).

In 1978 she founded Our Ultimate Investment, a non-profit organization focused on conception and infant life and dedicated to the "nurturing of the possible human."

Maggie Kuhn (1905 –   )

Born in Buffalo, New York, Kuhn is best known as a founding member of the Gray Panthers, a 60,000-member social activist organization whose motto is "Age and Youth in Action."

In the 20s and 30s, as an employee of the YWCA, she became interested in women's rights and her subsequent twenty-five-year career as editor, writer, and program coordinator for the United Presbyterian Church of the United States broadened her advocacy to include race relations, housing, medical care, and the elderly.

Following their mandatory retirement in 1970 Maggie Kuhn and five others established the Gray Panthers to work for social justice including the right of all ages, young and old, to be considered of equal dignity and value.

In 1978 she was honored as Humanist of the Year.

Her writings include: *You Can't be Human Alone: A Handbook on Group Procedures for the Local Church* (1956), *Get Out There and Do Something About Injustice* (1972), *Maggie Kuhn on Aging: A Dialogue* (1977).

George Ignatieff (1913 – 1989)

Born in St. Petersburg, Russia, Ignatieff, Rhodes Scholar (1936), was one of Canada's most distinguished diplomats — a member of the Department of External Affairs for over thirty years and the Department's first foreign-born Canadian ambassador.

Among his many postings Ignatieff was private secretary to the high commissioner for Canada in London (1940-44); diplomatic advisor to the United Nations Atomic Energy Commission (1945-46); advisor to the Canadian delegation to the United Nations (1946-47); permanent Canadian representative to NATO (1963-65) and to the United Nations Security Council (1965-68). From 1980-89 he was Chancellor of the University of Toronto.

George Ignatieff was the recipient of more than ten honorary degrees, the Companion of the Order of Canada (1973) and the Pearson Peace Medal (1984).

He contributed to many scholarly journals including "Nato, Nuclear Weapons and Canada's Interests" (1980) and he is the author of *The Making of a Peacemonger: The Memoirs of George Ignatieff* (1985).

Dorothy Livesay (1909 –   )

Born in Winnipeg, Manitoba, Livesay, B.A., M.A., M.Ed., D. Litt., began writing poetry as a child and published her first book of poems, *Green Pitcher* (1929), at nineteen.

After graduation from the University of Toronto, she earned a Diplôme d'études supérieures from the Sorbonne in Paris. Politicized by the ferment in Europe, she became deeply involved in 30s left-wing politics on her return to Canada and wrote committed social poetry such as *Day and Night* (1944).

Livesay has been a social worker, the European correspondent for the *Toronto Star* (1946), teacher, and, after the death of her husband (1959), UNESCO Program Assistant (Education) in Northern Rhodesia.

She was founder and editor of the influential poetry journal *CVII*, a founding member of the League of Canadian Poets, Amnesty International (Canada) and the Committee for an Independent Canada. She twice won the Governor General's Award for Poetry (1944, 1947).

Dorothy Livesay's range of interests as seen in her poetry is, according to her, "personal, sexual, social, educational and political." It includes: *Selected Poems, 1926-1956* (1957), *The Unquiet Bed* (1967), *The Documentaries* (1968), *Plainsongs* (1969), *Collected Poems: The Two Seasons* (1972), *Ice Age* (1975), *The Woman I Am* (1977), *The Raw Edges* (1981), *The Phases of Love* (1983), *Feeling the Worlds* (1985), *The Self-Completing Tree* (1986).

Her non fiction books are *A Winnipeg Childhood* (1973) and *Right Hand Left Hand* (1977).

Hugh MacLennan (1907 – 1990)

Born in Glace Bay, Nova Scotia, Rhodes Scholar MacLennan, B.A., Ph.D., was Classics Master, Lower Canada College (1935-45) and professor of English Literature, McGill University (1951-82).

Although he spent much of his working life teaching, Hugh MacLennan wrote seven nonfiction books and seven novels, winning the prestigious Governor General's Award five times — for the novels *Two Solitudes* (1945), the title of which has become a watchword for the relations of English and French in Quebec, *The Precipice* (1949), *The Watch That Ends the Night* (1959), and in nonfiction for *Cross Country* (1950) and *Thirty and Three* (1955). Elspeth Cameron, his biographer, called his final novel *Voices in Time* (1980) "MacLennan's greatest novel."

He is a Companion of the Order of Canada, a Fellow of the Royal Society, the recipient of twelve honorary degrees and the subject of no fewer than seven books.

Critic Edmund Wilson described Hugh MacLennan as "a scholar of international culture and a man of the great world."

Gordon Nakayama (1900 –   )

Born in Kura Kawa, Ozu, Ehime-Ken, Japan, Nakayama entered Ritsumeikan University (1918) and emigrated to Canada (1919). Born into the Buddhist faith, he converted to Christianity (1920), entered the Anglican Theological College of British Columbia (1929), and was ordained a deacon (1932) and a priest (1934).

After WWII, Nakayama was sent to start a mission in southern Alberta, the relocation site of 4,200 Japanese and Japanese-Canadian evacuees. He remained in southern Alberta for thirty years and retired after fifty years in the Anglican Church.

He is the author of *Issei: Stories of Japanese Canadian Pioneers* (1984).

Linus Pauling (1901 –   )

Born in Portland, Oregon, Pauling, B.S., Ph.D., always excelled in research, writing the landmark book *The Nature of the Chemical Bond* (1939), producing, with colleagues, the first synthetic antibodies (1942), discovering the cause of sickle cell anemia (1949), and publishing, with R.B. Corey, the first complete description of the molecular structure of proteins (1951).

In 1954, he received the Nobel Prize in Chemistry.

With the increased public profile of a nobel laureate and the encouragement of his wife, Pauling devoted time to humanitarian issues connected to science. He wrote the best-seller *No More War!* (1958) and presented an anti-nuclear weapons petition, signed by 11,000 scientists, to the United Nations. Concerned about radioactive fallout because of his research on the molecular basis of genetic disease, he monitored atmospheric radioactivity and proved the drastic effects of atmospheric bomb tests. He wrote a draft of a superpower treaty to suspend atmospheric testing.

In 1962, on the very day that the United States/Soviet Union treaty suspending atmospheric testing, went into effect, Pauling was awarded the Nobel Peace Prize.

In 1967 he worked on the molecular basis of memory and this interest in orthomolecular medicine led to his founding the Linus Pauling Institute of Science and Medicine (1973). In the latter part of his career, his humanitarian concerns focused on the role of micronutrients, especially vitamin C, in the physiology of the organism. He is the author of twelve books including: *Vitamin C and the Common Cold* (1970), *Cancer and Vitamin C*, written with Ewan Cameron (1979), and *How to Live Longer and Feel Better* (1986).

Linus Pauling includes among his distinctions 36 honorary degrees. He has written over 600 scientific articles and 200 political and social articles. He has received the most prestigious scientific honors of the United States and the Soviet Union — The National Medal of Science and the Lomonosov Gold Medal.

Lea Roback (1903 –   )

Born in Montreal and raised in the small town of Beauport, Quebec, Roback grew up in a family of nine children speaking English, French and Yiddish.

At 15 she worked in a dry cleaners, then at the box office of Her Majesty's Theatre in Montreal. While there a Parisian actress suggested she study in Grenoble, France. She borrowed the money for a one-way boat passage and tutored English to live. In 1924, she joined her older brother, a medical student, in Berlin, and studied languages and sociology at the University of Berlin where "everyone was either far left or joining the Nazis." Roback joined the Communist Party and remained in Germany until 1932 when "I couldn't even give out leaflets without being beaten by the Nazis."

In Montreal she worked as a youth group worker, YMHA, and then ran the first and only Marxist bookstore in Quebec, smuggling illegal books across the border from New York in defiance of Premier Duplessis's Padlock Law.

In 1936 she became a labor organizer for the International Ladies Garment Workers in the "dog-eat-dog shmata trade." During WWII she was business agent for the United Electrical Workers Union. In the McCarthy period, radicals were driven out of the unions but Roback continued organizing for the Voice of Women, and also for the repeal of the Padlock Law. In 1956, with Khrushchev's revelations about Stalin, she left the Communist Party "to screw up their own heads." She continues to organize and demonstrate publicly, for refugees, against poverty, supporting public sector strikes, and women's issues — "there is so much work to do among the people."

Roback is the subject of the films *La Turlutte des Années Dur*, and *Des Lumières dans la Grandes Noirceur* (1990). She is featured in many books including *The Strangest Dream: Canadian Communists, the Spy Trials and the Cold War* (1983).

In March 1986 hundreds of women from l'Intersyndicale des femmes feted this pioneering feminist and unionist in a stirring Hommage à Lea Roback.

Ruth B. Weg (1920 –   )

Born in New York City, Weg, B.A., M.S., Ph.D., engaged in research on the molecular bases of physiological phenomena at the University of Southern California, Department of Biological Sciences, and then joined the Andrus Gerontology Center (1968) as Associate Professor of Biology.

As well, she is Professor of Gerontology, Leonard Davis School of Gerontology, USC, where her research focuses on change through the lifespan — sexual behavior in later life, nutrition, morbidity, and longevity.

Weg is active in numerous scientific and professional societies and is a frequent lecturer on the biology and physiology of aging. She is editor of and contributor to *Sexuality in the Later Years: Roles and Behavior* (1983) and author of *Nutrition in the Later Years* (1979).

Edith Wallace (1909 –   )

Born in Offenbach, Germany, Wallace, M.D., Ph.D., worked with C.G. Jung and Mrs. Emma Jung in Zurich. She counts J.G. Bennett, a disciple of Gurdjieff and Sufi teacher, as her second great teacher. She has been a practicing Jungian analyst in New York City since 1951, and teaches at the Pratt Summer Institute for Expressive Analysis.

Wallace is editor emeritus of the *Journal for the Arts in Psychotherapy*, and contributes articles about healing through the visual arts to books and journals including *Approaches to Art Therapy*, edited by Judith Aron Rubin (1987), *Impressions* (Summer 1988). She is the author of, *A Queen's Quest: A Pilgrimage for Individuation* (1990).

Bibliography

Books and Articles

Adelman, Marcy, ed. *Long Time Passing: Lives of Older Lesbians.* Boston: Alyson Publications, 1986.

Ambroise-Rendu, Marc. "Sex After 60." *The Guardian,* 20 March 1988, 15.

Anderson, Jessica. *Tirra Lirra by the River.* Melbourne: Macmillan of Australia, 1978.

Andrus Center Volunteers. *Aging: Today's Research and You: A Lecture Series.* Los Angeles: The Ethel Percy Andrus Gerontology Center, University of Southern California, 1978.

Bair, Deirdre. *Simone de Beauvoir: A Biography.* New York: Summit Books, 1990.

Bannerman, R. Leroy. *Norman Corwin and Radio: The Golden Years.* University, AL: University of Alabama Press, 1986.

Barbach, Lonnie Garfield. *For Yourself: the Fulfillment of Female Sexuality.* New York: New American Library, 1976.

Barber, H. et al. "Sexual Problems and the Elderly, I: The Use and Abuse of Medications: A Panel Discussion." *Geriatrics* 44, no. 3 (March 1989): 61.

Barlow, Wilfred. *The Alexander Technique.* New York: Warner Books, 1973.

Beauvoir, Simone de. *The Coming of Age,* translated by Patrick O'Brian. New York: G.P. Putnam's Sons, 1972.

————. *Old Age*, translated by Patrick O'Brian. London: Andre Deutsch, 1972.

Berger, Raymond M. *Gay and Gray: The Older Homosexual Man*. Boston: Alyson Publications, 1984.

Birren, James E. *The Psychology of Aging*. New York: Prentice-Hall, 1964.

Birren, James E. and K.W. Schaie, eds. *Handbook of the Psychology of Aging*. 2nd ed. New York: Van Nostrand Reinhold, 1985.

Birren, James E. and R. Bruce Sloane, eds. *Handbook of Mental Health and Aging*. New York: Prentice-Hall, 1980.

Blythe, Ronald. *The View in Winter: Reflections on Old Age*. San Diego: Harcourt Brace Jovanovich, 1979.

Brecher, Edward M. *Love, Sex and Aging: A Consumers Union Report*. New York: Consumers Union, 1984.

Bragger, Lydia, Sylvia Friedman and Sudie George. *Report of the Mini-Conference on Challenging Age Stereotypes in the Media*, 1981 White House Conference on Aging. Mini-conference convened by Maggie Kuhn, New York: Department of Health and Human Services, 1981.

Brookdale Institute. *Aging: An International Perspective*, conference proceedings. New York: Columbia University Press, 1982.

Bulcroft, Kris and Margaret O'Conner-Roden. "Never too Late." *Psychology Today* 20 (June 1986):66-69.

Butler, Robert N., and Myrna I. Lewis. *Love and Sex After Sixty*. New York: Harper and Row, 1977.

Callaghan, Morley. *A Wild Old Man on the Road*. Don Mills, Ont.: Stoddart, 1988.

Canada. *Canada's Seniors: A Dynamic Force*. Ottawa: Supply and Services Canada, 1988.

Canada. Statistics Canada. *The Elderly in Canada*, based on the 1981 Census. Ottawa: Supply and Services Canada, 1984. Cat. no. 99-932.

Casper, Ursula Hodge. *Joy and Comfort Through Stretching and Relaxing, for Those Who are Unable to Exercise*. New York: Seabury Press, 1982.

Cohen, Leah. *Small Expectations: Society's Betrayal of Older Women*. Toronto: McClelland and Stewart, 1984.

Cole, Thomas R. "Aging and Meaning." *Generations* (Winter 1985):49-52.

Comfort, Alex. *Ageing: The Biology of Senescence*. New York: Holt, Rinehart and Winston, 1964.

———. *Practice of Geriatric Psychiatry*. New York: Elsevier, 1980.

———. *The Process of Ageing*. London: Weidenfeld and Nicolson, 1965.

Corwin, Norman. *Overkill and Megalove*. Cleveland: World Publishing Company, [1963].

Cousins, Norman. *Anatomy of an Illness as Perceived by the Patient: Reflections on Healing and Regeneration*. New York: W.W. Norton, 1979.

———. *Head First, The Biology of Hope*. New York: Dutton, 1989.

Cowley, Malcolm. *The View From 80*. New York: Viking Press, 1980.

Csikszentmihalyi, Mihaly and Isabella Selega Csikszentmihalyi, eds. *Optimal Experience: Psychological Studies of Flow in Consciousness*. Cambridge; New York: Cambridge University Press, 1988.

Cunningham, Imogen. *After Ninety*. Seattle: University of Washington Press, 1977.

Doress, Paula Brown and Diana Laskin Siegel. *Ourselves, Growing Older: Women Aging with Knowledge and Power*. New York: Simon and Schuster, 1987.

Dychtwald, Ken and Joe Flower. *Age Wave: The Challenges and Opportunities of an Aging America*. Los Angeles: J.P. Tarcher, 1989.

Eckstein, D. "Common Complaints of the Elderly." In *The Geriatric Patient*, edited by William Riechel. New York: H.P. Publishing, 1978.

Edel, Leon. *Stuff of Sleep and Dreams: Experiments in Literary Psychology*. London: Chatto and Windus, 1982.

El Nassar, Haya. "As USA Ages, Mags Want In on Action." *U.S.A. Today*, 9 February 1988:1-2B.

Ellis, Havelock. *From Rousseau to Proust*. Boston: Houghton Mifflin, 1935.

Erikson, Erik H. *The Life Cycle Completed: A Review*. New York: Norton, 1982.

Erikson, Erik H., Joan Erikson and Helen Q. Kivnick. *Vital Involvement in Old Age*. New York: W.W. Norton, 1986.

Erikson, Joan. *Wisdom and the Senses: The Way of Creativity*. New York: W.W. Norton, 1988.

Farber, Norma. *How Does it Feel to be Old?* New York: Dutton, 1979.

Feldenkrais, Moshe. *Awareness Through Movement: Health Exercises for Personal Growth.* New York: Harper & Row, 1977.

Felsteen, I. *La Sexualité du Troisième Age.* Paris: Robert Laffont, 1971.

Fisher, M.F.K. *Sister Age.* New York: Knopf, 1983.

Frankl, Victor E. *Man's Search for Meaning.* New York: Simon and Schuster, 1984.

Friedan, Betty. *The Feminine Mystique.* New York: W.W. Norton, 1983.

Gatz, Margaret and Charles Emery. "The Effect of Physical Exercise on Cognitive and Psychological Functioning in Community Aged," *Andrus Annual Report,* University of Southern California, 1984-1985.

Goleman, Daniel. "Erikson, In His Own Old Age, Expands His View of Life." *New York Times,* 14 June 1988, 3:1.

"Gray Panther Power." *Center Magazine* 8 (1975).

Gutmann, David. *Reclaimed Powers: Toward a New Psychology of Men and Women in Later Life.* New York: Basic Books, 1987.

Hartwig, Heyman. "Letters to the Editor." *Gray Panther Network* (Fall 1985):11.

Heilbrun, Carolyn G. "Women Writers: Coming of Age at 50." *New York Times Book Review* 93 (4 September 1988):1.

Higbie, Les. *To Understand the Aging Process: The Baltimore Longitudinal Study of the National Institute on Aging.* Bethesda: U.S. Dept. of Health, Education, and Welfare, Public Health Service, National Institute of Health; Washington, D.C.: G.P.O., 1978.

Hite, Shere. *The Hite Report: A Nationwide Study of Female Sexuality.* New York: Macmillan, 1976.

Huxley, Laura. *You Are Not the Target: Transforming Negative Feelings Into Creative Action and Harmonious Relations.* Los Angeles: J.P. Tarcher, 1986.

Ignatieff, George, with Sonja Sinclair. *The Making of a Peacemonger: The Memoirs of George Ignatieff.* Toronto: University of Toronto Press, 1985.

Kaplan et al. "Mortality Among the Elderly in the Alameda County Study: Behavioral and Demographic Risk Factors," *American Journal of Public Health* 10 (1987): 7.

Kay, Billye and Neelley James. "Sexuality and the Aging: A Review of the Current Literature." *Sexuality and Disability* 5, no. 1 (Spring 1982):38-46.

Keough, Carol, ed. *Future Youth*. Emmaus, PA: Rodale Press, 1987.

Koestler, Arthur. *The Act of Creation*. London: Hutchinson, 1964.

———. *From Bricks to Babel*. New York: Random, 1980.

Kra, Siegfried. *Aging Myths: Reversible Causes of Mind and Memory Loss*. New York: McGraw-Hill, 1986.

Kramer, Sydells and Jenny Masur. *Jewish Grandmothers*. Boston: Beacon Press, 1976.

Lahr, John. *Automatic Vaudeville: Essays on Star Turns*. New York: Knopf, 1984.

Layton, Elizabeth. *Through the Looking Glass: Drawings by Elizabeth Layton*. Kansas City: Mid-America Art Alliance, 1984.

Lesnoff-Cravaglia, Gari, ed. *Values, Ethics and Aging*, Frontiers of Aging Series, Vol. 4. New York: Human Sciences Press, 1985.

Levinson, Daniel J. et al. *The Seasons of a Man's Life*. New York: Ballantine Books, 1986.

Livesay, Dorothy. *Collected Poems: The Two Seasons*. Toronto: McGraw-Hill Ryerson, 1972.

———. *The Phases of Love*. Toronto: Coach House Press, 1983.

———. *The Self-Completing Tree: Selected Poems*. Victoria: Press Porcépic, 1986.

McCrae, Robert R. "Age Differences in the Use of Coping Mechanisms." *Journal of Gerontology* 37, no. 4 (1975):454-460.

Macdonald, Barbara and Cynthia Rich. *Look Me in the Eye: Old Women, Aging and Ageism*. San Francisco: Spinsters/Aunt Lute, 1983.

McLeish, John A.B. *The Ulyssean Adult, Creativity in the Middle and Later Years*. Toronto; New York: McGraw-Hill Ryerson, 1976.

MacLennan, Hugh. *Voices in Time*. Toronto: Macmillan, 1980.

Macniven, Ian S., ed. *The Durrell-Miller Letters, 1935-1980*. New York: New Directions, 1988.

Marshall, Doris. *Silver Threads: Critical Reflections on Growing Old*. Toronto: Between the Lines, 1987.

Masters, William and Virginia Johnson. "Sex and the Aging Process." *Journal of the American Geriatrics Society* 29, no. 9 (1981):385-390.

Miller, Henry and Brenda Venus. *Dear, Dear Brenda: The Love Letters of Henry Miller to Brenda Venus*, edited by Gerald S. Sindell. New York: William Morrow, 1986.

Mitchell, Marietta. "Preface." In *After Ninety*, by Imogen Cunningham. Seattle: University of Washington Press, 1977.

Money, Miriam C. et al. "Evaluation of a Supervised Exercise Program in a Geriatric Population." *Journal of the American Geriatrics Society* 37, no. 4 (April 1989).

Montagu, Ashley. *Touching: The Human Significance of the Skin*. New York: Columbia University Press, 1971.

Myerhoff, Barbara. *Number Our Days*. New York: Dutton, 1979.

"New Care Service is Launched With a Hug." *Viewpark Community Hospital: In the News*, 27 March 1980:1-2.

O'Brien, Beatrice, ed. *Aging: Today's Research and You*. San Diego: University of California Press, 1977.

Olds, Sally W. *The Eternal Garden: Seasons of Our Sexuality*. New York: Random House, 1985.

Oriol, William E. *Getting the Story on Aging: A Sourcebook on Gerontology for Journalists*. New York: The Brookdale Institute on Aging and Adult Human Development and Columbia University Press, 1984.

Pauling, Linus. *How to Live Longer and Feel Better*. New York: W.H. Freeman, 1987.

Painter, Charlotte. *Gifts of Age: Portraits and Essays of 32 Remarkable Women*. New York: Chronicle Books, 1985.

Phillipson, Chris. *Capitalism and the Construction of Old Age*. New York: Macmillan, 1982.

Powys, John Cowper. *The Art of Growing Old*. London: Jonathan Cape, 1944.

"Report of the American Society of Plastic and Reconstructive Surgeons." *Newsweek* 105 (27 May 1985):64-68.

Russell, Bertrand. *The Autobiography of Bertrand Russell, 1914-1944*. Vol. 2. Toronto: McClelland and Stewart, 1968.

Rhys, Jean. "Whatever Became of Old Mrs. Pearse?" *The Times*, 21 May 1975, 16.

Sarton, May. *At Seventy: A Journal.* New York: W.W. Norton, 1984.

———. *The Magnificent Spinster.* New York: W.W. Norton, 1985.

Schaie, K. Warner, ed. *Longitudinal Studies of Adult Psychological Development.* New York: Guilford Press, 1983.

Scott-Maxwell, Florida. *The Measure of My Days.* New York: Knopf, 1968.

Selye, Hans. *The Stress of Life.* New York: McGraw-Hill, 1956.

———. *Stress Without Distress.* Philadelphia: Lippincott, 1974.

Shaw, Bernard. *Collected Letters 1926-1950,* edited by Dan H. Laurence. London: Max Reinhardt, 1988.

Shock, Nathan W. et al. *Normal Human Aging: The Baltimore Longitudinal Study of Aging.* U.S. Department of Health and Human Services, NIH Publ. no. 84-2450, 1984.

Skinner, B.F. and Margaret Vaughan. *Enjoy Old Age.* New York: W.W. Norton, 1983.

Stearns, Peter N. *Old Age in European Society: The Case of France.* Baltimore: Croom Helm, 1977.

Strachey, Lytton. *Eminent Victorians.* San Diego: Harcourt Brace Jovanovich, 1961.

Taguchi, Yosh. *Private Parts: An Owner's Guide,* edited by Merrily Weisbord. Toronto: McClelland and Stewart, 1988.

Thomas, Dylan *The Poems of Dylan Thomas,* edited by Daniel Jones. New York: A New Directions Book, 1971.

"Timing is Everything to Playwright." *The Montreal Gazette,* 2 January 1989.

United Nations. Department of International, Economic and Social Affairs. *World Demographic Estimates and Projections, 1950-2025.* New York: United Nations, 1988.

Ward, Russell A. *The Aging Experience: An Introduction to Social Gerontology.* New York: Harper and Row, 1984.

Weil, Andrew. *Health and Healing.* Boston: Houghton Mifflin, 1988.

Welty, Eudora. *One Writer's Beginnings.* New York: Warner Books, 1984.

White, Charles B. "A Scale for the Assessment of Attitudes and Knowledge Regarding Sexuality in the Aged," *Archives of Sexual Behavior* 11, no. 6 (1982):491-502.

White, Katherine S. *Onward and Upward in the Garden*. New York: Farrar, Straus and Giroux, 1979.

Women and Aging: an Anthology by Women, edited by Jo Alexander et al, Corvallis, OR: Calyx Books, 1986.

Writers Guild of America. *The Journal*, Los Angeles, November 1989.

Yourcenar, Marguerite. *Memoirs of Hadrian*, translated by Grace Frick. New York: Farrar, Straus and Young, 1954.

————. *With Open Eyes: Conversations with Matthieu Galey*, translated by Arthur Goldhammer. Boston: Beacon Press, 1984.

Television

"René Dubos: The Despairing Optimist at 80," *Bill Moyers' Journal*, Show #711, Journal Graphics Inc., New York, 2/20/81.

"Sex and Aging," Gary Hochman, Producer/Writer/Director, A Production of the Nebraska Projects Unit Network, University of Nebraska-Lincoln Television, KUON TV, 1987.

"Stanley Kunitz: Dancing on the Edge of the Road," *The Power of the Word with Bill Moyers*, Show #5, Journal Graphics Inc., 13/10/89.

"Young at Heart," Sue Marx and Pamela Conn, Producers, Detroit, PBS, 1986.

Index